BUSHRANGERS

A PICTORIAL HISTORY

BUSHRANGERS

A PICTORIAL HISTORY

Harry Nunn

URE SMITH PRESS

SYDNEY • HONG KONG • CHICAGO • LONDON

ACKNOWLEDGEMENTS

Acknowledgements are made to the staff of the La Trobe Library, Melbourne, for their assistance in locating illustrations and in particular to Miss Leonie Mills, Library Photographer of the State Library of Victoria, to the Public Record Office, Victoria, and to the Police Museum of the Victoria Police Force.

Published by Ure Smith Press
an imprint of Weldon International
372 Eastern Valley Way, Willoughby, NSW 2068, Australia

First published by Lansdowne Press 1979
Reprinted by Ure Smith Press 1991

Typeset in Australia by G.T. Setters Pty Limited
Printed in Singapore by Kyodo Printing Co (S'pore) Pte Ltd

National Library of Australia Cataloguing-in-Publication data

Nunn, Harry W. (Harry Wilfred), 1916–
Bushrangers, a pictorial history.

Includes bibliographical references and index.
ISBN 0 7254 0843 X.

1. Bushrangers — Australia — Pictorial works. I. Title.

364.15520994

Contents

Preface

The term 'bushranger' is distinctively and indigenously Australian and to Australians, 'bushranging' has more connotations of skill in bushcraft and horsemanship and of heroic romanticism in 'roaming the bush free and bold' in defiance of authority than of the theft, robbery under arms and murder that was associated with it.

Bushranging belongs to the late eighteenth and nineteenth centuries and extended over a period of ninety-one years mainly on the Eastern seaboard in Van Diemen's Land where between the years 1805 and 1842 there appears to have been twenty discernible gangs, some of them large, and about sixteen other bushrangers who operated either in pairs or as loners, and in New South Wales where between 1789 and 1879 nearly thirty four gangs and over fifty two other bushrangers were active, either singly or in pairs.

It is ironic that Victoria should have become famous as the epic bushranging colon around which the quintessence of folklore has centred. At the height of the State's traditional rivalry with New South Wales, there were only ten smaller gangs and about fifteen other bushrangers who engaged in robbery under arms over a shorter period of approximately thirty-eight years while New South Wales suffered a greater intensity of three times as many bushrangers over a much longer period. This is undoubtedly due to the mystique surrounding Ned Kelly, who despite the small numbers in his gang has become almost immortalised in Australian romantic folklore.

The origins of the bushrangers were inextricably linked with eighteenth-century England and its criminal laws, the convict system and early administration of the penal settlements, the colonial gold rushes and problems of land settlement in New South Wales and Victoria.

The penal system and its 'convict bolters', the gold rushes and intoxicating new liberty, gold escorts and hold-ups and the 'new' native bushrangers provided a prolific source material for Australian writers adopting the conventions of early Victorian Romantic literature. The bushrangers became linked with tales of the bush and rollicking highwaymen who were either alternatively gallant or remorseful or sometimes both, or just defiant over the life which circumstances forced them to live.

There were three distinct eras of bushranging in Australia. The first was that of the 'convict bolters' or escapees from the penal settlements in New South Wales and Van Diemen's Land who took to plundering for survival. The second was that of the Wild Colonial Boys with armed robbers accompanying the Gold Rushes and who operated in Victoria in the 1850s and in New South Wales in the 1860s. The third era brought the 'new' native born bushrangers who were associated with cattle duffing, horse thieving and bank robberies both in New South Wales and in Victoria and which culminated in the end of bushranging with the Kelly gang.

Almost without exception, bushrangers were shot dead during confrontations with soldiers and police or were hanged or imprisoned and all gangs were ultimately broken up. The colonial community also paid a price with loss of life by soldiers, police and civilians. The superiority of the 'bush telegraph' and horsemanship declined with the advent of the electric telegraph and the railway and the year 1880 saw the demise of almost a century of bushranging.

Although bushrangers were a small minority of the population that settled in the eastern areas of Australia, estimated at possibly between three hundred and fifty to four hundred and sixty, and although they were of considerable nuisance to colonial society and administration, nevertheless they were a distinctively indigenous element of an emerging Australian society in the nineteenth century and have become part of its history as well as its legendary folklore.

Introduction

Callous Killers to Gentlemanly Wrongdoers

When Ned Kelly, Australia's most famous bushranger, was captured at Glenrowan in north-eastern Victoria on 29 June 1880, this self-confessed horse-thief and bank robber was destined to become a hero and part of an Australian legend.

In the dubious fashioning of national heroes which developed in the classical romantic fashion of the nineteenth and early twentieth century, many more heroic, less violent men such as early Australian explorers have taken second place to Ned Kelly. He has even become part of the Australian language, such phrases as 'as game as Ned Kelly', 'to walk out on his mates' and 'to be a nice kind of dingo' have entered into everyday life in Australia.

The demise of the 'bold' Kelly gang was the culmination of almost a century of bushranging which began with John 'Black' Caesar, a Negro born in Madagascar and transported from Kent to New South Wales for a minor crime. A 'First Fleeter' and an escapee, he took to the bush on 13 May 1789.

Unable to live off the land with the mastery and adaptability of the Aborigines, he took to prowling round settlements and stealing. Joined by other runaways in January 1796 he was declared an outlaw with a price of five gallons (twenty-three litres) of rum on his head and within a few weeks was shot dead by a settler who sought the reward.

Caesar was the first of a variety of characters, once officially estimated at possibly 350 and later as 456 men, who were classed as bushrangers. These characters ranged from prowlers in the bush stealing from settlements, to footpads, highwaymen, bank robbers, gold escort robbers and murderers.

Some were loners or operated in pairs, but the majority were in organised gangs ranging from three to fifteen members. One exception was the largest and earliest of them all in Van Diemen's Land led by escaped convict John Whitehead which reached over one hundred members. When he was killed in 1814, the gang was reorganised by Michael Howe and survived in reduced numbers till Howe also suffered the same fate in 1818. The gang had terrorised Van Diemen's Land for thirteen years and became so notorious that Governor Macquarie of New South Wales named Howe in official correspondence as 'the Chief of the Banditti of Bush Rangers in Van Diemen's Land' and Howe grandiloquently called himself 'Lieutenant-Governor of the Woods' and 'Governor of the Ranges'.

Most gangs of bushrangers were, however, small and many itinerants sporadically joined them for short periods. The activities of bushrangers reached peaks in different periods in each colony and a summary of bushrangers in each colony in the different eras is given in

Table 1 (page 11). In Van Diemen's Land the main activity took place between 1805 and 1842 when there appear to have been twenty definable gangs, and sixteen men who operated in pairs or as loners. In New South Wales there were thirty-four gangs between 1796 and 1879 as well as fifty-two men working in pairs or alone. In Victoria, Bushranging did not really begin until the 1840s. There were ten gangs and fifteen men acting in pairs or as loners between 1842 and 1880. In Norfolk Island there were two gangs prior to its occupation by the Pitcairners. In Queensland, South Australia and Western Australia there were only two loners in each colony.

Throughout the ninety-one years of bushranging in Australia, almost without exception, bushrangers were shot dead during confrontations with soldiers and the police or were hanged or imprisoned, and all gangs were ultimately broken up. The majority were in their twenties or under and only three of those shot dead or hanged had reached the age of thirty. With one exception they all died poor — 'Darkie' Gardiner was able to buy a saloon in San Francisco but died there in a brawl.

They varied from callous killers, rapists, or those whose use of guns inevitably resulted in fatalities, to those educated gentlemanly wrongdoers like Ben Hall and Andrew George Scott (Captain Moonlite) whose tragic careers ended inexorably in violent death or the rope.

The life of a bushranger was in fact, as Steve Hart said when he joined the Kelly gang, 'no life at all' and after the demise of the Kelly gang bushranging, defeated by the electric telegraph, the railway and developments in law and order, ceased to be popular.

There were three distinct eras of bushrangers in Australia. The first bushrangers were the 'convict-bolters', escapees from the penal system who plundered to survive from Aborigines and white settlers alike and who roamed about mainly in small gangs in New South Wales and Van Diemen's Land from 1789 until the 1840s.

In the second era were the Wild Colonial Boys, the Gold Rush or Gold Escort bushrangers who operated in Victoria in the 1850s and in New South Wales in the early 1860s.

The third era brought the 'new', native-born bushrangers, associated with cattle duffing, horse thieving and bank robberies from the 1860s to the 1880s in both New South Wales and Victoria, culminating in the end of bushranging with the Kelly gang.

'BUSHRANGER', AN AUSTRALIAN TERM

The term 'bushranger' is indigenous and distinctly Australian. The *Concise Oxford English Dictionary* defines 'the bush' as 'woodland' or 'untitled district especially in the colonies'; to 'take to the bush' is to 'become a bushranger'. A 'bushman' is defined as a 'dweller, farmer or traveller in the Australian bush.' Further, a 'bushranger' is defined as an 'Australian brigand (at first an escaped convict) living in the bush'.

In early official correspondence the word 'banditti' was frequently used especially for the early large band of bushrangers led by John Whitehead and Michael Howe, a 'banditti' being a 'gang of brigands'. A 'brigand' is defined as a 'bandit or robber', and a 'bandit' as 'an outlaw, a lawless robber or a brigand (usually in organised gangs).'

These terms are quite clearly related to the 'Australian brigand' or 'bushranger' but to Australians, bushranging has more connotations of skill in bushcraft, knowledge of the bush, horsemanship and the heroic romanticism of 'roaming the bush, free and bold' in defiance of authority and less emphasis on banditry, organised robbing, plundering and murder.

TABLE 1

NUMBER OF BUSHRANGERS IN THE THREE ERAS

	FIRST ERA Convict Bolters 1788-1840	SECOND ERA Wild Colonial Boys and Gold Rush Bushrangers 1850s	THIRD ERA New Native-Born Bushrangers 1860s-1880s	Total
New South Wales and Norfolk Island	14 Gangs (5 Pirate Gangs) 6 Pairs 5 Loners		20 Gangs 21 Pairs 20 Loners	34 Gangs 27 Pairs 25 Loners
Van Diemen's Land	20 Gangs (4 Pirate Gangs) 12 Pairs 4 Loners			20 Gangs 12 Pairs 4 Loners
Victoria		7 Gangs 8 Pairs 2 Loners	3 Gangs 1 Pair 4 Loners	10 Gangs 9 Pairs 6 Loners
Queensland		2 Loners		2 Loners
South Australia	1 Pair			1 Pair
Western Australia		1 Loner	1 Loner	2 Loners

The First Era-
Convict Bolters Escape from Misery

VAN DIEMEN'S LAND

Bushranging in Van Diemen's Land was almost entirely confined to 'convict bolters' as a result of the convict system and its geography, and the term was more commonly used there than in New South Wales.

Founded as a penal settlement in 1803, Van Diemen's Land remained the chief penal establishment of New South Wales until it became an independent colony in 1825. By 1820, out of a total population of 6,198, there were 3,477 convicts — over half the population. The military establishment was represented by one company of the 48th Regiment at Hobart Town and one at Port Dalrymple.

Convict bolters rarely tried to acquire the Aborigines' knowledge of how to live in the bush and instead took to plundering for survival. By 1832, of the one hundred and twelve who escaped from Macquarie Harbour Penal station, sixty-two had perished in the bush, nine had been cannibalised for food by their companions and the rest either were captured or had given themselves up voluntarily.

Within five years runaway convict bushrangers infested the settlement and a contemporary observed 'there was no species of outrage and atrocity in which these marauders did not indulge'[1] Their brutality in raiding Aboriginal tribes in pursuit of women quickly alienated the friendly Aborigines and had much to do with the ensuing conflict that saw the demise of the Tasmanian Aborigines. The convict bolters operated in gangs or pairs and occasionally as loners. A summary of the main convict bolters in Van Diemen's Land is given in Table 2 (page 13).

NEW SOUTH WALES

Bushranging flourished in New South Wales in all three eras from 1789 to the 1870s. However, the main peaks of intensity were the convict bolter era and the later vintage era of the new native-born bushrangers of the 1860s and 1870s. During the period of the Wild Colonial Boys and the Gold Rush bushrangers the main turbulence shifted to Victoria.

Although the gangs in New South Wales never reached the proportions of those in Van Diemen's Land, of the total number of bushrangers along the eastern seaboard of Australia, over half were in New South Wales.

The increase in the number of transported convicts, the harsh discipline and inefficiency of the penal system led to increased numbers of escapees which in turn created the need for more easily policed and more secure penal settlements. Settlements were made at Norfolk Island (1788-1813, and re-opened 1824-56) and Newcastle (1801-22), and at Macquarie Harbour and Port Arthur in Van Diemen's Land (1803). An abortive attempt was also made to establish a penal settlement at Sorrento, Port Phillip, in 1803. A summary of the main convict bolters in New South Wales is given in Table 3 (page 16).

NORFOLK ISLAND

At the Norfolk Island penal settlement the discipline and conditions were so harsh that death was frequently sought as a release from the misery. Many bushrangers from Van Diemen's Land as well as New South Wales were sent to the Island. In 1846 the unrest at the settlement culminated in a riot led by the bushranger William Westwood. Of the thirteen prisoners that were hanged after the riot was put down, the majority were bushrangers. Martin Cash, however, the notorious bushranger from Van Diemen's Land refused to take part in the riot.

TABLE 2

CONVICT BOLTERS IN VAN DIEMEN'S LAND

Gangs

1805

Escapees **Rush** and **Hunter** led gangs of up to 14 convict bolters.

The famine year. Convicts sent foraging for food did not return and turned 'banditti'.

Rush and Hunter killed by police. Hunter decapitated.

1805-14

The largest gang ever, over 100 convict bolters led by **John Whitehead** and later **Michael Howe.** It included **Edward Bageant, Charles** and **George Baxter, George Bould, Thomas Burrell, James Campbell, John Cresswell, James Dalton, John Davis, William Elliott, Moses Davis, Bartholemew Foley, Randel Fore, Richard Forrest, Morris Healey, John Lee, George Moore, John Ricketts, John Rose, William Russell, Thomas Starkey, Thomas Stewart,** and **William Taylor.**

An original forager, Whitehead raided native tribes for women for his banditti.

1813 bolters declared outlaws. Whitehead shot dead by soldiers 1814. Decapitated by Howe to avoid bounty payment.

1808

The **Watts, Brown** and **Lemon** gang.

Port Dalrymple bushrangers.

Watts and Brown Life sentences. Lemon decapitated for the bounty.

1810

Gang of bushrangers referred to by *Hobart Gazette.* Offer of rewards and indulgences to convicts for capture of bushrangers.

1813-17

Dalrymple Gang led by **Hector MacDonald.** Gang included **Peter Mills** (ex Deputy Surveyor), **George Williams** (ex Deputy Commissary), **Peter Geary** (military deserter), **Peter Sefton, John Jones, Richard Collyer, Thomas Cormes, Brown** or **Brune** (French), **John Smith, James Tull, Denis Currie** and **Matthew Keegan.**

MacDonald shot. Mills captured, discharged—lack of evidence. Williams flogged and imprisoned. Deary shot. Jones shot and decapitated. Holmes, Smith, Tull, Currie, Keegan, White, Johnson—all imprisoned.

1814-18

Michael Howe's Gang. Took over from **Whitehead** in reduced numbers. Ultimately only **Browne, Watts, Hillier, Currie** and **Keegan.**

Self-styled 'Governor of the Woods', officially named 'Chief of the Banditti'.

Howe shot 1818. Browne surrendered, Hillier killed in quarrel, others all captured.

1821

Twenty-six bushrangers sentenced to death, 10 executed at Hobart Town and another 9 at Port Dalrymple.

1822

Alexander (Cannibal) Pierce escaped from 'Hell's Gates' with 7 others: **Bob Greenhill, Matthew Travers, Thomas Bodenham, Bill Cornelius** or **Kennelly, James Brown, John Mathers** and **Alexander Dalton.**

Bushed on landing on the mainland and turned cannibal.

Dalton, Greenhill, Travers, Bodenham, Matthews, all murdered and eaten. Pierce joined Cheetham and Davis and all three imprisoned. Pierce escaped with Cox. Cox cannibalised. Pierce hanged 1826. Brown prison sentence. Cornelius died in hospital.

1822

Jeffries, Hopkins and **Russell.**

Bolted from Macquarie Harbour. Cannibalism and bushranging.

Russell shot and eaten. Jeffries and Hopkins captured by John Batman. Both hanged 1826.

1824-26

Matthew Brady's Gang. **Brady** with 14 other convicts escaped from Macquarie Harbour. **Patrick Connolly, James McCabe, James Bryant, John Burns, John Downs, James Crawford, John Griffiths, George Lacey, Jeremiah Ryan, John Thompson, Charles Rider, Isaac Walker, James Tierney, James Dunne.** The gang grew to 25, including **Jeffries** the cannibal.

Great Western Tiers hide-out. Raided Hobart, South Esk Valley, Launceston.

Dunne shot. Brady was captured by John Batman, (Cowan turned informer). McCabe and Brady executed with his gang, three by three 29 April 1826.

1825-26

Over 100 bushrangers hanged by Governor Arthur.

Mid-1820s

Gang of four, **Gregory, Hodgetts, McKenney** and **Tilley.**

Bushranged near Hobart.

All sentenced to death, 1826.

1837

Martin Cash & Co. Cash joined **Lawrence Kavanagh, Thomas Jones** and later added **James Dalton** and **John Liddell** to his gang. **Jones** also paired with **Moore.**

Mt Dromedary and New Norfolk.

Cash received death sentence but was reprieved and ultimately pardoned. Kavanagh life, but hanged for participating in Norfolk Island riot, 1846. Moore, Liddell, Dalton, life sentences; Jones hanged.

Martin Cash

1838

James Atterill, James Reegan, William Davis and **Anthony Banks.**

Bushranging round Richmond and Brown Mountains.

Atterill, Davis and Banks life sentences; Reegan hanged.

1839

The **'Boy Bandit' Rares**, aged 16, escapee from Point Peur, joined **Lawlor** and **Cowden.**

Robbery around Launceston.

Rares hanged at Launceston, 1839.

1841

James Bloomfield, Jonas Hopkins and **James McCallum.**

Robbery under arms, New Norfolk.

All received life sentences.

1842

George Griffiths, Thomas Hurn, William Lambeth, Samuel Harrison and **John Gunn.**

Bushranging and robbery under arms.

Death sentence commuted to life imprisonment for all.

1852-53

Maberly, Pickson and **Poulson.**

Robbery under arms in Sandy Bay area.

Life sentences.

Pairs

1822

Cheetham and **Davis.**

Sheepstealing before joining up with 'Cannibal' Pierce.

Life sentences.

1823

Musquito and **Black Jack.**

Bushranging and murder.

Both hanged in Hobart, 1825.

1842

Armytage and **Hogan.**

Robbery under arms.

Armytage disappeared, Hogan sentenced to Norfolk Island.

1843

John Conway and **Riley Jeffs.**

Bushranging, shot Constable Ward.

Both hanged.

1844

Michael Cogan and **Richard Gordon.**

Highway robbery around Hobart.

Both life sentences.

1846

'Dido' (William Timothy) and **Wilson.**

Robbery near Piper's River.

Caught and imprisoned.

1846

Henry Ford and **Henry Smart.**

Esk River district.

Life sentences.

1846

George Jamieson and **Jones.**
Tamar River district.
Life sentences.

1853

Moses Birkett and **Peter Perry.**
Near Lake Crescent. Murder.
Both hanged.

1853

Dalton and **Kelly.**
Campbelltown. Highway robbery.
Long sentence.

1853

John Price and **Tom Roberts.**
Highway robbery.
Life sentence.

1855

Peter Connolly and **John Whelan.**
Bushranging and murder.
Both hanged in Hobart.

Loners

1824

Broughton
Murder and cannibalism.
Captured by John Batman. Hanged 1824.

1842

George Cumsdon
Robbery under arms.
Hanged.

1846

Henry Jenkins alias **'Billy from the Den'.**
Highway robbery.
Life sentence, 1846.

1852

John Jones
Operated near Launceston.
Captured.

Note: There were only a few loners who were convict bolters turned bushrangers and those listed above were amongst the most notorious.

TABLE 3

CONVICT BOLTERS IN NEW SOUTH WALES

Gangs

1789

John Caesar, First Fleeter, escaped to the bush 13 May, and joined by 6 or 7 other bolters formed the first gang.

Operated near Sydney. Outlawed in 1796.

Shot dead 14 February 1796 at Liberty Plains.

1816

Raid on Women's Prison at Parramatta by bushrangers seeking mistresses.

1816-23

Three assigned servants with spurious names of English statesmen, **Edmund Burke, Charles Fox, William Pitt.**

Highway robbery.

All hanged at Parramatta, 1823.

1822

Governor Macquarie hanged 34 bushrangers within 12 months.

1820-32

The Underwood Gang. **William Underwood, John Donahoe, George Kilroy, William Smith, John Walmsey, John Webber** and others.

The Nepean, Hawkesbury and Parramatta districts with Burragong as their headquarters.

Donohoe and Webber shot by police 1830. Underwood shot 1832. Walmsley turned informer, Smith and Kilroy hanged 1832.

1833

Six Maitland prison rioters escaped and became bushrangers.

Five hanged, the other sent to Norfolk Island.

1833

James Ryan, John Poole, James Riley, Anthony Hitchcock, Sam Parrot and **David Jones.**

Hunter River District.

Jones, life sentence at Norfolk Island. The other five hanged.

1834

Emmanuel Brace, John Jenkins, Thomas Tatterdale.

Robbery under arms, murder of Dr R. Wardell.

Brace turned informer. Jenkins and Tatterdale hanged.

1834

The Monaro Plains Gang. **Arthur Keys, Boyd** and **Bull.**

Monaro Plains. Robbery under arms, wounding with intent.

Boyd shot dead by police, Bull and Keys hanged.

1838-41

The 'Jewboy Gang'. **Edward 'Jewboy' Davis, James Bryant, Robert Chitty, James Everett, John Shea, John Marshall, Richard Glanvill** and **Thomas Maguire.**

New England, Liverpool Ranges.

All hanged, 16 March 1841.

1838

Hall, Mayne, Maynard and **Welsh.**

Robbery under arms, murder, around Yass.

All hanged for murder, 1838.

1842

John McCann, William Lynch and **James O'Donnell.**

Bushranging around Liverpool.

All received life sentences.

Pairs

1840-41

Scotchie and **Whitton.**

Operated around the Lachlan River area.

Two of the few to retire into obscurity.

1841

Henry Steele and **Charles Vaut** (assigned servants).

Armed robbery.

Life sentence on Norfolk Island.

1841

James Berry and **Paddy Curran.**

Bushranging and murder of Constable Maguire. Curran was also associated with William Westwood in 1840.

Berry hanged. Curran hanged for rape as well as murder.

1842

John Morgan and **John Wilkinson.**

Berrima area, armed robbery.

Life sentences.

1844-45

Nowlan Cashan and **McIntyre.**
Robbery under arms, and mail hold-ups.
Both sentenced to death.

1846

John, Booth, an accomplice of **William Westwood.**
Murder of Constable John Morris.
Both hanged 1846, Westwood, both for this murder and murder in the Norfolk Island riot of 1846.

Loners

1833-34

Jack the Rammer.
Monaro Plains. Was also associated with Keys and Boyd.
Shot dead by his intended victim.

1836

William Hutchinson
Escapee turned bushranging.
Recaptured 1840.

1838-46

William (Jacky Jacky) Westwood
Robbery under arms. Rode with Paddy Curran whom he sacked as a rapist.
Life sentence. Gaol breaks at Darlinghurst Gaol, Cockatoo Island, Port Arthur and a fatal one at Norfolk Island. Hanged 1846.

1841

Thomas Willmore
Highway robbery and 2 murders.
Hanged 1841.

1842

John Lynch (alias **Dunleavy**)
Confessed to 10 lurid murders.
Hanged 1842.

Bolters Turn to Piracy

As most of the early penal settlements were on the coast and surrounded by harsh bushland where bolters found it hard to survive, it was inevitable that some managed to escape by sea and took to piracy. The main occurrences in Van Diemen's Land and New South Wales are given in Table 4 (this page).

TABLE 4

BUSHRANGER PIRATES IN NEW SOUTH WALES AND VAN DIEMEN'S LAND

Van Diemen's Land

1806

Venus

Seized at Hobart by convict bolters.

Seen in New Zealand waters, fate unknown.

1829

Cyprus

Carrying 33 convicts, seized at Research Bay by 15 mutineers. Crew and rest put ashore.

Four of the fifteen reached London. George Davis (alias Huntley), William Watts (alias Williams), Alex. Stevenson (alias Telford), John Beveridge (alias Anderson), all received the death sentence. Swallow (alias Waldron) returned to Van Diemen's Land to finish his sentence.

1840

Schooner *Edward*

Six bushrangers attempted seizure.

All captured.

1840

Schooner *Waterwitch*

Seized by three bushrangers.

Amicably put ashore at Sealer's Cove.

New South Wales

1808

Brig *Harrington*

Seized in Sydney Cove.

Captured in Indian Ocean.

1814

Argo

Seized by bushrangers.

Recaptured near New Zealand.

1820s

Brig *Wellington*

Bound for Norfolk Island, seized by 60 convicts.

Ringleaders hanged in Sydney, rest sent to Norfolk Island.

1842

Brig *Governor Phillip*

Seized at Norfolk Island. Six convicts charged with piracy and intent to murder Sgt Whitehead.

Henry Sears hanged. Life sentences to Thomas Whelan, John Jones, George Beavors, Nicholas Lewis and James Woolf.

1853

Lord Auckland

Seized by eight convicts at Norfolk Island, sailed to Queensland. Captured near Brisbane after bush-ranging the coastal areas.

Fifteen years each for Denis Griffiths, James Clegg, Thomas Clayton, Robert Mitchell, Joseph Davis, Patrick Cooper, Jeremiah O'Sullivan and John Naisk.

The Second Era–
Gold Fields Produce Armed Stick-ups

In Victoria there were two peaks of intense activity of bushrangers: Wild Colonial Boys and the Gold Rush bushrangers between 1852 and 1854, and the new 'native-born' bushrangers during the 1870s.

Hold-ups and robberies began in 1842 with 'Yankie Jack' Ellis and his gang. Separation from New South Wales in 1850 and a sudden ten-fold increase in population with the gold rush, brought a new vigour and a new vulgarity to the colony. These elements coupled with development of self government and acquisition of landholdings influenced the character of bushranging, which was also given impetus with an inflow of 'Vandemonians', ex-convicts from Tasmania, during the early days of the gold rush.

These bushrangers were characteristically linked with gold fields, gold escorts and bank robberies, with horse thieving for mobility as well as 'flashness', cattle duffing, highway stick-ups and the inevitable fatalities that followed from armed stick-ups, no matter how heroic their motives may have been. A summary of the main bushrangers and their operations in Victoria during this period is given in Table 5 (this page).

TABLE 5
WILD COLONIAL BOYS AND GOLD RUSH BUSHRANGERS IN VICTORIA

Gangs

1842

John Ellis (Yankie Jack), 'Vandie' Jepps, Young Fogarty and **Jack Williams.**

Hold-ups and robberies in Dandenong Hills near Melbourne.

Captured by police and volunteers. As a volunteer, Fowler, was killed, all were hanged for murder, 1842.

1852

The Keilor Plains Gang. **James Duncan, John James** and **James Morgan.**

Operating in the Black Forest they raided the ship *Nelson* for gold 8,183 ounces (230kg) worth £25,000.

Fifteen years each, the first three in irons.

1852

The Eureka Gang. **John Donovan, John Finegan, John Baylie, Henry Johnston** and **Charles Bowe.**

Highway robbery on Melbourne-Bendigo gold fields road. Captured at Bunninyong gold field.

Donovan 15 years, Finegan 12 years, Baylie, Johnston and Bowe, 6 years.

1853

George Melville, William Atkins, George Wilson and **John** and **Jeremiah Murphy.**

Ambushed McIvor to Kyneton Gold Escort. Driver killed, three troopers wounded.

Melville, Atkins, and Wilson hanged 1853. John Murphy suicided and Jeremiah escaped to Queensland and informed.

1853

William Young, William Simpson, William Rogers, Thomas Stroud and **William Layworth.**

Highway robbery round Melbourne, raided ship *Strathedon* for £100,000 in unsigned bank notes.

Caught cashing cheques. Layworth informed, the rest received long sentences.

1854

Thomas Quinn, John Boulton, Henry Marriott and **Henry Garrett.**

Robbery, Bank of Victoria, Bakery Hill, Ballarat £14,300 and 350 ounces (10kg) of gold.

Quinn informed, Boulton, Marriott and Garrett, 10 years. Garrett escaped to London but was extradited.

1857

Fifteen bushranger prisoners mutinied at Williamstown quarry.

Inspector-General of Police, John Price murdered.

John Young, John Smith, James Anderson, Daniel Donovan, John Chesley, Francis Brannigan, William Brown, Richard Bryant, Thomas Maloney, Henry Smith, Thomas Williams, hanged. James Kelly, William Jones, Richard Jones, and John Williams acquitted.

1851

Owen Suffolk and **Christopher Farrell.**

Highway robbery Geelong-Portland road.

Ten years each.

1852

Richard Bryant and **William Mack.**

Minor robbery under arms.

Twelve years each.

1852

Frank McCallum (alias **Captain Melville**) and **William Roberts.**

Ballarat gold fields, highway robbery Ballarat and Geelong roads.

McCallum cumulative sentences of 32 years. Convicted of murder of warder on hulk Success. Found dead in cell at Pentridge. Roberts sentenced to 12 years.

Frank McCallum
(alias Captain Melville)

1853

Connor and **Brady.**

Two escapees from Tasmania, murdered farmer at Kilmore. In one week three other murders.

Both hanged.

1853

William Bryan and **John Douglass.**

Highway robbery, Muddy Creek, Geelong-Ballarat road.

Five years each.

1853

William Edwards and **James Hammond.**

St Kilda Road, Emerald Hill (South Melbourne).

Ten years each.

1853

Alfred Barrow and **William Garroway.**

Highway robbery Ballarat district.

Both gaoled.

1853

Chris. Goodison and **Alfred Stallard.**

Highway robbery Bendigo road to goldfields.

Both gaoled.

Loners

George Ellison

Robbed a digger in Melbourne.

Gaoled.

1855-69

Harry Power

Wounded a policeman when questioned on horse stealing 1869. Highway robbery.

Sentenced to 14 years, escaped. Sentenced to another 15 years, on 4 counts of highway robbery. Drowned in Murray River, 1891.

Harry Power

The Third Era–
The Rise and Fall of Bushranging in the 1860's and 70's

NEW SOUTH WALES — THE CLASSICAL 'GENTLEMAN' BUSHRANGERS

The 1860s and 1870s saw the most intense period of bushranging in Australia. Although the 'gentleman' bushrangers Frank Gardiner, Johnny Gilbert and Ben Hall of the classical 'vintage' bushranging gangs, have been overshadowed by the stark fascination and notoriety of the Kelly gang, in New South Wales during the five years from 1862 to 1867 twenty-three bushrangers were either killed or hanged, twenty police and civilians were killed by bushrangers and almost twenty police were wounded.

During the 1850s there had been a lull in New South Wales as the colony was busy with economic and pastoral development and a three-fold increase in population, but in 1860 news of fresh gold strikes in New South Wales attracted thousands of diggers across the border from Victoria.

In the quest for gold and adventure were many who turned to bushranging. These new bushrangers were usually either native born or sons of immigrants. They were not convict bolters driven by desperation or ignorance, but were driven by a restless inability to settle down to the frustrations of a harsh environment and were enticed by the lure of easy riches and adventure in the bush.

Cattle duffing and horse stealing became almost a common trademark of adventurous young bush labourers and were often the first steps to highway and bank robbery and outlawry. They became romanticised as independent, bold and free, and stirring tales of stick-ups, racing horses and secret hide-outs are still a source of idealism in Australian literature. The main gangs, pairs and loners of the vintage era who operated in New South Wales are summarised in Table 6 (page 26).

VICTORIA — NED KELLY AND HIS IRISH SYMPATHISERS

It is ironic that the colony of Victoria at the height of its traditional rivalry with New South Wales should have become universally famous as the epic bushranging colony around which the quintessence of folklore has centred, when during the entire bushranging era, New South Wales had three times as many bushrangers.

This is undoubtedly due to the mystique surrounding Ned Kelly and his gang of three whose activities only lasted just over two years. Bushranging in Australia culminated in the classic shoot-out of Kelly with the police which became well known throughout the world and has become immortalised in classical romantic folklore in books, films, paintings, ballets and rock operas.

Nevertheless, the development of communications, the electric telegraph and the railway, inexorably destroyed the supremacy of both the bush telegraph and the stolen, well-bred, sure-footed horse that enabled the bushranger to elude and mock the mounted troopers. Together with a centralised police force they saw the end of the bushrangers.

During the 1860s bushrangers of the new breed were relatively quiescent in Victoria compared with the activity in New South Wales, and there was only one small gang. However, loners such as Harry Power and Dan Morgan became notorious and in north-eastern Victoria, a feud between the Quinn, Kelly and Lloyd families and the police was smouldering. Cattle duffing and horse stealing flourished.

In the north-east, the Kellys were part of a close-knit clan of Irish kinship with problems of land settlement. There was an inherited Irish frustration of tilling a hard soil with limited horizons of fine horses and small holdings rather than large sheep runs of the pastoral economy that the geographical environment dictated.

It is not without significance that a Royal Commission was appointed in 1879, the year of the Jerilderie Bank hold-up by the Kellys, to inquire into the progress of land settlement under the *Victoria Land Act* of 1869. The Commission revealed a sad story of selectors beaten by ignorance and poverty, and of men attempting to eke out a miserable existence on small blocks a third of the size necessary for an economic holding. To this were added the uncertainties of climate — drought or flood could ruin a man in one season. The same applied to New South Wales where in 1883 a report stated 'the social effect of the system has been to bring into the country many of the poor and unthrifty who must inevitably be a burden on the community'.

The forces of adversity and kinship of outlook and blood developed a population of closely knit sympathisers who had links with cattle and horse stealing in an area in which it was difficult to enforce law and order.

The second period of intense activity in Victorian bushranging began with the hunt for Edward Kelly in late 1878. Early in 1879 Captain Moonlite (Andrew Scott), freed from prison, raised his gang of young desperadoes and the violent Kelly period burst with many passions and sympathisers from a ground swell of hard-core Irish clanship. This was coupled with an increasingly mature, humanitarian public opinion towards capital punishment and the severity of long penal sentences for young offenders.

Apart from the Kelly gang there were only two other discernible gangs and a few other bushrangers in this period in Victoria (see Table 7 (page 31).

The Romantic Outlook Brings Heroism to Bushranging

The nineteenth century revolt against traditional imperial systems took two related forms: romanticism and nationalism. Romanticism admired strong, bold passions, irrespective of social consequences, and this can be seen in the psychology of nineteenth century Australian bushrangers and the folklore that has grown up about them. The establishment in 1880 of the *Bulletin* with its bush school of writers reflected the growing feelings of Australian nationalism.

The twentieth century philosopher, Bertrand Russell drew attention to the divisiveness in the aim of Romanticism 'of freeing man from social convention and morality'[2]. 'Its elements of resentment, hate, jealousy, remorse, despair, outraged pride, the fury of the oppressed and martial ardour'[3] are evident in the story of the Australian bushrangers and their sympathisers.

The penal system, squatting, gold rushes and intoxicating new liberty, land selectors and tales of bushrangers, oral and written, provided prolific material for some Australian writers adopting the conventions of early Victorian Romantic literature.

The first pamphlet published in Van Diemen's Land in 1818 was a romanticised life of *Michael Howe, Bushranger* and in 1844, James Tucker mingled fact and fiction with episodes featuring bushrangers and Aborigines in *The Adventures of Ralph Rashleigh, a Penal Exile in Australia, 1825-44* and in 1870 J. L. Burke romanticised the life of Martin Cash.

In 1874, many years after transportation had ceased, Marcus Clarke published *For The Term of His Natural Life.* Using official documents to study the inhumanity possible where authority is unchecked, he wrote a bloodcurdling Romantic-style ironic melodrama. His semi-moronic Gabbett is based on Alexander Pierce, the cannibal escapee, and it is conjectured his Maurice Freers was based on 'Bloody Tyrant Price' an Inspector General of Prisons murdered in 1857 by convict bushrangers who remembered him from Norfolk Island and Port Arthur days.

The early reactions of first settlers to a harsh, alien and melancholy bush were reflected in Marcus Clarke, and early pioneers yearned for the beauties of the 'Old Country'. It was not till the 1860s and 1870s that idealisers of the Australian landscape revealed its beauties and crystallised a love of the country and a feeling of patriotism; in literature Henry Kingsley and Adam Lindsay Gordon's rhythms of galloping hooves and Lawson's gospel of bush mateship; in painting Tom Roberts' life on stations and shearing sheds and mail hold-ups by bushrangers, Streeton's blue distances of the purple noon's transparent light and Heysen's intimate foreground beauty of that most constant feature of the bush, the gum tree.

Although Henry Kingsley was only in Australia for five years from 1853-58, he was on the goldfields, worked on a sheep station and with the police, and in his novel *Geoffrey Hamlyn* there is an appreciation of the honesty and independence essential to 'mates' in the bush.

Thomas Alexander Browne (Rolf Boldrewood) lived on the land till 1869, became a police magistrate and a goldfields' warden and having met Henry Kingsley similarly became a chronicler of squatters. His admiration for Sir Walter Scott, a master storyteller and a great figure of the English Romantic movement, was such that he took his pen-name from Scott's *Marmion* and imitated his romantic style. His mining, bushranging and pastoral novels use incidents from records, legends and personal experiences.

Influenced by the mythical Captain Starlight of Henry Kingsley's galloping bush writings, he wrote of the idealised bushranger and of the hardy Australian bushman gradually slipping into wrongdoing by a combination of circum-

Bailed Up, the famous painting by Tom Roberts inspired by the Eugowra Rocks Robbery.
Courtesy Art Gallery New South Wales.

stances and his own weakness. In *Robbery Under Arms,* serialised in 1882, two years after Ned Kelly's execution, Starlight, a gentleman bushranger, joins Dick and Jim, boys led astray by their convict father on a cattle-duffing scheme. They are regretful and self-reproachful and it is only circumstances that force these daring bushrangers to act as they do. Starlight enjoys the kind of reputation of Ben Hall and his gang in the Weddin Mountains and a siege of Knightley's house is based on the attack by Ben Hall on Assistant Gold Commissioner Kneightley's house.

Browne himself reflects the divisiveness of the Romantic; on the one hand, there is a certain respect for the Australian as a manly, heroic bushman and on the other, he is aristocratic in outlook wishing to perpetuate English class distinctions in Australia. *Robbery Under Arms* has as much English as Australian sentiment and Starlight is always the gentleman even if down and out.

In *Nevermore,* the Lawless family are persecuted by police and Ned Lawless is modelled on Ned Kelly and Kate Lawless on Kate Kelly. Browne himself was bailed up by 'Bluecap' Cotterall near Wagga Wagga and Redcap (Bluecap) appears in *Ups and Downs.* In the *Sphinx of Eaglehawk* a barmaid is kidnapped by bushrangers who are caught by local vigilantes.

The *Bulletin* was established in 1880, the year of Kelly's execution. It stimulated an aggressively Australian spirit. Henry Lawson, Joseph Furphy and Banjo Paterson delighted in bush characters and eulogised the bush, the galloping hooves and the pioneering spirit.

Bushrangers became linked with tales of rollicking highwaymen either alternately gallant or remorseful or sometimes both, or just heroically defiant over the life which circumstance had forced them to follow.

Australian artist Tom Roberts painted *Bailed Up* in the 1890s, a famous picture inspired by the Eugowra Rocks robbery by the Gardiner gang and painted near the actual site. In heroic vein it depicts a coach held up by bushrangers in the halcyon bush landscape of the nineteenth century.

Roberts was one of the Heidelberg set, a quartet with Streeton, McCubbin and Condor of Romantic Impressionists who created the first distinctive school of Australian painting. Their object was to express the true character of Australia by painting in the open air and to interpret the magnitude of the scene, its age, remoteness and its contrasting strong light and shadow.

The romanticism of coach and horses and daring bushrangers were part of Roberts' vivid canvases just as bustling shearing sheds and Streeton's landscapes with the blue distant haze added to the love of the bush and patriotism.

The writers and painters of the nineteenth century depicted elements of the emerging Australian society, of which a distinctively indigenous one was bushranging, and interpreted Australians to themselves. The twentieth century painting of Ned Kelly by Sydney Nolan crystallises Kelly as heroically defiant.

More perceptively, however, Bertrand Russell wrote 'the type of man encouraged by romanticism is anti-social and violent; either a conquering tyrant or an anarchic rebel'[4]. It is not insignificant that bushranger Darkie Gardiner carried a tattered volume of the poems of that great Romantic poet Byron on his adventurous raids in some vague affinity with Byron's 'noble pirates'.

Other aspects of the Romantic outlook can be seen in the philosophy of the bushrangers. Wrote Russell 'the poor were supposed to possess more virtue than the rich' and they 'always had a few paternal acres and lived on the produce of their own labour without the need of external commerce. True they were

always losing the acres in pathetic circumstances'[5]. Many bushrangers had an affinity with small selectors and their most frequent targets were rich squatters and big landholders. Furthermore, to the anarchic rebel 'truth is what *he* posits, duty what *he* commands'. This attitude so clearly stated in Russell's phrase could almost be straight out of Ned Kelly's Jerilderie, Cameron, and other letters. He believes that there is no other truth but his and his Jerilderie letter concludes 'I am a widow's son outlawed and my orders *must be obeyed*'.

Russell pointed out 'Romantics did not aim at peace and quiet but a passionate individual life'[7] and this the bushrangers restlessly sought irrespective of any cost to the society around them. The impact of the railway, the telegraph and increasing commerce and industrialism also brought a romantic nostalgia for the vanishing era of bold raids, escapes and chases on horseback.

In politics, Romanticism is closely allied to nationalism and the 'Bushman's Bible', the *Bulletin,* stood for the poor against the privileged — labour against capital. Republican and anti-British, in its first edition it carried eight thousand words on bushrangers Scott and Rogan in mockery of capital punishment, and included a passionate mixture of local history.

The perpetuation of bushranging folk lore in literature, balladry and painting had much to do with the Romantic revolt of the nineteenth century and the ghost of the ethic of Rousseau, the philosopher of the French Revolution from which it sprang. It may explain, in part, why the Ned Kelly saga is still legendary and emotive.

Although bushrangers were a small minority of the population that settled on the eastern seaboard of Australia during the late eighteenth and nineteenth centuries, apart from being source material for Romantic writers and Impressionist painters, they were also a considerable danger and 'nuisance' cost to society and the colonial administrators.

Their origins are inextricably linked with the major influences and events of early Australian history, the criminal laws in England the convict system, the early administration of the penal settlements under naval and military authority, the colonial gold rushes and problems of land settlement in Victoria and New South Wales.

TABLE 6

NEW NATIVE-BORN BUSHRANGERS IN NEW SOUTH WALES

Gangs

1861

Henry Keene, William Watson and **Michael Lawler.**

Billabong. Shot a station hand.

Keene hanged. Watson and Lawler, 15 years.

1862

The Three Jacks. **Jack Connors, Jack McGuiness** and **Jack Davis.**

Forbes area.

Connors, death sentence. McGuiness shot by police tracker. Davis, death sentence, commuted to life.

1862-64

The Frank Gardiner Gang. **Daniel Charters, John Bow, Henry Manns, Alexander Fordyce, Johnny Gilbert, Johnny O'Meally, Ben Hall, Patrick Daly** and **John Piesley.**

Burrangong District, Eugowra Gold Escort, £14,000 gold and banknotes.

Gardiner, two 10 year and one 12 year sentence, cumulative, 32 years. Pardoned after 10 years. Manns, hanged. Fordyce and Brown, death sentence, commuted to life, served 12 years. Daly, 15 years, Gilbert, shot dead by police, also later both Hall and O'Meally. Charters turned informer. Piesley hanged, 1862.

Frank Gardiner

1862

The Gilbert Gang became Gilbert and Hall then the Ben Hall Gang 1863-65. **Ben Hall, Johnny Gilbert, Johnny O'Meally, James Mount, John Dunleavy, Jim Gordon, John Vane, Michael Burke** and **Johnny Dunn.**

Emu Flat, Gundagai, Binalong, Binda, Collector, Araleun etc.

Hall shot dead, 1865. Gilbert shot dead, 1865. O'Meally shot dead, 1864. Mount, 10 years, Dunleavy, death sentence, Gordon, death sentence. Vane surrendered, 15 years, Burke shot dead, 1863. Dunn, hanged, 1866.

John Gilbert

Ben Hall

1862

Charles MacKay, James MacKay and **George Williams.**

Lithgow, Blue Mountains, highway robbery.

The MacKays 15 years each, Williams 10 years.

1862

William MacKie, John MacMahon and **Charles Ross.**

Held up the Northern Mail.

MacKie and MacMahon, 7 years, Ross, 5 years. Charles Ross was later hanged with his brother Alexander (1863) for murder of storekeeper.

1862

Robert Smith, Aaron von Ehrstein and **Michael Davis.**

Armed highway robbery.

Smith and Ehrstein 10 years. Davis, death sentence commuted to life.

1862

The French Gang. **Louis Deuchef, Auguste Rivet** and **Charles Robardi.**

Mail coach stick-up. Driver killed.

Rivet life sentence. Robardi hanged, 1863. Deuchef, captured 1868, death sentence.

1862-3

William O'Connor, Charles and **Alexander Ross.**

Fish River. Robbery under arms, murder.

O'Connor, death sentence, 1863. Ross brothers both hanged, 1863.

Frederick Ward
(Captain Thunderbolt)

1863-70

Frederick Ward (Captain Thunderbolt), **William Monckton** and **John Thompson** (aged 16).

Highway robbery, horse stealing.

Ward shot dead by Constable Walker 1870. Thompson shot dead 1865. Monckton 3 years.

1863-64

James Crookwell, George Lynham, Michael Seary, John Southgate and **Dan Matthews.**

Goulburn area, often operated in pairs.

Crookwell, 15 years, but death sentence after Bargo Brush mutiny. Lynham, Seary, Southgate, Matthews all 15 years.

1865

The Clarke Gang. **John Clarke, Thomas Clarke, James Clarke, William Fletcher, Tom Connell** and **Patrick Connell.**

Southern New South Wales.

John and Thomas hanged, 1867. James, 7 years. Fletcher shot dead. Tom Connell sentenced to death, commuted to life imprisonment. Patrick Connell shot dead by police.

The Clarke Brothers

1865

Sullivan Gang. **Daniel Sullivan, Joe Clarke** and **Amos Donnelly.**

Central New South Wales, Orange.

Sullivan and Clarke, 10 years. Donnelly shot by police.

1866

Patrick Fitzgerald and **Edward Kelly** (no relation to Ned).
Castlereagh River area.
Fifteen years each.

1866

John and **Larry Cummings.**
Horse stealing and robbery, Abercrombie area.
John accidentally shot dead by Larry in rescue bid. Larry gaoled, pardoned 1874.

1866

Patrick Foran and **James Kelly.**
Lambing Flat area.
Ten years each.

Daniel Moran
(alias Morgan)

1867

John Egan and **Patrick Ryan**.
Orange district, robbing teamsters.
Fifteen years each.

1867

John Kerr and **John Shepherd**.
Cowra roads, Emu Creek.
Ten years each.

1867

H. Moran and **Tom Smith**.
Western district.
Seventeen years each.

1868

John Baker and **William Bertram**.
Mount Murchison and Barrier Ranges. Murder and robbery.
Baker hanged 1869, Bertram extradited from South Australia, hanged 1871.

1868

Charles Johnson and **William Miller**.
Mudgee district.
Gaoled.

1869

John Bollard and **Joseph Horne**.
Bank Robbery, Australian Joint Stock Bank, Braidwood.
Ten years each.

Loners

1860-5

James Boyd
Horse stealing and hold up of Singleton mail coach.
Five years, 1860, and later another 9 years.

1861

Benjamin Allerton
Billabong. Robbery and murder.
Hanged at Goulburn, 1862.

1862

George Williams
Cowra mail robbery.
Ten years.

1862

John Paisley
Bush telegraph, murder during hotel quarrel.
Hanged, Bathurst 1862.

1862

Jack Bullfrog
Murder.
Hanged, Bathurst 1862.

1863

Frank Stanley
Goulburn district.
Twelve years.

1865

Richard Middleton, John Wilson and **Thomas Tracey**

Forbes area.

All imprisoned.

1866

James Booth, Thomas Hampton and **William Willis**

Campbelltown and Muswellbrook mail

Booth and Hampton 8 years. Willis, 10 years.

1866

Bargo Brush Mutiny. **James Crookwell, William Bland, William Lee, Thomas Berryman, John Ovens** and **Michael Slattery.**

During the transfer of bushranger prisoners from Berrima prison to Sydney, Constable Raymond shot dead.

All sentenced to death.

1867

James Baldwin, Henry Brown, Charles Gough and **Thomas Cunningham.**

Highway robbery.

15 years each.

1867

William Brookman, John Williams, Edward Kelly (no relation to Ned) and **John Payne.**

Stuck up race meeting at Willandra. Constable McNamara wounded.

Death sentence commuted to life. All pardoned 1874.

1879

Thomas Gorman, Bill Kaye, Charles Jones and **'Hoppy' Bill Hobbs.**

From brumby catching to bushranging round Murrumbidgee district.

All death sentences, commuted to life.

Pairs

1855-60

Thomas and **Henry Dargue**

Robbery under arms.

Both received 14 years, 1860; pardoned 1867.

1862

John Brownlow and **Charles Foley**

Abercrombie district.

Seven years each.

1862

Frederick Britton and **George Willison**

Bathurst mail coach robbery.

Ten years each.

1863

John Foley and **Frederick Lowry**

Hold up Fish Creek race meeting (New Year's Day).

Foley, 15 years. Lowry escaped, later shot by police.

1863

George Bermingham and **William Dunne**

Robbery, Cooma mail.

Ten years each.

1863

German Bill and **Dan Morgan**

North of Wagga Wagga.

German Bill shot dead by police, Morgan later shot by a station hand.

1864

Jim Hill and **Jim Jones**

Twofold Bay.

Fifteen years each.

1864

John Taylor and **Thomas Webb**

Abercrombie district, raided Chinese camp.

Two years each.

1864

Charles Jones and **Frank Stanley.**

Goulburn area.

Twelve years each.

1865

Robert Johnstone and **William MacKie.**

Northern Mail coach hold up.

Gaol.

1865

Charles Stanmore and **Jimmy Boyd.**

Walgett mail stick-up.

Twelve years each.

1866

Charles Rutherford and **William MacKie.**

Robbery under arms.

Rutherford, 7 years, escaped and shot by civilian at Cannonbar, Mackie gaoled.

1863

Francis Foley
Campbells River, Chines gold camp stick-up.
Ten years.

1864

Johnny Foster
Mail coach stick-ups. Sydney-Bathurst, Orange-Wellington.
Ten years.

1864

Harry Wilson
Culgoa. Murder.
Hanged, 1864.

1865

Dan Shea
Central New South Wales. Horse stealing.
Eight years.

1866

Samuel Clarke
Robbery under arms.
Five years.

1866

James Kennedy
Highway robbery.
Fifteen years.

1866

John Weekes
Murder at Grenfell.
Hanged, Bathurst, 1866.

1866

James Smith
Horse stealing and robbery.
Seventeen years, 1867; released after 7 years, (1874).

1867

'Blue Cap' Robert Cotterall
Highway robbery.
Ten years, 1867; released after 7 years (1874).

1867

William Johnson
Goulburn area. Robbery under arms.
2 years.

1867

John Foran
Bathurst district.
15 years. Released after 6½ years (1874).

1867

John Kelly
Wellington. Highway robbery.
14 years.

1867

Walter Maher
Southern district.
10 years.

1867

John Miles
Orange district. Stick-up at Chinese gold camp Mookerawa.
10 years.

TABLE 7

NEW NATIVE-BORN BUSHRANGERS IN VICTORIA

Gangs

1862

James Regent and two accomplices.

Robbed Traveller's Rest Hotel at Yall-y-poora.

Sentenced to gaol at Ararat.

1869-79

Andrew G. Scott (Captain Moonlite).

Robbed London Chartered Bank, Mount Egerton. Led escape from Ballarat Gaol, recaptured.

Ten years.

In 1879 Scott recruited a gang of **Thomas Rogan, James Nesbit, Gus. Wernick, Graham Bennett** and **Tom Williams**.

Raid on Wantabadgery station. Gun battle with 9 police at McGlede's property. Constable Bowen shot dead.

Scott and Rogan hanged. Nesbitt shot dead. Wernick died of wounds. Bennett and Williams, death sentences, commuted to life.

Andrew G. Scott
(Captain Moonlite)

1878-1880

The Kelly Gang. **Edward Kelly, Daniel Kelly, Steve Hart, Joe Byrne.**

Sergeant Kennedy, Constable Lonigan and Scanlan shot dead at Stringybark Creek, 27 October 1878.

Euroa Bank hold-up, 9 December 1878, Jerilderie Bank hold-up 10 February 1879. Murder of Sherritt and Glenrowan gun battle, June 1880.

Edward Kelly hanged, November 1880, Hart shot dead at Glenrowan June 1880, Daniel Kelly and Joe Byrne shot dead at Glenrowan, possible suicide.

Ned Kelly

Pairs

Robert Shanks, James Sharks.

Held up Australasian Bank at Moe.

Captured at Trafalgar Railway Station. Convicted.

Loners

1854-65

Daniel Moran (alias **Morgan**).

Armed robbery, Castlemaine Goldfields.

1854 Sentenced as John Smith. Released 1860.

Bushranging near Wagga Wagga, NSW, shot two police, one civilian.

Killed by station hand Peechelba station Victoria, 1865.

1864-68

Robert Bourke

Horse stealing. In 1868 he robbed between Wondonga and Wangaratta, murdered Station owner's son, Diamond Creek, near Melbourne.

Sentenced 3 years 1864. Hanged 1868.

1870

Patrik Stanton (alias **Jack Muck**).

Attempted stick-up Rutherglen.

Gaoled 1870.

The First Era

The celebrated pickpocket and thief Jack Shepherd.

English Highwaymen, Precursors of Australian Bushrangers

The cradle of Australia's first settlers and of its brigands and banditti was eighteenth century England. The English love of liberty and suspicion of police forces as instruments of political oppression, particularly the police force of France, had resulted in professional law and order enforcement being almost two centuries behind other European countries.

Many foreign observers admired individual and political liberty in England and one of them, de Saussare, asserted 'they value this gift more than all the joys of life and would sacrifice everything to retain it'[1]. Another foreign observer, Du Muralt, thought that this liberty 'is the source of the many extraordinary characters among them, *Heroes in Evil as well as Good*'[2]. Based on the doctrine of the sanctity of the individual, the English ideal was individual freedom within a disciplined structure to be achieved by the supremacy of law, an enforceable contract based on assent freely given.

When the word 'police' was introduced in the eighteenth century it was viewed with suspicion as an omen of the sinister force in France where supervision, spying, files, dossiers and arbitrary powers of detention were used to mould opinions and for political offences. They did not accept one Frenchman's view 'that its only object consists in conducting mankind to the most perfect happiness that may be enjoyed in this life'[3].

The English system of law enforcement depended upon Parish Constables and Justices. It worked reasonably well while England was mainly rural, but the growth of population, towns and wealth in the early stages of the Industrial Revolution led to a deterioration of law and order. Increasing the number of offences for which the death penalty applied to well over two hundred and transporting offenders to other countries did not deter the increasing numbers of robbers, pickpockets, footpads and highwaymen although all punishments applied equally to men, women, adolescents and children, and children were actually sentenced to death and executed.

The infestation of robbers and assassins was such that an illuminative prose writer of the eighteenth century, Horace Walpole, wrote that 'one is forced to travel, even at noon, as if one were going into battle'[4] and another great writer of the same period, Tobias Smollett, thought that 'this defect, in a great measure, arose from the absurd notion that laws necessary to prevent those acts of cruelty, violence and rapine would be incompatible with the liberty of British subjects', and also from 'want of police in the interior government of the country'[5].

Nevertheless, England had the lowest ratio of murders relative to its population of all European countries and another contemporary writer, Charles Lewis, Baron de Pöllnitz, observed 'even the highwaymen seem to be more humane here than abroad; for they generally content themselves with what is given them, without shedding of blood'[6].

One of the most notorious of the English laws was the *Waltham Black Act* of 1722. Covering more felonies than any law framed before, it extended the death penalty over a wide range of offences and persons. It was aimed at stopping highwaymen near Waltham in Hampshire who had blacked their faces in disguise, and was framed to prevent their technique of using a base headquarters. Operating from the forests of Waltham, these precursors of Australian bushrangers modelled their activities on the famous band of Roberdsmen or followers of Robin Hood who committed great outrages in the reign of Richard I in the twelfth century on the border between England and Scotland.

Two aspects of the circumstances that led to the *Waltham Black Act* may be related to the romance and notoriety of Australian bushrangers.

First, the activities of Robin Hood and his followers were directly responsible for severe penal statutes. Coke, a brutal Attorney and Chief Justice of the early seventeenth century, but nonetheless one of the most important champions of the individual's liberties who held that judges were umpires between King and subject, had said that: 'the statutes ... cannot well be understood unless it be known what this Robin Hoode was that hath raised a name to these kine of men called Roberdsmen'. He described Robin Hood as nothing more than 'a brigand' who lived

> in woods and deserts, by robbery, burning of houses, felony, waste and spoile and principally by and with vagabonds, idle wanderers, night walkers and draw-latches ... and albeit he lived in Yorkshire, yet men of his quality took their denomination of him and were called Roberdsmen throughout all England[7].

Similarly, the excesses of bushrangers in Van Diemen's Land, New South Wales and Victoria resulted in severe penal legislation, such as the *Felon's Apprehension Act,* and outlawry.

Coke however took no account of the social background of the crimes of Robin Hood and his followers and it may well be that any attempt to enshrine Ned Kelly as Australia's Robin Hood should take into account Ned's Quinn-Lloyd-Kelly background, as well as the social and economic circumstances of nineteenth century Australia in which the perpetuation of the ideas and social order of eighteenth century England had not yet fully reacted with the new environment and its vast spaces to emerge as a distinctively Australian way of life.

Second, the relation of deer stealing in eighteenth century England to cattle stealing in nineteenth century Australia. Referring to the *Waltham Black Act,* a contemporary English writer, Gilbert White, had declared:

> though the large herds of deer do much harm to the neighbourhood, yet the injury to the morals of the people is of more moment than the loss of the crops ... most men are sportsmen by nature ... hence towards the beginning of this century *all this country was wild about deer-stealing*. Unless he were a *hunter,* as they effected to call themselves, *no young person was allowed to be possessed of manhood or gallantry*[8].

Some of the 'flashness' of young gangs of cattle duffers and cattle stealers, their dress and the 'larrikin heel' or high boot to give the impression of tallness can be seen in this psychology. It can also be seen in the police, as

'Mad' Dan Morgan's avowed impulsive aim in crossing the border from New South Wales into Victoria where he met his end was 'to take the flashness out of the police'.

In England, the severe laws, the Justice of the Peace and the soldier often stood alone between the riotous mob and the people. The English who otherwise preserved their wealth did little to secure it against robbers, preferring 'to be ruled by wretches of desperate fortune than to be persecuted by the executive'[9].

The underworld of London had become highly organised. Theft and robbery had been reduced to a regular system and London was notorious for its lawlessness and immorality. Despite this the severity of the laws was eased by English common sense.

The generous use of the Royal Prerogative of mercy helped redress the balance between the antiquated criminal law and modern notions of guilt and punishment which were beginning to take shape, and a pardon could either be a free one or one conditional on transportation or service in the Fleet or Army. The practice of giving pardons began in 1655 and by the middle of the eighteenth century, one capital felon was transported for every two executed.

The magistrates and judges also showed surprising leniency. An accused person could claim 'benefit of clergy', a plea originally intended for clerks but available for anyone who could recite a verse of the Lord's Prayer in Latin. This entitled an offender to have his sentence commuted to transportation for a specific term. Also many capital charges were eliminated by 'pious perjury', that is, the accused being found guilty and convicted of a lesser offence not carrying the death sentence. This virtually suspended the operation of many capital statutes. Lord Mansfield, a judge of the time, not known for his leniency, advised the jury to find a gold trinket, the subject of a capital indictment, to be of less than its value of 40 shillings. The prosecution complained, 'under forty shillings my Lord: why the fashion alone cost me more than double the sum'. Lord Mansfield calmly observed, 'God forbid, gentlemen, we should hang a man for fashion's sake'.

A considerable number of those committed for trial were not prosecuted and this was generally as high as one in four and sometimes over fifty per cent and by 1817, of 13,932 people committed for trial in England and Wales only 9,056 were convicted. Highway robbery was the seventh most 'popular' crime on the list with 276 offences in that one year.

BALLADRY

The balladry that sprang up around bushranging in Australia and in particular the Kelly balladry had its precursors in eighteenth century England. Although distinguished as an 'Age of Pleasure: her altars are erected in every street and corner: the common people are initiated into her mysteries'[10], ballad singers were regarded as a threat and nuisance and the glorification of the exploits of notorious rogues in books, songs and on the stage was seen as an incitement to vice and crime and the songs they sang were generally regarded as immoral and obscene.

Henry Fielding's *History of the Late Mr Jonathan Wild the Great,* a biography of a notorious thief, partly a political satire, was also an attempt to destroy by irony the hero worship of a dangerous criminal whose exploits were remembered but whose villainy was forgotten In a report on education in Wales in the early nineteenth century evidence was given that around 1788, when transportation to Botany Bay began, songs were 'sung about the streets in praise of housebreaking, *highway robbery* and thieving'.

M'Clean, the gentleman highwayman. Son of a Scottish Presbyterian minister, he aped the 'beau' and occupied fashionable lodgings in St James's Street in between plundering ventures.

There was a song sung in a place in Pall Mall called the Shades kept by an old thief who wrote it and sang it: the chorus was 'then who would work and not go thieving'. The song pointed out 'the difficulties of labour and getting on in the world and the superior advantage of thieving and was sung almost every night'[11].

The doctrine of enforced subordination and contentment had many adherents and the poor were taught to accept responsibility for their misfortunes. The lower classes especially suffered from an inherited situation, which also governed the fortunes of the English upper classes. At a time when England's population growth outstripped her food resources and England was forced to trade to provide further food, there were those who held that the distresses of the poor arose nearly as much from their own bad mismanagement as from the hardships of the time. Of the same school of thought were 'The Society for the Reformation of Manners' whose self-imposed task was to correct depravity. Their advocacy of moral police and the use of informers was, however, condemned as encouraging vice rather than diminishing it, and encroaching on individual liberty. Constables of a 'reforming kind' were accused of hiring people to perform 'the worst of all work, the dirty work of eaves dropping and lurking in corners to collect matters for an information'[12].

Along with suggestions for the suppression of ballad singers who were described as 'this cradle of filth' and as a training school for 'infant mendicants and juvenile thieves from the ages of six to sixty', there was a suggestion that the police fight fire with fire and issue to ballad singers literature conveying moral lessons on the advantages of 'industry, frugality, the happiness of a good husband, an honest man and the pleasures of abstention from public houses'[13].

There was a schism in community attitudes

(*Top*) Leg irons worn by Jack Shepherd are similar to those used in the penal colonies of New South Wales, Norfolk Island and Van Diemen's Land.

(*Below*) Jack Shepherd in special irons — he held *levées* in gaol, entertaining persons of rank, and was renowned for his zestful accounts of his misdeeds.

and moral attitudes towards liberty and highway robbery, theft, debauchery and licentiousness similar to that in nineteenth century Australia between the developing forces of law and order on the one hand and intoxicating liberty, bold, free bushrangers, their bush telegraphs and sympathisers and anti-police and anti-authoritarian sentiments on the other. A central element in these attitudes in the Australian colonies was the struggle for the possession of land in a new country not only as a source of wealth but also of individual integrity, independence and stability.

Although the restraints of the police of eighteenth century England were slight and there were differences in moral attitudes, nevertheless there was a general love of order and a willingness by people to earn their living by industry.

ROMANCE OF THE HIGHWAYMEN

The eighteenth century public took an intense interest in the life of great criminals and contributed more than any other period to the romance of crime, particularly that of highwaymen.

In 1750, Sir Horace Walpole wrote that 'on the Sunday after the condemnation of M'Clean, a notorious highwayman, three thousand people visited him in his cell'[14]. He added further, 'I have been in town for a day or two and heard no conversation but about M'Clean, a fashionable highwayman, who is just taken ... his history is very particular for he confesses everything and is so little a hero, that he cries and begs'[15]. Despite this lack of heroism 'there are as many prints and pamphlets about him as about the earthquake'[16]. (At Lisbon.)

Jack Shepherd, a highwayman who died on the gallows before he was twenty-three years old, became a *cause célèbre*. Sir James Thornhill painted his portrait, a pantomime was played at the Royal Theatre of Drury Lane called 'Harlequin Shepherd' and a drama was published entitled *The Prison Breaker* and a great number of pamphlets appeared.

A few days before his execution, Richard Turpin 'bought himself a new fustian frock and a pair of pumps'[17] and after his execution the people whom he had selected as his mourners 'took all possible care to secure his body which they deposited in a grave'[18] and took further steps to prevent it being stolen from the grave and anatomised, that is, being sold for dissection.

One of the effects of public hangings was to encourage superstition, adulation and romance. After the execution of Colonel Wall in 1802, the hangman was selling the rope at a shilling an inch and at the same time a woman was selling the 'authentic' rope at a reduced price elsewhere in London. According to a newspaper report, the rope that hanged Ned Kelly is still the proud possession of a Melbourne collector and Kelly relics fetch a high price. These together with the Kelly ballads, films, ballet and paintings are in the British romantic tradition.

'The Drop', the method of hanging used for most Australian bushrangers, was first used in the execution of Earl Ferrers in 1760, but was not adopted as the general mode of execution until 1783, when the 'new' drop, covered with black, was used to hang ten offenders in front of Newgate prison. Of primitive construction, it was improved and in 1828, the new drop set up at Northampton County Gaol was described as adequate for hanging twelve persons 'comfortably'. There was 'a temporary platform with a falling leaf supported by bolts'. The bolts were fixed 'so as to be removed in an instant and as instantaneously the victim of his own crime would be launched into eternity'. Above the platform was a cross beam to which the fatal cord was to be affixed and the platform was approached by a short flight of steps.

Seven o'clock on a Sunday evening was a popular time for highwaymen, according to a French scientist visiting England, and this was 'about the time when highwaymen usually come upon the road to rob the imprudent traveller. They are known to be dangerous and to carry on their dangerous profession upon horseback often mounted upon hunters'[19]. Thieves and receivers of stolen property worked in gangs employing spies and armed confederates.

Highwaymen were often polite, begging to be excused for being forced to rob and retiring if they gained a reasonable contribution. This politeness associated with robbery, which some of the Australian convict bolters and bushrangers affected, appears to have been almost a tradition in England. When transportation to New South Wales was just beginning, a contemporary traveller in England, von Archenholtz, wrote of highwaymen: 'these men are generally very polite; they assure you *they are very sorry that poverty has driven them to that shameful recourse* and end by demanding your purse in the most courteous manner'[20]. He thought that they were not 'in the least dangerous as they never proceed further than a menace never making use of their pistols but in case of resistance'[21].

Footpads, however, were much more dreaded than highwaymen. Of a lower social origin, they were far more dangerous, brutal in manner and often maimed or even killed. Pickpockets were legion and these juvenile offenders were immortalised by Charles Dickens in *Oliver Twist.*

Along with popularising of petty offences, although deliberate murder was unpardonable to the English and thought to be the 'greatest and most heinous of crimes', this contrasted

The 'Drop' method of hanging was used for most Australian bushrangers, and was approved for general use first in 1783 in England, when it was used to hang ten offenders outside Newgate prison.

(Above) Newgate, London's Metropolitan Prison, erected by "Dick Whitington", Lord Mayor of London to "re-edify the jail". Of all London prisons, except the Tower it alone had an imposing aspect.

(Below) Tread wheel and Oakum shed at the City Prison, Holloway. The tread wheel was used in early days in Victoria.
The Great World of London, vol. 1.

(Above left) A less imposing entrance to Newgate Prison. *(Above right)* Inside the Debtor's Doors, Newgate.

(Below) The exterior of Newgate.

(Above) En route for the new penal colonies of New South Wales and Van Diemen's Land. Convicts embarking at Millbank Stairs.

(Left) Convicts leaving the Old Bailey after being sentenced.

(Right) "Transportees under convoy".
Rex Nan Kivell Collection, courtesy National Library of Australia.

with their liking for brutal exhibitions of physical force and shocking spectacles. The popularity of public hangings may have been an expression of this desire, like that of the ancient Romans, to witness scenes where courage and indifference to death could be displayed.

BOTANY BAY CHOSEN FOR TRANSPORTEES

With the victory of American colonists in 1783, England's main outlet for offloading her convicts was cut off. Industrialisation and a growing population led to an increasing number of the very poor and, with inadequate measures for their relief, to increasing numbers of vagrants and robbers. The expediency of transporting undesirables out of the country made it easier to relinquish reliance on the death penalty.

It was probably Sir Joseph Banks who first suggested Botany Bay for transportees and Lord Sydney took the action in August 1786 which led to the foundation of the colony with a letter to the Treasury recommending the 'sending out of this kingdom such of the convicts as are under sentence of transportation'. He felt that New South Wales was a suitable penal colony because of 'the fertility and salubrity of the climate connected with the remoteness of its situation'. Another advantage was that of forestalling other European powers from occupying Norfolk Island with its potential of flax and pine trees for sails and spars for the Royal Navy.

The "First Fleet", 1788 under Captain Phillip. The *London* was the last convict ship to leave England, reaching Gibralter in 1871.
Rex Nan Kivell Collection, courtesy National Library of Australia.

Penal Settlements Produce Convict Bolters

HARSH CONDITIONS OF THE FIRST FLEET

With the arrival of the First Fleet came those values and ideas of eighteenth century England which influenced the founding fathers of Australia. The ideals and characters of the 1 124 people who arrived with Captain Arthur Phillip doubtless reflected the circumstances into which they had been born.

It was no mean endeavour to bring eleven ships of sail that 'had never sailed in that distant and imperfectly explored ocean' without accident to safe anchorage within forty-eight hours of each other in Botany Bay, the other side of the world, in those summer days of 18-20 January 1788. On January 26 Phillip unfurled the British flag and work began.

The first settlers were surrounded by an alien bush and could not foresee the hardships of settlement and exploration. Within ten months famine struck and there were reduced rations for two long years. Hunger and disease were endured by convicts and free settlers alike.

Difficulties arose because the convict work force was in the main lazy and incapable and because the supply ships from England, on which the colony depended, were irregular and inadequate.

When the women convicts were landed from the ships on 6 February it was recorded 'the scene of debauchery and riot that ensued during the night may be better conceived than expressed'. The next day the entire population, bond and free, were mustered to hear Judge Advocate Collins read Phillip's Commission and Letters Patent constituting civil and criminal courts. In his address Phillip warned that theft would be considered a crime and only those who worked would eat.

The first criminal court on 11 February 1789 sentenced a convict to 200 lashes for hitting a marine with an adze, another to 50 lashes (in the event remitted) for stealing some wood and a third who had stolen bread was put in irons and marooned for a week on a small island in the harbour, still popularly known as Pinchgut, on a diet of bread and water.

Phillip's task was not easy. Few convicts were used to manual labour and most of the provisions had deteriorated badly on the sixteen months voyage out.

Many convicts and marines went down with scurvy or dysentery, convicts strayed in the woods and became lost; some sheep died of disease and the settlement's few cattle escaped through the carelessness of the convict tending them and were not seen again. The Commander of the Marines, Major Ross, was difficult and refused to allow his marines to oversee working parties, claiming that such work was not part of their duties, and Phillip had to appoint overseers from among the convicts themselves.

In that first ten months fifty-five died from sickness. In addition four convicts were killed by natives, five were hanged and fourteen were lost in the bush and presumed dead through lack of bushcraft. These were the first of the 'convict bolters'.

CRUELTY ON NORFOLK ISLAND

Before leaving England, Phillip had been instructed to colonise the island which Cook had discovered some 900 miles north-east of Sydney to prevent it being occupied by any other power. Three weeks after landing at Botany Bay he sent Lieutenant King there accompanied by a party of twenty-two which included fifteen convicts, and a penal settlement was established.

On Norfolk Island the new settlers found that prospects were good and the harvests bountiful, and in 1790, to ease the situation at Sydney, a further 118 convicts and 27 children were sent there with two companies of marines. It was not long before a marine, John Batchelor, found guilty of stealing rum, received public punishment of 'one dozen lashes for quitting his work, one dozen lashes for breaking into ye King's stores and one dozen for theft'. Three days later, Charles MacLennan, a convict boy aged fourteen, received three dozen lashes for stealing rum from the surgeon's tent, and on 10 May, a further three dozen for 'uttering some very seditious and threatening words'. These were the first moderate punishments in a long chapter of cruelty on Norfolk Island.

By October 1792, the population on Norfolk Island had grown to over a thousand and with ground under cultivation the initial uncertainty was over. However, the number of convict bolters had increased to the extent that King had to issue arms to settlers to protect themselves against these early bushrangers and James King, their ringleader, was finally shot.

DISCONTENT INCREASED BY SECOND AND THIRD FLEETS

The arrival of the Second Fleet under appalling conditions brought 750 more convicts to the colony. Two hundred and fifty convicts had died on the journey through neglect, brutality or deliberate starvation and almost two-thirds of the survivors were ill on arrival. With the arrival of the Third Fleet with another 1,820 transportees of whom 600 went down with dysentery, the colony was brought face to face with starvation.

Even before the arrival of the Second and Third Fleets, Phillip's greatest problem had been to feed the Sydney settlement and the theft of food was a major crime. Six marines who had systematically plundered stores for eight months were sentenced to death and hanged by the 'drop' immediately. The seventh escaped by turning King's evidence.

The stealing of food, particularly by plundering gardens and hen coops at night, became such a serious problem that Phillip formed a regular night watch from trusted convicts, dividing the settlement into four areas, each patrolled by three men. Appointments of constables were also made from among convicts of good behaviour but the system proved as inadequate as it had been in England and, while the night watch met with some success, the rate of crime still gave cause for alarm.

The Second Fleet brought the first one hundred members of the New South Wales Corps, a unit specially recruited in England to take over garrison duties from the marines and a second detachment arrived in February 1792, but a convict writing home thought:

> in all the Crusoe like adventures I ever read or heard of, I do not recollect anything like it ... we fear the troops and they are not contented with seeing those who live better than themselves nor with us who live worse'[22].

By early 1792 discontent was so rife that a muster at Parramatta revealed forty-four men and nine women missing. Most had wandered off to the bush, deluded into the belief that they would reach China or some other land of refuge. Few were ever heard of again.

THE ABORIGINES SUFFER

The Aborigines, living as their forefathers had for centuries, presented to the settlers a unique if uncomprehended view of intelligent stone age life. Phillip scrupulously observed his own instructions 'to live in amity and kindness' with them, but difficulties in communications

ABORIGINAL
Photo

Relics of convict discipline in the Penal Colonies.
Rex Nan Kivell Collection, courtesy National Library of Australia.

caused unfortunate misunderstandings and all diarists of early days refer to tension and clashes.

Phillip declared he had 'not the slightest doubt of the convicts being the aggressors' and, in a brush between Aborigines and convicts in March 1789, he had to restore order after one convict was killed and seven wounded plundering Aborigines' fishing tackle and spears at Botany Bay. He punished seven convicts with 150 lashes each.

The introduction of smallpox to the Aborigines was a much more serious and destructive force and spread remorselessly till Phillip estimated that as 'much as one half of those who inhabit this part of the country' were dead.

The original occupation of Sydney and Hobart and a few points of coast did not have a great effect on most Aborigines but when the new settlers pushed deeper into the interior and along the coast they began to feel a major impact. Their first contacts were often with convict bolters, particularly in Van Diemen's Land.

The Aborigines were very vulnerable to gunpowder and to imported diseases, and their social and economic life was tragically shattered.

STARVATION, DISEASE AND INHUMANITY

Miserable gangs of convicts built the Sydney settlement. It was a gaol, the walls of which were the Pacific Ocean to the east, the Blue Mountains to the west and the unexplored wilderness to the north and south-west.

Most of the male convicts were organised into gangs to carry out timber collecting, tile making, building huts, farming and general labour. They were controlled by convicts chosen as overseers and some of the penalties meted out were savage.

Though at first, banishment on Pinchgut Island on bread and water was the main penalty, the lash and the cat-o'-nine-tails soon became the regular punishment, the only variant being the number of lashes. A convict was tied to a stake and a marine administered from 200 to 300 lashes or even 2,000 spread over several days to prolong the agony. Leg irons were only used in isolated cases and the two extremes of punishment were the pillory and the stocks on the lighter side where a convict was placed for varying periods to be stoned or abused by settlers and soldiers, and on the other more severe side the noose or hanging used for murder or, in times of crisis, for special circumstances.

The worst of the early crimes were those committed by marines rather than convicts. Nevertheless despite starvation, disease and inhumanity, the colony not only prospered but grew.

AUSTRALIA'S FIRST BUSHRANGERS

The career of Australia's first bushranger, the huge negro John 'Black' Caesar, was spread over seven years. He was reputed the 'hardest working man in the colony ... but in his intellects he did not very widely differ from a brute'.

Sentenced at Maidstone Assizes on 14 March 1785 to transportation for seven years on a minor crime, he stood out for his remarkable physique and strength but his ravenous hunger drove him to theft during the famine years in the colony. With another Negro, 'Black Jemmy', he was caught in the act of stealing food and on 29 April 1789 Jemmy received 500 lashes and Caesar's term of seven years was extended to life. Escaping, he stole a musket and ammunition and took to the bush, but

Iron Punishment of the hulk *Success*.
Courtesy La Trobe Library, Melbourne.

unable to live off the land, prowled around the outskirts of the settlement in armed robbery. Caught by a convict, William Saltmarsh, he escaped again in a native canoe and complete with musket, provisions and a cooking pot, set off inland towards Parramatta (Rose Hill) to live with natives but he 'offended them' and, wounded by spears, staggered into Rose Hill to give himself up. Transported to Norfolk Island he was imprisoned for four years and returned to New South Wales in July 1794. Still incorrigible, he again went into the bush and took to plundering. Captured, he once more escaped and terrorising settlers was joined by other runaways and finally declared an 'outlaw' with a price of five gallons of rum on his head. A man named Winbow set out to get the rum, tracked Caesar to his hide-out on Liberty Plains (now Concord) and shot him in the early hours of the morning. Thus Black Caesar died as many of his successors were to die. Governor Collins wrote 'he had given more trouble than any other convict in the settlement'.

Other famous 'bolters' were William and Mary Bryant, two transported convicts who had married four days after the first landing at Sydney Cove. They were two of the many convicts who sought to escape the near starvation conditions of 1791. With their two children and seven other male convicts they set out in a stolen small six-oared boat, the Governor's cutter, on an incredible journey. Slipping out of harbour at ten o'clock on the night of 28 March, with remarkable skill, they crossed the Arafura Sea, skirted Timor and after nine weeks in seas 'often mountainous high', tied up at Coupang (Keopang) on 5 June.

Arrested and transported to Batavia, six of them died from disease contracted at fever-ridden Batavia, and Mary Bryant, James Martin, John Butcher, William Allen and Nathaniel Kelly reached Portsmouth on 18 June 1792. Mary Bryant's other child, Charlotte, sadly died on the way home.

IRISH REBELS, BITTER ENEMIES OF THE BRITISH

Irish rebels also disrupted the colony. Two hundred and thirty-five 'seditious people' were sent from Ireland after the 1798 Irish rebellion. Early in 1801, five plotters, suspected of planning to overthrow the Government, received 100 lashes each, seven received 200 lashes, and four received 500 lashes. In March, a second plot resulted in the banishment of the ringleaders to Norfolk Island. Again in 1804, 250 convicts, mostly Irish, took part in armed insurrection at a Government Farm, Castle Hill. Fifteen were killed and one ringleader summarily hanged from a staircase of the public store. Eight more ringleaders were subsequently hanged, three at Castle Hill, three at Parramatta and two at Sydney. Nine others were sentenced to floggings ranging from 200 to 500 lashes and thirty-four were sent to the coal mines at Newcastle.

Bitter enemies of the authority that exiled them, these Irish rebels, who numbered almost two thousand, were more troublesome than all the forgers, burglars and thieves with whom successive Governors had to deal. There were many attempts at escape.

17
THE IRON PUNISHMENT
PRISON HULK "SUCCESS". 497B. BEATTIE, HOBAR

A convict team ploughing the ground at the Farm, Port Arthur. The convict driver used a whip at the end of a thong having a bladder attached to it.
Rex Nan Kivell Collection, courtesy National Library of Australia.

Brutalized Convicts Turn Bushranger

POLICING OF CONVICTS

The increase in the volume of transported convicts, the inefficiency of the imported system of constables and night watchmen and the number of escapees from the intolerably harsh discipline led to the need for additional penal settlements that could be more easily policed and more secure.

There was no real police force in Sydney till 1810. The development of police in Van Diemen's Land began at Sorrento in Port Phillip in 1803 when Lieutenant Colonel David Collins, newly arrived from England with nearly three hundred convicts, a guard of marines and a civil staff, appointed a night watch there in October of that year. The night watch was then transferred with the rest of the settlers to Hobart and formed the nucleus of the Hobart Night Watch.

As in Sydney, the watch proved ineffective and a military patrol was established three years later. In 1818, the police came under a unified command when A.W.H. Humphrey, formerly a minerologist with Collins at Sorrento, became the first police superintendent for the colony. However, the main function of the police was still that of assisting with the administration of the penal system.

Until 1823, the government of New South Wales was vested entirely in the Governor who worked under the control of the British Secretary of State for the Home Department or later the Secretary for War and the Colonies. He was an autocrat and the first four Governors were naval captains, three of them from the First Fleet. When settlement was extended, Lieutenant Governors were appointed.

KING LASH OF NEWCASTLE

The first extension of penal settlements after Sydney and Norfolk Island was at Newcastle and for more than twenty years after its establishment in 1801 it was the most dreaded name among the convict population. Here, the most incorrigible sweated it out as coal miners, cedar cutters and lime burners. 'King Lash was master here', wrote Commander Mark Currie. Lieutenant Charles Menzies controlled the Irish recalcitrants firmly, stamped out an assassination plot and sent the leaders Neason and Smith back to Sydney 'double-ironed and handcuffed'.

The miners, naked, hewed out the coal in fearsome pits, but there were tougher commandants to follow. Miners guilty of petty misdemeanours were double leg-ironed and flogged at the triangle to the beat of the drum, two floggers beating alternately.

Not surprisingly, convicts braved the perils of the bush and the likelihood of slow death from starvation in the forests. One such runaway, Craig, found a skeleton propped against a tree, musket at his side. As Craig said, 'a bushranger like himself'.

Runaway convicts and settlers opened a track overland from the Hunter River and over Mangrove Mountain to Windsor. Some convict bolters used the sea as an escape route and in 1814 the *Speedwell* (Captain Pattern) was seized by four desperate bolters and sailed north.

The notorious Major James Morisset was fanatically devoted to his job of commandant over more than a thousand convicts and was so ready to swing the cat-o'-nine-tails that his other name became King Lash. Women convicts with heads shaven had iron bands clamped around their necks and Morisset had the habit of lining up the convicts and taking out every second or third man to be given 50 lashes for the sake of good discipline.

Commissioner Bigge in 1819 said the penal settlement had to go since there were too many 'bolters' and too many interruptions to the smooth flow of coal production and by 1822 convicts began to be moved north to Port Macquarie, and by 1825 emancipated settlers began to move into the rich Hunter Valley. There are few traces today of the Newcastle penal settlement of over a century and a half ago.

BANDS OF DESPERADOES

In 1803 a settlement was made at Sorrento, Port Phillip, under the command of Lieutenant Colonel David Collins. An officer, Lieutenant Tucker, wrote of the settlement 'I behold a second Rome arising from a coalition of *banditti*', but six months later Collins withdrew to the River Derwent (Hobart) in Van Diemen's Land. Depredations at Sorrento by convicts and marines had been just as acute as elsewhere, even 'the sick being plundered of their provisions in their tents'. Convicts were organised into work gangs with overseers and a 'civil association' was formed, each man with a 'brace of pistols' to patrol at 'such hours as not to interfere with military rounds or patroles'[23]. Convict bolters were common. A gang of nine escaped, one named Shaw was wounded and all recaptured. One of them, William Buckley, a giant standing six feet six inches (198 centimetres), escaped again, walked about one hundred miles (160 kilometres) around the Bay across the Yarra and lived with Aboriginals for thirty-three years. The original crime for which he was transported was of receiving a roll of stolen cloth.

The discipline of the Collins' convict expedition at Sorrento was as severe as elsewhere but most bolters were either shot or recaptured or returned to receive a flogging.

The Port Phillip District had scarcely been resettled in 1836 before Sergeant King set off for two reported bushrangers, but although crime was prevalent and fifty lashes the order of the day, it was not till 1842 that the English treadmill was introduced as a deterrent to felons and the first hanging was carried out on 20 January of that year.

The execution at Sorrento in 1842 of Bob and Jack, two Aborigines from Van Diemen's Land who had been convicted of the murder of two sailors, was a crude affair and after the manner of Tyburn in England publicly witnessed by a crowd of some six thousand inhabitants after a procession of the death cart through the streets. The 'drop' was not far removed from the 'bucket', the kicking of which was the original form of hanging, as piled bricks supporting the hinged plank had to be clumsily pulled away by rope. Death was grotesquely not instantaneous, another instance of the inhumanity of the times.

The execution of three of a four man bushranging gang, the first real gang in the Port Phillip district, 'Vandie' Jepps, aged twenty-seven of Boston, USA, and an ex-whaler from Van Diemen's Land, 'Yankie Jack' Ellis, also twenty-seven, an ex-English migrant cook, and Young Fogarty, a bounty migrant, was more expertly carried out some months later. It was also a public affair before seven thousand people after another death march in a large open cart, the three prisoners seated on their coffins with an escort of military and mounted police. The leader of the gang, Williams, an Irish bounty migrant aged nineteen, had been shot dead in the gunfight that led to the capture of the gang after it had plundered nine homesteads. The gang faced twenty-four charges of armed robbery and the capital charge of wounding with intent to murder.

They had come together at a promiscuous lodging house in Little Flinders Street which acted as a receiving house with a 'fence' named Cam, but in May 1842, they were hunted down by 'Gentleman Volunteers' from the 'Club House, Melbourne' who surrounded them at Mr Campbell Hunter's homestead one

Saturday morning. By early afternoon the four volunteers were reinforced by twenty-four other armed citizens and by three o'clock the remaining three bushrangers, fairly intoxicated, had surrendered. Having run short of paper, they were using £1 notes as gun and pistol wadding. The cavalcade back to Melbourne on the Sunday morning emptied St Francis's morning church service of its congregation. The 'Gentleman Volunteers' were subsequently banqueted and a toast drunk: 'Health to our Gallant Guests who so nobly distinguished themselves by the capture of a band of desperadoes'.

A group of convict bolters escaped from the Melbourne Gaol in 1843 with the aid of a soldier sentry, William Beacroft. William Duncan, James McGuire and William Rafter were joined by Beacroft and they went bushranging around Geelong. None were captured, but two skeletons were later found, reputedly of two of them murdered by the others who were then thought to have disappeared into South Australia.

A practice in the late 1840s was smuggling female transportee convict bolters from Van Diemen's Land to Port Phillip in wooden beer casks with the bung open. It ceased when a convict called Nancy was found dead in a cask by the Captain of the ship with an empty bottle of gin near her head and in 'incipient decomposition' thrown overboard.

BUSHRANGERS GAIN NOTORIETY

The extension southwards came not only from the need for more effective and distant penal settlements but also from the fear of French occupation. Collins' settlement at Hobart was followed by Lieutenant Colonel Patterson settling Port Dalrymple (Launceston) with 150 in November 1804. News of Nelson's victory at Trafalgar the following year was celebrated with 'great joy and jubilation' for British sea power guaranteed the integrity of Australia as a field of exclusive British settlement.

Later on, during the years 1824 to 1827, three more strategic ports were selected; in the south at Westerport, west at Albury and in the north at Melville Island. The pre-eminence of British sea power in the Napoleonic Wars made it possible to declare the whole of Australia British in 1829.

With poor equipment and a reluctant labour force of convicts whose outlook was that the administration owed them sustenance, it was not long before famine struck Collins' settlement and he was forced to organise convicts into foraging parties. By hunting kangaroos and using the meat to feed hungry convicts, famine and resultant anarchy was avoided, but a new terror threatened. Many hunting parties refused to return and soon gangs of roaming convicts turned 'banditti' and their raids became so severe that they were outlawed. They grew to such an extent as to challenge the whole authority of government. A summary of the main convict bolters in Van Diemen's Land is given in Table 2 (page 13).

Escapees Rush and Hunter burned down farmhouses in bushranging sorties but in 1805, meeting with another gang in the bush, each mistook the other for police and fought till both bands were demoralised and several men were killed.

Wrote diarist the Reverend Bobby Knopwood, 'the police coming in at the finish made short work of the remainder'. Hunter was decapitated and his head taken to Hobart and exhibited on a pole.

Brutalisation was of such a degree as to be hardly equalled elsewhere and punishments became very severe. When convict strikes became common during the famine years such deterrents as three to five hundred lashes for

(Top) The Reverend Bobby Knopwood, Van Diemen's Land's first chaplain.
Rex Nan Kivell Collection, courtesy National Library of Australia.

(Below) Eaglehawk Neck, the approach to Port Arthur.
Rex Nan Kivell Collection, courtesy National Library of Australia.

killing a goat or stealing food were common and three soldiers who stole meat received seven to fourteen year sentences and for the same offence a convict was hanged.

'Bushranging' by convict bolters grew naturally out of the conditions of the violent and profligate society, but bushrangers were not always successful at survival for from time to time 'skeletons moss greened and crumbling to decay' came to light telling how the forest had taken its toll.

Up until 1807, communication between Northern (Port Dalrymple) and Southern (Hobart) settlements was by water, but early in February driven 'by scarcity of provisions' a party of five, led by Lieutenant Laycock of the New South Wales Regiment, braved dangers of the bush and 'armed against natives and *bushrangers*' made their way to Hobart Town.

Knopwood listed 'prisoners who are bushrangers at this time and they are all armed and have plenty of dogs—Carrot, Story, Fernander, Watts, Williams alias Rush, Grover, Meyers, Russell, Tomlins, Marsh, Brown, Duff, Parish and Bowers—14'. Eight of these ultimately returned[24].

By 1808, a band of 'Port Dalrymple bushrangers' was notorious and a sergeant with a party of seven set off after them. Watts was captured and imprisoned, Brown sentenced in Sydney and Lemon, whose ambush gave his name to Lemon Springs, was killed by a settler named Mansfield and his head brought to Hobart Town.

It was not only the settlers who found the bushrangers dangerous. The Deputy Surveyor, General G.W. Evans, writing in 1822, quoted an earlier observer, Lieutenant Jeffreys, 'that those pests of society, the bushrangers ... attacked at different times these poor creatures [the Aborigines] many of whom ... they have basely murdered ... barbarous excesses have been laid to their charge' and 'they have incensed the males by familiarities with the females ... no wonder therefore ... that the natives of this island should dislike and shun the presence of Europeans'[25].

Sent to relieve famine in Hobart Town in 1806, the ship *Venus* was seized by convict bolters. One of them, named Lancashire, had previously attempted to stowaway with two other convicts on the ship *Tillicherry* and was being transported on board *Venus* to serve his sentence in Van Diemen's Land. This time he was successful and with two women convicts and three others, stole the ship at anchor at

TASMANIAS FIRST CLERGYMAN — REV. ROBERT KNOPWOOD M.A. J.P.
BEATTIE-HOBART.

EAGLE HAWK NECK, FROM FORESTIER'S.
711.
BEATTIE, HOBART.

Hobart. Reportedly seen in New Zealand waters, the fate of both the ship and its convict pirates is unknown.

Bushranger pirates were plentiful (see Table 4, page 18) and a diarist recorded 'more vessels disappeared than were accounted for by the winds and waves'. The *Cumberland* was one of these and all that was found of her after her disappearance was one of her ship's buckets found on a pirate vessel.

The man who had to govern when the bushranging terror was at its height was Lieutenant Governor Tom Davey who held office from 1813 to 1817. He was succeeded by Colonel William Sorrel in 1817 and a year after Colonel George Arthur became Governor in 1824, Van Diemen's Land became independent of New South Wales with a seven-man Legislative Council and an Executive Council. At the same time the island was divided into police districts.

Nevertheless the groups of marauders, formed earlier, flourished unchecked. Their numbers increased when doubly convicted prisoners sent down from Sydney became a positive menace. The worst were sent to the George Town penal station where 'no one died a natural death'.

Such was the strength of the numerous banditti that during the luckless Davey's regime they were known to have marched in file through bush settlements as if they owned them. Peter Mills, the Deputy Surveyor, and George Williams, the Deputy Commissioner, both deserted and with several convicts formed their own gang of bushrangers and even Martin, the Reverend Bobby Knopwood's servant, succumbed to the lure of bushranging only to be recaptured and punished.

In Sydney, in May 1814, Governor Macquarie ineffectually offered a pardon to named bushrangers for all their crimes except murder. This virtually guaranteed bushranger outlaws immunity to commit as many crimes as they like other than murder. The following year even the races on St Patrick's Day had to be cancelled 'on account of so many bushrangers being in the woods'. A few days later after a settler named Carlisle had been killed and four others

Arrival of Lieutenant Colonel Collins from Port Phillip in 1803, at present site of Hobart.
Rex Nan Kivell Collection, courtesy National Library of Australia.

wounded in a pitched battle, at the request of settlers, after meeting with all the officers both civil and military, Davey proclaimed martial law on the basis of virtual war between settlers and bushrangers. As a result of this vigilant law-making, several bushrangers were then caught and hanged.

The first to lead a big gang was John Whitehead, one of the convicts set loose to hunt for kangaroo meat for the starving colony during 1805, but he soon changed to bush-ranging on a massive scale leading a gang of over one hundred. Even when provisions finally arrived many released forager convicts failed to return and, when Michael Howe, an ex-highway robber from York, England, and the most notorious of them all, joined White-head there were still at least twenty-three in the gang. Under the easy-going rule of Governor Tom Davey discipline had become lax and 'the woods abounded with bushrangers'. The banditti were so powerful that some settlers formed liaisons with the gangs to safeguard their flocks, store keepers became allies as the result of 'standover' threats and some left their holdings to live more safely in the towns. Even then, at one point, Howe's gang plundered the town of New Norfolk.

Bushrangers were outlawed in 1813, but Whitehead's gang continued on their way. They tortured John Hopkins, whom they accused of trying to betray them, by tying bullock hide moccasins filled with 'soldier ants' to his feet, from which he died in agony. Finally, Whitehead was shot in a skirmish with police in October 1814 and his lieutenant Howe cut off his head to prevent the person who had killed him from getting 'blood money'. Howe, closely pursued, threw the head into a bush from where it was recovered and taken with the body to Hobart Town and exhibited.

Howe surrendered to 'Captain Nairn, H.M.46' under Macquarie's amnesty but soon broke his parole and was declared an outlaw with a price of one hundred guineas on his head. He organised a raid on a tribe of Aborigines for wives for himself and his banditti. In revenge, not the camps of bush-rangers but the houses of settlers who had no connection with the raiders were attacked and conflict between black and white intensified. Some of the Aboriginal women, however, became reconciled to the change and 'Black Mary' lived with Howe for several months at 'Michael Howe's Marsh'. A free pardon was offered for any man who could take Howe, alive or dead, and though he killed two of his gang whom he suspected of designs on his life and the reward, two other pardon seekers, Stambo, alias Drew, and Watts, were still tempted. Watts, a prisoner who had absconded from Coal River, was a fine looking man and a noted bushranger with a price of eighty guineas on his own head and thought the chance of a pardon too good to miss. The pair of them caught Howe off guard, but in bringing him in to Hobart, Howe was able to wrench his tied hands free and with a secreted knife stab Watts in the back, grab his gun, shoot Drew dead and escape.

The banditti were highly organised. Howe drew up his articles of discipline with fidelity sworn on a prayer book. Transgressors had to cut wood and were often flogged. Often a chapter of the Bible was read aloud to the gang. A mixture of criminality and piety was not uncommon and reached its acme of incongruity with John Lynch, the New South Wales bushranger who, having prayed to Almighty God 'to assist him and enlighten him', felt strengthened to commit his diabolical murders.

With his escape and management of the gang Howe developed delusions of grandeur, he called himself 'Governor of the Ranges' and in an insolent letter to Davey called him 'Governor of the Town'. Under increasing attack from

(Top) Mess Room, the Model Prison, Port Arthur. *Rex Nan Kivell Collection, courtesy National Library of Australia.*

(Below) Isle of the Dead, Port Arthur, Van Diemen's Land. *Rex Nan Kivell Collection, courtesy National Library of Australia.*

settlers, the gang fell out in 1817. Various plans were laid to bring Howe to justice. Either a former accomplice Warburton betrayed him, or the convict Worrall was really behind his capture. The plan was that Worrall and a soldier named Pugh should wait in Warburton's hut while Warburton lured Howe to it. Howe, becoming suspicious, ran off but fell down a hidden bank into a creek. He was covered in kangaroo skin, carried a powder horn and wore a beard. Worrall's beard was grey. Cried Howe: 'Black beard against grey beard for a million'. Both fired and Howe leapt for the opposite bank but Pugh catching up smashed his skull with his forelock. Howe's head was later exhibited at Hobart Town.

The year before Howe's gang was broken up, Lieutenant Governor Sorrell had made a determined effort to enforce law and order and on 5 July 1817, issued a Proclamation offering a 'reward of 520 guineas for the apprehension of the bushrangers who under Peter Geary, a deserter from the 73rd Regiment, had attacked and plundered the store at George Town and escaped with two boats in which they were afterwards cast ashore at Port Dalrymple'[26].

George was also charged with murder with a price of one hundred guineas on his head. Others included were Peter Sefton, John Jones, eighty guineas each, Richard Collyer, Thomas Coines, Brown or Brune a Frenchman, fifty guineas each.

Three days later, Sergeant McCarthy and his party caught up with the 'bushrangers of the Port Dalrymple party' at T-Tree Brush. Geary, 'the ringleader of the Banditty or Bushrangers' was shot dead and John Smith and James Tull wounded. The remaining eight of the eleven man gang escaped, but Dennis Currie and Matthew Keegan, two of the original Howe gang, surrendered within days. The surgeon Mr Hood, Lieutenant Nairn and Ensign Ross and a party of the 46th brought Geary's body and the wounded in to Hobart. White and Johnson were also caught by McCarthy after being led to their haunts by 'Black Mary', Howe's former mistress. Later, on 5 August, a party of soldiers shot Jones, whose decapitated head worth eighty guineas was brought to Hobart Town. Another bushranger, Holmes, was also brought in wounded.

Sorrell's drive had been prompted by an article in the Sydney *Gazette:* 'the accounts of robberies by the banditti of bushrangers of Van Diemen's Land present a melancholy picture of the distresses to which the most respectable classes of the inhabitants are constantly exposed'[27] and a public meeting was called for the 'purposes of considering the most effectual measures of suppressing the banditti'.

MESS ROOM PENITENTIARY, PORT ARTHUR.
BEATTIE, HOBART.

Hell Hole, MacQuarie Island. Convicts rafting logs for ship building near Grumnet Island.
Rex Nan Kivell Collection, courtesy National Library of Australia.

Bushranging Becomes Rife

'DISTANT BANISHMENT'

With the breaking up of Howe's gang it was thought bushranging in Van Diemen's Land had been suppressed. Sorrell's drive against bushrangers had tightened up the convict system with the use of passes and convicts absent without leave were sentenced to hard labour. Commissioner J.T. Bigge, sent to New South Wales to enquire into the state of the colony, recommended places of 'distant banishment' and as a result Norfolk Island was re-established and prisons established at Macquarie Harbour and Port Arthur in Van Diemen's Land.

MACQUARIE HARBOUR — BLEAK AND DESOLATE

The penal system was to undergo a metamorphorsis as the colonists sent their most hardened criminals to the bleak and desolate Macquarie Harbour fronted by a sea constantly subject to the fury of the Antarctic gales. Here the dangerous entrance cost many boats and lives and the harbour was frowned over by huge, desolate mountain passes so that escape either by sea or land was perilous. The 'canaries', the incorrigibles, were clad in yellow with black, broad arrows; ordinary convicts wore black or blue.

Gangs laboured at felling huge trees which grew in swampy areas and many fine boats were built. Men however, worked in freezing water up to their waists for most of the day on empty stomachs with one meal in the evening. A hundred lashes was the most common punishment and men regarded solitary punishment as a relief from unremitting labour. A line of posts was established across the neck of the land between Pirates Bay and Storm Bay and watch dogs, not hunting dogs as often rumoured, were chained there to give the alarm.

Escape attempts were frequent but few were successful. Violent death was common and of eighty-five deaths at the settlement over a period of eleven years, only thirty-five were natural; twenty-seven were drowned while escaping, eight killed accidentally, three shot by the military and twelve murdered.

MURDER AND CANNIBALISM

Cannibal escapee Alexander Pierce escaped over 'Hell's Gates' with seven others by boat in 1822, but got bushed on landing. With him were Bob Greenhill, Matthew Travers, Thomas Bodenham, Bill Cornelius or Kennelly, James Brown, John Mathers and Alexander Dalton.

After eight days wandering, Bill Cornelius declared that he was so hungry 'I could eat a piece of man'. Dalton was first to go and four others were murdered and eaten in turn. After roaming and being fed in a shepherd's hut Pierce fell in with two other bushrangers named Davis and Cheetham who had stolen 126 newly marked sheep. Ultimately they were

MacQuarie Harbour, 1830. Commandant's Quarters, Sarah Island.
Rex Nan Kivell Collection, courtesy National Library of Australia.

captured by soldiers, Davis being wounded in the arm. Pierce again escaped from Macquarie Harbour with Thomas Cox, whom he also murdered and cannibalised. Of the original eight, Bill Cornelius and Brown, who had managed to go their own way after going ahead to survey a route after the cannibal episode, returned, Cornelius to be punished as a 'bolter' and Brown to die in hospital. Pierce was eventually caught and hanged.

Three others who escaped were Jeffries, Hopkins and Russell. They lived well by the gun for a few days, but game soon failed and they tossed for their lives. Russell lost and was shot by Jeffries and afforded food for five days till they came on a sheep station and stole two sheep. Jeffries and Hopkins then turned bushrangers. Jeffries had few rivals for brutality; he shot a stockman employed by a Mr Tibbs, dashed Mrs Tibbs' young baby's brains out against a sapling, shot Tibbs and left Mrs Tibbs with her dead. At George Town, he shot a Mr Baker dead without apparent cause. In the meantime, John Batman had been officially engaged to track and capture bushrangers as a 'bounty hunter' and was soon on the trail catching both Jeffries and Hopkins. They both hanged in April 1826. Batman also caught Broughton, another escapee convicted of both murder and cannibalism.

MATHEW BRADY, 'GALLANT BUSHRANGER'

The bushranging evil, far from being suppressed, monopolised a great deal of Governor Arthur's efforts on his appointment in 1824. For two years his soldiers, police and bounty hunters tried to capture the 'gentleman convict' Matthew Brady. High in his mountain hide-out, Brady and his gang were virtually impregnable.

Transported for forgery, retransported to Van Diemen's Land for insubordination, he was one of a gang of fourteen who escaped from Macquarie Harbour in a stolen whale boat across the Hell's Gates sand bar in pitch blackness. With a keen sense of humour, Brady was the classic bushranger. Like Ned Kelly, he talked a lot about himself and claimed he was a 'gallant bushranger' who only hurt when he had to and treated his women prisoners properly. Indeed, he expelled several of his gang for molesting women, including the vicious Jeffries, mass murderer and cannibal.

Governor Arthur was not impressed and ordered extra efforts for his capture to be made. Not only was the Brady gang broken up but more than a hundred bushrangers were hanged during the two years 1825 and 1826.

For two bloodstained years, however, from his hide-out among the crags of Great Western Tiers, Brady became king and he went so far as to answer Arthur's offer of a reward of twenty-five pounds for his apprehension with a counter proclamation:

> Mountain Home, April 25th. It has caused Matthew Brady much concern that such a person as Sir George Arthur is at large. Twenty gallons [ninety litres] of rum will be given to any person that will deliver his person unto me. (Signed) M. Brady[28].

His first highway robbery was more significant than any others for the victim was the personal servant of Lieutenant William Gunn. Gunn, an ex-officer and farmer, a giant of a man, henceforth became Brady's implacable enemy and relentlessly pursued him. He captured five of Brady's men. Most settlers armed themselves since the *Bushranging Act* now enabled them to legally shoot armed convicts on sight and Brady's gang, now about thirty strong, repeatedly struck on forays from their mountain stronghold. Brady made his biggest raid when he virtually captured the town of Sorrell, freeing prisoners from gaol and locking the local police in. Gunn was wounded in the arm in the shoot-out and his arm was later amputated. This impudent assault intensified the hunt, and McCabe, Brady's close friend and first lieutenant, was captured and went to the gallows.

In December 1825, Brady made an unsuccessful attempt to flee from Van Diemen's Land by seizing the ship *Glory* anchored in the River Tamar. He had previously eluded capture at Elizabeth River when an informer led two troopers to his hide-out. Colonel Balfour with ten soldiers and some civilians drove off the gang during a robbery attempt near Launceston and although Brady always tried to stop his men from murder, they used violence and two of the civilians were killed. John Batman got in before Gunn and tracked Brady four thousand feet up the Tiers. Brady, shot through the ankle in the previous raid, handicapped, alone and on foot, surrendered on 17 March 1826.

Singer of sentimental ballads, Brady bowed to the crowd as he reached the scaffold and ladies wept, but he was denied the privilege of holding the stage alone, as the scaffold was built to accommodate six; Jeffries the Cannibal, whom he despised, and four other convicts, hanged with him.

Although popular fiction has cast a kind of

glamour over bushranging, in the same way as English poetry and romance gilded the deeds of the highwaymen, there was little chivalry in the deeds of the convict bolters dangerously at large. Bushranging in the mainland colonies never reached the proportions of Van Diemen's Land where the number of convicts only just exceeded the number of free emigrants. Governor Arthur had a tremendous task in checking crime and reforming convicts to fit into the social order.

GOVERNOR ARTHUR

Bushrangers were partly responsible for the conflict which led to the extermination of the Tasmanian Aborigines. Unaggressive and good humoured, when left in peace the Aborigines were not likely to cause any trouble.

In 1813, Lieutenant Governor Thomas Davey declared 'the resentment ... has been provoked by a most barbarous and inhuman mode of proceeding viz, the robbing of their children'[29] and the depredations of the bushrangers aggravated this resentment. It was natural for the Aborigines to turn upon their oppressors.

Governor Arthur formed the Aborigines Protection League but the Aborigines could no longer distinguish between friend and foe. When Arthur tried to ease the situation by offering rewards for the capture of uninjured Aborigines, this led to the formation of capture gangs who hunted them like game.

Finally Arthur organised a drive to sweep all the Aborigines into the centre and south. The force employed about 2,000 soldiers and civilians and cost £35,000 but all but two Aborigines escaped the net. Subsequently the Aborigines were removed to Flinders Island under the care of missionaries but they gradually died out.

Very few turned bushranger. The Sydney Aborigine, Musquito, transported to Van Diemen's Land for the murder of an Aboriginal woman in 1823, was employed as a tracker and aided soldiers in capturing some bushrangers but turned bushranger himself roaming the bush for over two years. He claimed that in killing two settlers he was only defending himself, but he was hanged in Hobart in 1825.

PORT ARTHUR CONVICTS

Macquarie Harbour had proved difficult to manage. Conditions were so bad and forbidding at Hell's Gates that violence was aggravated and prisoners bolted in desperation and as the sand bar was creeping up to an even less shallow draft, making entry even more difficult, it was abandoned.

In 1830, a new model prison was built at Port Arthur to confine second offenders and incorrigibles in one safe place. Its only escape route inland was by way of the peninsula which narrowed at Eaglehawk Neck to less than one hundred feet and was constantly patrolled and had a barrier of eleven dogs chained at the narrowest sector.

In the first five years, over seventeen hundred convicts passed through Port Arthur, each in their yellow-dyed 'canary' clothing. All were subject to hard labour in gangs and chains under overseers, but the convicts received the same rations as the officers who guarded them, regular evening schools were held and after one-third of his term, a convict could, if he merited it, receive lighter work and after the second third of his term, could petition for work outside in settled districts. For convicts in solitary confinement, however, twelve cells under one roof were each seven feet (2.1 m) by four feet (1.2 m) and eight feet (2.4 m) high, a small hole in the door providing light and

Prison Guard at Port Arthur, Van Diemen's Land.
Rex Nan Kivell Collection, courtesy National Library of Australia.

Martin Cash.
Rex Nan Kivell Collection, courtesy National Library of Australia.

ventilation. A medical officer had to supervise floggings.

On the 'Iles des Morts' where dead convicts were buried is a pathetic epitaph over a grave: 'He hath died in a place whither they led him captive and he shall see the land no more'.

CASH, 'GENTLEMAN BUSHRANGER'

One of the convict bolters from Port Arthur was Martin Cash who had been transported from England to New South Wales in 1828 at the age of nineteen.

An Irish farm boy and a fast talker, after an involvement in cattle stealing, he hurriedly escaped to Van Diemen's Land in early 1837 with his mistress, Bessie Clifford, the wife of a British army officer.

Although he had been transported for housebreaking Cash's story was not robbery under arms but putting some buckshot into the buttocks of a man stealing the affections of his then sweetheart. However, within two years of escaping to Van Diemen's Land with his new love Bessie, he was sentenced to seven years for larceny and had escaped and been recaptured three times.

It was in the cells at Port Arthur that he associated with some other twelve hundred incorrigibles, including Thomas Jones and Lawrence Kavanagh, both of whom had had some earlier success as bushrangers in New South Wales.

Cash, Jones and Kavanagh together swam naked from Eaglehawk Neck to the mainland to establish a log fort on Mount Dromedary. From here 'Cash & Co' filled the local newspapers with their armed exploits.

Although known as the 'polite gentleman bushranger' Cash, as well as his gang, was always armed. However, Bessie, 'Mrs Cash', tired of life at the log fort, packed up and left for brighter lights in Hobart only to incur a gaol sentence for possession of 'her jewelry' which was unfortunately stolen. When Cash wrote a letter to the Governor, Sir John Franklin of later Antarctic exploration fame, 'that a very respectable person, Mrs Cash, is now falsely imprisoned', Bessie was released, not because Sir John was impressed but as a bait to lead troops to Cash & Co. In the event, Cash, learning that Bessie had become unfaithful, came to town in company with Kavanagh, both disguised as sailors, seeking vengeance on 'her companion and her paramour'. Recognised, in escaping, Cash fatally shot Constable Peter Winstanley through the chest and that was the beginning of the end for Cash & Co.

Cash, sentenced to death for the murder of Constable Winstanley, was reprieved at the eleventh hour because of strong public opinion and sent to Norfolk Island on a life sentence, where he became a model prisoner. After serving ten years he was allowed to marry an Irish convict, Mary Bennett. Soon afterwards he got his ticket of leave and returned to the mainland. He worked for a while as an overseer of Government gardens and was given a conditional pardon. He went to New Zealand for four years but returned in 1860 to farm at Glenorchy and was one of the few bushrangers to die in his own bed. A romanticised version of his life written by an ex-convict, J. L. Burke, became a best seller.

His partners were not so fortunate. Kavanagh surrendered and sentenced to life imprisonment on Norfolk Island was hanged for his part in the 1846 'Jacky-Jacky' Westwood riot. Jones tried to form a new gang with John Liddell and James Dalton, but both were captured by police. Jones, on the run with another bushranger, Moore, and with fifty guineas on his head, was betrayed, captured and hanged without delay. Moore's death sentence was commuted to life imprisonment.

Prison Establishment at Norfolk Island.
Drier Collection, courtesy La Trobe Library, Melbourne.

NORFOLK ISLAND REFORMS

In 1824, Lord Bathurst, Secretary of State for Colonies, decided a 'secure place for lapsed criminals' had to be found away from New South Wales and in 1825 Norfolk Island, uninhabited since 1813, was re-established as a penal settlement. Intended by Governor Darling to be a place of 'the extremest punishment short of death', there was an uprising within eighteen months in which a soldier was killed, a convict shot and two others drowned while attempting to escape. Two ringleaders were hanged in Sydney and others sentenced to hard labour in chains. Conditions were appalling and homosexuality was rife.

Even at sea there was mutiny. The brig *Wellington* with sixty convicts on board was taken by force just before she reached the island, but was recaptured near New Zealand. The ringleaders were hanged and the rest sent back to the island.

Colonel James Morisset became commandant of Norfolk Island in 1829, and in 1833, a series of murders resulted in the setting up of a court on the island and the execution of three murderers before a parade of the whole convict population. In January of the following year, a riot in the prison compound led to several guards and convicts being killed or wounded and at the same time at the agricultural station at Longridge, one hundred and sixty convicts were charged with rioting, fifty-eight were tried and thirteen sentenced to death. They were glad to die and kissed the feet of the executioner in gratitude.

When he became Commandant in 1840, Captain Maconochie wrote: 'a more demoniacal assemblage could not be imagined'. He described conditions for:

> 1400 double convicted prisoners, the refuse of both penal colonies ... rigorously coerced all day and cooped up at night in barracks which could not decently accommodate half the number. In every way their feelings were habitually outraged and their self-respect destroyed ... for the merest trifle they were flogged, ironed and confined in gaol for successive days on bread and water ... they were also fed more like hogs than men. Neither knives nor forks ... were allowed. They tore their food with their fingers and their teeth and drank for the most part out of water-buckets. Not more than two-thirds of them could even enter their mess shed at a time; and the rest, whatever the weather were required to eat as they could in an open shed beside a large privy[30].

He cites the words of an unhappy victim himself 'when a prisoner was sent to Norfolk Island he lost the heart of a man and got that of a beast instead'[31].

Maconochie was able to carry out some amazingly liberal reforms, but newly arrived convicts from Ireland contributed to his downfall. His system was condemned and he was dismissed. Norfolk Island became almost a 'Devil's Island' as his successor Childs transported most of 'Maconochie's convicts', that is those contaminated by liberal humaneness, to Van Diemen's Land replacing them with new convicts from Britain and doubly convicted men from New South Wales. 'Kangaroo courts' were set up and convicts punished by their fellows in secret cells. Childs' successor John Price was 'caught up with' later in Williamstown penal quarry where he was stoned to death.

The last of the convicts left Norfolk Island in 1856.

THE SUPPRESSION OF BUSHRANGERS

After the breaking up of Matthew Brady's gang, both the activities of bushrangers and

COPYRIGHT.
MURDERERS MOUND, NORFOLK ISLAND.
BEATTIE, HOBART.

Murderer's Mound, Norfolk Island, contains the remains of eleven or twelve convicts hanged for mutiny in 1847. *Brier Collection, courtesy La Trobe Library, Melbourne.*

their executioners moved to the mainland. A summary of the main convict bolters in New South Wales is given in Table 3 (page 16).

GOVERNOR DARLING'S MEASURES

In 1825 a Corsican, Captain F.N. Rossi, was appointed Principal Superintendent of Police in New South Wales, although he never effectually became more than head of the Sydney police, since by 1828, Sydney's population had grown to 35,000, of whom about sixty per cent were either convicts or emancipists. In the same year, 1825, Governor Brisbane formed a Horse Patrol especially to combat bushrangers. There was some similarity between this body of mounted police, in New South Wales and the Royal Irish Constabulary formed in 1822, as both were basically a military police force. The Royal Irish were regarded as repressive and unsuitable for England and Wales but the size of the Australian environment, the rugged bush terrain and difficulties of communication were great obstacles to an effective police force and favoured a military-type mounted force. As bushranging increased, the force numbered over one hundred by 1830 and recruitment was from the Army whereas Governor Arthur's Mounted Field Police in Van Diemen's Land, formed in 1826, came from the best behaved convicts. The *Sydney Police Act* of 1833 was partly modelled on the *English Metropolitan Police Act* of 1829 and New South Wales and Van Diemen's Land both developed the guide lines for the establishment of police forces in other colonies.

In April 1830, Governor Darling proclaimed an Act for the suppression of bushrangers. It gave police powers to arrest on suspicion and to enter and search premises without a warrant and caused many complaints.

Commissioner Bigge had reported as early as 1819 that in New South Wales 'the offences termed bushranging or absconding in the woods and living upon plunder and robbery of orchards are most prevalent' and it became serious in 1822 when although thirty-four bushrangers were hanged in that one year, hanging was no deterrent. In March 1826, in a clash between mounted troopers and seven bushrangers near Bathurst, the leader Morris Connell was shot dead by Corporal Brown but the others escaped. The *Sydney Monitor* accused the Principal Chaplain of New South Wales, Reverend Samuel Marsden, who was also an ex-officio magistrate, of handing down too severe sentences of flogging of desperadoes, thereby 'helping manufacture bushrangers'.

Assigned servants began taking to the bush. One group, John Poole, James Ryan and James Riley, attacked a prisoners' escort and released the prisoners to make up an armed gang using single and double barrelled guns, fowling pieces and pistols as well as a musket. When captured by Trooper Daniel Craddige and his party of six which included civilians, Poole, Ryan and Riley subsequently hanged with two of the escaped prisoners, Hitchcock and John Perry who had joined them. Another of the escaped prisoners, Jones, was acquitted of the capital charge but sent to Norfolk Island for life. An inquiry into the alleged ill usage of the assigned servants which caused them 'to go bush' cleared Mr John Larnack and his son-in-law, Major James Mudie, of Castle Forbes estate in the Hunter River district, but did not bring back to life the assigned servants and their comrades in arms.

The story of Jack the Rammer illustrates the relationship of assigned servants to bushrangers. An aggrieved servant named Bull was involved in an attack on his master by Jack and two others, Boyd and Arthur Keys, but his master, Shepherd, survived fourteen slugs in various parts of his body. Police followed the bushrangers and shot Boyd as he was trying to escape by swimming the Snowy River. Keys and Bull were soon captured and hanged. Jack the Rammer, whose stamping ground was the Monaro Plains, escaped for a time, but was shot a few months later.

DONOHOE, POPULAR BUSHRANGER

The famous gang of Will Underwood and 'Bold Jack' Donohoe operated on the roads round Campbelltown, Liverpool, Penrith and Liberty Plains for nearly twelve years. Other members were Walmsley, Webber, Kilroy, Smith and some itinerants.

Their camp in the valley of Burragong, about sixty miles (100 kilometres) from Sydney, was a favourite and secure base for bushrangers of the 1820s. There are tales of quarrels and murder, even one of a captured settler being burned to death at the stake. Certainly the first troopers, in discovered relics, broken shackles, handcuffs and skeletons and bones of men who had died violently.

In September 1830, Donohoe, aged twenty-one, was killed in a running fight with Trooper Maggleton and the ballad *Bold John Donohoe* sung in the early 1830s glamorised his fictional deeds and heroic death. It was banned only to re-emerge, with minor variations, as the *Wild Colonial Boy* narrating the equally fictitious deeds of one Jack Doolan. Donohoe, popularly known as 'The Stripper' was less violent than most bushrangers, gallant to women and had a sense of humour enough to make him a popular hero. To a certain extent it was Donohoe's influence that induced the New South Wales Legislative Council to pass the notorious Bushranging Act, in the same way that the Roberdsmen of Old England had brought about severe penal statutes.

JOHN LYNCH, MURDERER OF TEN

John Lynch, alias Dunleavy, was in sharp contrast to 'Bold Jack'. Transported from Ireland for 'false pretences', he worked in a road gang before being released as an assigned servant. Arrested in 1835 for stealing a saddle from his employer, although he was acquitted, he 'bolted'. Shortly afterwards a witness in a highway robbery, Thomas Smith, was found dead in the bush. Lynch and two others were arrested on suspicion and although the two were hanged for the murder, Lynch was again acquitted. Later he spent a year in gaol for harbouring bushrangers, and on 21 February 1841, was arrested at Mulligan's farm for the murder of Kearns Landregan who was found battered on the head and strangled. Lynch had 'acquired' Mulligan's farm, but Mulligan, his wife and two children had disappeared. When sentenced to death, Lynch made the astonishing confession: he had stolen eight bullocks to sell in Sydney but on the way he met a teamster with an Aboriginal boy with goods that were a better haul. He killed both. In his rambling confession he also told how he ran into a Mr Fraser and his son with a dray and horse team and killed both after praying to 'Almighty God to assist and enlighten'. He had asked for similar assistance in murdering the Mulligans and their sixteen-year-old son and then violated and killed their daughter aged fourteen. Lynch lived on the farm for six months before engaging a labourer Kearns Landregan for fencing work whom he also killed. Lynch was particular in pointing out that his murders were accomplished with one blow of a tomahawk but that Landregan, a powerful man, took 'two chops'. Lynch himself was only five feet three inches (160 centimetres) in stature, but was emphatic that he had Divine direction. His confession omitted numerous bushranging robberies. Aged twenty-nine, he was executed at Berrima on 22 April 1842 for ten murders.

DAVIS, 'HERO OF THE ROAD'

Edward Davis, 'Teddy the Jewboy', in contrast was more of the popular 'hero of the road' and next to 'Jacky Jacky' Westwood and perhaps Matt Brady, more bushranging folklore surrounds him than any other early bushranger. His gang, which varied with runaways joining him from time to time (although one Thomas Maguire was said to be a free man), plagued the area between Maitland and the New England and Liverpool ranges for nearly two years.

Often they were accompanied by Davis's mistress, an Aboriginal girl who became an expert in fast reloading of guns and whose job it was to stand guard over prisoners. The gang dressed up as gentlemen in clothes stolen from victims, which enabled them to get close to unsuspecting victims. From their headquarters at Doughboy Hollow, they stole only the best horses and it was not uncommon for them to take over the Great Northern road for a whole day. Davis usually treated his victims well and on one occasion, after a mock trial, dealt out thirty-six lashes to an overseer noted for harsh treatment of assigned convict servants. Four of the Jewboy gang were captured in June 1839, but it had little effect on their continuous robberies of homes as well as on the highways. On one occasion they captured a party of pursuers, a Chief Constable, some troopers and settlers and 'yarded them like cattle' and took their horses and arms.

Law and order finally caught up with Davis and his gang. In December 1840, they raided Captain Horsley's homestead at Hexham. Citizens, roused by a local settler, Edward Day, formed a posse and after two days hard riding cut them off before they reached Doughboy Hollow and after a violent battle, Davis and five others surrendered. Glanvill was captured next day and all seven, Davis, Jack Everett, John Shea, Bob Chitty, Jim Bryant, Jack Marshall and Richard Glanvill, were hanged on 16 March 1841. Citizen Edward Day was given a public testimony for organising the pursuit and capture which was both an expression of community service as well as of public irritation with lawlessness.

WESTWOOD 'RUINED BODY AND SOUL'

A direct victim of the transportation system, William 'Jacky Jacky' Westwood was a bushranger with a difference. Convicted at sixteen for forging a receipt for a few shillings, he was transported and became an assigned servant. Returning with goods purchased for his master he was robbed by a bushranger, disbelieved and sent for trial accused of the loss of the goods. He absconded and went bush with the notorious Paddy Curran, an established bushranger. They subsequently raided Westwood's overseer, Phillip King, but Westwood attacked Curran when he attempted to rape King's wife. Westwood then worked on his own and became famous as the 'polite bushranger'. He stole racehorses, 'blacked' his face in the tradition of the 'Waltham Blacks' and for two years pillaged on roads and in stores, hotels and houses. In 1841 he was captured and escaped no less than three times. But he was not so lucky at the Black Horse Inn on the Berrima road; when recognised by the publican's wife, he was knocked unconscious by a carpenter with a hammer. He was sentenced to life imprisonment but escaped again from Darlinghurst Gaol. Caught, he was this time sent to the prison for incorrigibles at Cockatoo Island. There he led twenty-five other fellow convicts in a desperate attempt to swim to Balmain but

John Batman was a farmer in Van Diemen's Land, officially engaged to track and capture bushrangers as a bounty hunter. He caught Jeffries, Hopkins and Broughton, all convicted of murder and cannibalism, and captured the notorious Matthew Brady singlehanded and brought him to the gallows. He was rewarded by the post of special constable and poundkeeper and sizeable acres of land before becoming Melbourne's popular hero founder.
Courtesy La Trobe Library, Melbourne.

was arrested and sent to Port Arthur. A marked man by now he escaped from a work party but with his companion shot dead, he was recaptured within a few days. He finally escaped by swimming past Eaglehawk Neck and resumed bushranging but ultimately surrendered. His death sentence was commuted to life imprisonment on Norfolk Island under the harsh, reactionary Major Childs. Preferring death, Jacky Jacky led 1600 prisoners in a riot on 2 July 1846. Crying 'I'm going to the gallows', he personally clubbed two warders to death and his followers cut them to pieces. Two off-duty warders were also axed to death in bed.

With thirteen others, including Kavanagh, Martin Cash's partner in Van Diemen's Land, Westwood was hanged on 13 October 1846. Martin Cash, himself, refused to join the rebellion and remained in his cell. Westwood wrote before his execution:

> I welcome death as a friend ... the world or what I have seen of it has no allurement for me ... the spirit of the British law is reformation. Now sad years of experience should have taught them that instead of reforming the wretched man under the present system led by example on the one hand and driven by despair and tyranny on the other goes from bad to worse till at length he is ruined body and soul.

His letter from the condemned cell to a former chaplain at Port Arthur was so well written that it was published in England in the *Cornwall Chronicle*.

In the meantime, his ex-partner Paddy Curran, who had been tried with another prisoner Berry at Goulburn, killed one of their escorts, Maguire, on the way to Berrima gaol and they both escaped to continue bushranging until recaptured in September 1841, Curran being hanged for murder and rape and Berry for murder.

SHIPS SEIZED BY CONVICTS

In New South Wales some escaped convicts turned pirate. In 1808, convicts led by an ex-Royal Navy Lieutenant convicted of forgery and theft, seized the brig *Harrington* at anchor in Sydney Cove on the night of Sunday, 16 May 1808 and towed her down the harbour with rowing boats. The *Harrington* was finally captured in the Indian Ocean by the British frigate *Phoenix* and Stewart and some of the convicts were taken prisoner but others escaped when the *Harrington* ran aground and broke up during the affray. Again, in May 1814, prisoners escaped with the *Argo* pursued by a government schooner.

Several bushrangers also turned pirate in 1842 attempting to sieze the brig *Governor Phillip*. Sergeant Whitehead and the second mate Chris Lucas were wounded and three prisoners killed. When Henry Sears was hanged and the others, Thomas Whelan, John Jones, George Beavors, Nicholas Lewis and James Woolf, were sentenced to life imprisonment, the convict bushranging era in New South Wales almost completely receded. A summary of the main bushranger pirates in New South Wales and Van Diemen's Land is given in Table 4 (page 18).

The Second Era

V. R.

Chief Secretary's Office,
Melbourne, 8th July, 1857.

WILFUL MURDER.

£50 REWARD.

WHEREAS the HEAD of a MURDERED FEMALE has been found at the bottom of a hole situated in an abandoned gully known by the name of "*Paddy's Gully,*" a mile and a half from the township of Avoca, and in a neighbouring hole in the same locality a piece of canvas stained with blood has also been found: And whereas a skeleton without a head, and otherwise dismembered, with an axe lying alongside, has been discovered on an open piece of ground about four miles from the said gully: And whereas the said human remains are supposed to have belonged to the same individual: Notice is hereby given that a Reward of FIFTY POUNDS will be paid to any person who shall give such information as will lead to the apprehension and conviction of the person or persons who murdered the said female.

By His Excellency's Command,

WILLIAM C. HAINES.

PARTICULARS.

On Monday, 15th June, one of two miners working in an abandoned gully called "*Paddy's Gully,*" 1½ miles from Avoca, found the head of a European female at the bottom of a hole. The head was fractured in two places. It had been severed from the trunk by a sharp instrument. At the top of the forehead there is a bullet hole. The teeth are entire, except two, which are decayed. Some reddish brown hair lay beside the head. The deceased is supposed to have been about 30 years of age, and to have been dead about three months or more.

In a neighbouring hole had been previously found a tarpaulin or a canvas fly covered with blood: it appears to be a dray cover. The skeleton was found on an open piece of ground near the Four mile flat (on Mr. Bradshaw's run), it is destitute of the head, and otherwise incomplete. An American axe, rusted with blood, with a straight handle of iron bark, lay alongside the skeleton.

The murder appears to have been committed while the parties were camped for the night, and the head was carried four miles from the trunk in a direction leading up the country towards Avoca.

By Authority: John Ferres, Government Printer, Melbourne.

A group of Diggers panning for gold.
Fauchery Collection, courtesy La Trobe Library, Melbourne.

Robbers were mostly Callous Vandiemonians

By 1855, the transportation of convicts had virtually come to an end, except in Western Australia, where the last transport unloaded in 1868. It was there that the last of the convict bushrangers, Joseph Johns (Moondyne Joe), began horse-stealing in 1853, but he gained more notoriety as a gaol escapee than as a bushranger.

In the meantime gold was discovered in Victoria in 1851, and the population of Australia increased from 405,000 to 1,145,000 in the next ten years.

Although the independent digger was not typical of most Australian settlers since more than 100,000 assisted immigrants entered New South Wales alone during the Rush period, the gold rushes interrupted the steady growth of Victoria and New South Wales and brought a new kind of bushranger into existence with the 'Wild Colonial Boy'. He was a free, restless young man accustomed to open spaces and even had an established vocabulary with everyday terms such as mate, swag, coo-ee, bushwhacker, and the traps (a term which referred to the police).

Although the mining communities were generally orderly, persistent tension developed between diggers and police over the administration of the goldfields and this expanded into economic and political discontent. It was a period of restless mobility. Anti-authoritarianism was accompanied by racial antagonism towards Chinese gold-diggers and when alluvial gold declined, the unsuccessful and unemployed diggers shared the resentment of the labour force of stockmen, fencers and shearers towards the squatters. This resentment became bitter over legislation on land selection.

It was also a period of sturdy independence. The *Australian Colonies Government Act* of 1850 granted self-government to all the colonies. In Victoria, the sudden increase in population could hardly have come at a worse time for an inexperienced government, especially one in the hands of Crown nominees and pastoral representatives with half the population dependent, directly or indirectly, on the pastoral industry for a living. The squatters and the established gentry murmured against this invasion and the threat to their monopoly, and a Melbourne journal declared: 'the golden fleece of our pastures, waving fields of golden grain and golden oil obtainable from overseas are the true gold for us'[1].

Some improved conditions came from well-meaning if fumbling efforts of officials and from the common sense of the majority of miners but more specifically from the practical effect of rising gold revenue. However, some rebellious diggers, many of them directly from Europe or America, pressed for a more democratic constitution.

As gold fever raged, it was accompanied by crime by gold robbers, tent robbers, 'candle-light fossickers' who 'emu-picked' shafts while miners were asleep, highwaymen and confidence tricksters. It was estimated that about ten per cent of those flocking to the goldfields in Victoria were 'Vandiemonians' and by 1852 there were over 5,000 freed convicts in Victoria, half of them on 'conditional pardons'.

GOLDFIELDS POLICE

Police lived a dangerous existence on the goldfields and Lieutenant Governor La Trobe found it hard to recruit goldfields police, who were at all times below strength. Some diggers formed their own protective societies to pay back organised robbers. A 'Yankee kangaroo Court' hanged one ex-convict for murder after he had quarrelled with his partner, also an ex-convict, when they had struck it rich, and had put an axe deep into his skull.

A coachful of Chinese off to the Diggings, 1855.
Courtesy La Trobe Library, Melbourne.

While diggers laid waste the land, traders and merchants began to flourish, and squatters and sheep men, although short of labour, sold their meat and wool to the newcomers. Gold robbers, mostly callous Vandiemonians, strategically plundered the roads to the goldfields. The Black Forest became so notorious that not even mounted police could effectively patrol it.

In 1836 Captain William Lonsdale was appointed Police Magistrate for the Port Phillip District and brought with him three constables from Sydney. A Native Police Corps had been founded in 1837, disbanded, but reformed in 1842 and served till 1852.

The main role of the police had been as a mobile force for protection against bushrangers and Aborigines and to recapture escaped convicts, but when gold fever struck, forty of the fifty men that comprised the Melbourne Town Police, resigned to go off to the goldfields as well as fifteen men from the Rural Police. In the emergency 130 military pensioners from Van Diemen's Land were engaged.

There was no central direction and the seven distinct forces, the City Police, Geelong Police, Goldfields Police, Rural Bench Constabulary, Mounted Police, Water Police, and the Gold Escort, all operated independently of each other. Police were also stationed in twenty-six country areas.

In 1852 a Select Committee gave special emphasis to the alarm along the roads to the goldfields and the *Police Act* of 1853 created the post of Chief Commissioner and the police were re-organised under one central control. Chief Commissioner Mitchell engaged an Inspector, three sergeants and fifty police from the London Police Force for a period of ten years. In 1858, the Detective Force inaugurated in 1848 assumed more definite proportions and between 1858 and 1861 forty new stations were established by the Chief Commissioner Cap-

tain Standish. By 1860 the police force numbered 1,432 men but they had to cover a vast area of 87,884 square miles (227,620 square kilometres). At the time of the last of the bushrangers, the Kelly gang, the police force was still comparatively small.

After the Eureka uprising in 1854 Governor Hotham accepted the fact that the goldfields 'had been policed by young officers possessing no particular qualification for a very delicate duty'. In the event, 'the traps', the fledgling new police force, were off to an uneasy start in their part in the most difficult task of reconciling law and order in a young society with an intoxicating new liberty it had never dreamed of before.

Many of the legends of digger extravagance date from the early days of the rushes. The conservatives were horrified. The London *Times* thundered 'the flocks of Australia are on the verge of destruction' and a clergyman saw it as 'the French Revolution without the guillotine'. The *Geelong Advertiser* reported 'a most extraordinary demand for guns, pistols, powder, ball and even cutlasses', and by early 1852 it was reported 'the roads swarm with bushrangers, the streets with burglars and desperadoes of every kind'. Because of claim jumping and tent robbing, diggers at Mount Alexander were authorised to carry arms for their own protection.

As the rush for gold became a flood, the bullock dray and the horse and cart were soon inadequate. The English-style coaches on the route between Melbourne and Sydney were not suited for rugged frontier work and in 1853, Freeman Cobb imported American Concord coaches. Their success lay in replacing the hard springs with straps or 'through braces' of bullock hide which reduced bumpy shocks and gave a 'pleasant, regular rolling motion'. Frequently bogged, and frequently held up by bushrangers, Cobb & Co's coaches were for many years the only reliable means of transport.

Significantly in 1854, the first telegraph line was laid between Melbourne and Williamstown and within four years major towns in Victoria were linked and also Sydney. Faster than the bushrangers' 'bush telegraph' the 'electric telegraph' became an effective weapon against them.

There was little threat to the pastoralists' political power from the first diggers as most wanted to make a quick fortune and leave, but widening opportunities attracted more stable immigrants who were prepared to stay and wanted a greater say in affairs. The pastoralists were soon challenged by bitter disputes over land rights and as diggers increased their demands for land the battle cry of the 1860s and 1870s became 'unlock the land' and many of the sympathisers who aided bushrangers during the period were small selectors.

(Left) Corunquiam and Munight. Two troopers of the Port Phillip Native Police.
Courtesy Police Museum, Melbourne.

Digger "Justice" on the Gold Fields.
Courtesy Police Museum, Melbourne.

The Native Police Corps, reformed in 1842, served in the early days of the Gold Rush till 1852.
Courtesy Police Museum, Melbourne.

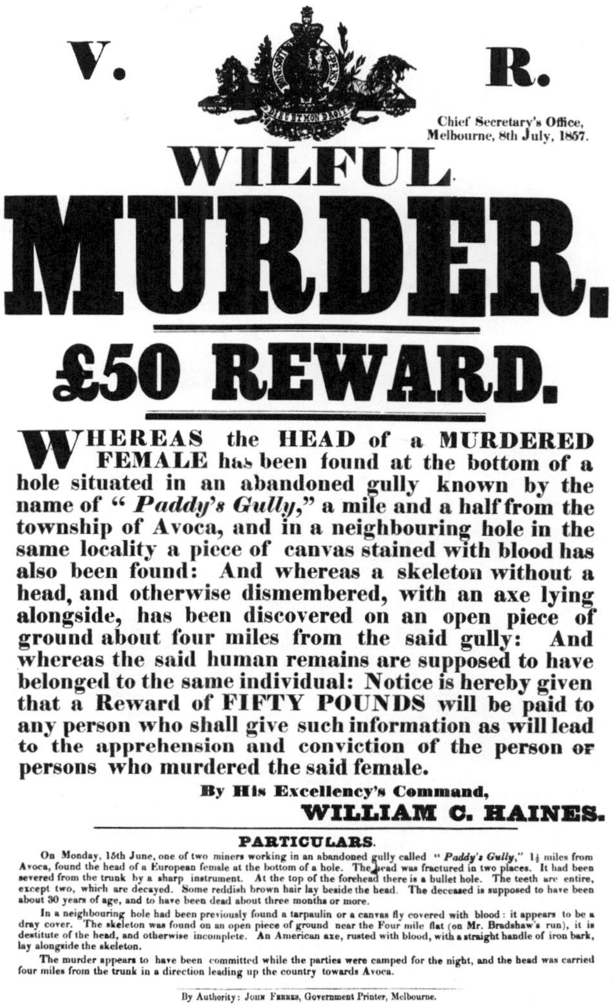

V. R.

Chief Secretary's Office,
Melbourne, 8th July, 1857.

WILFUL MURDER.

£50 REWARD.

WHEREAS the HEAD of a MURDERED FEMALE has been found at the bottom of a hole situated in an abandoned gully known by the name of "*Paddy's Gully,*" a mile and a half from the township of Avoca, and in a neighbouring hole in the same locality a piece of canvas stained with blood has also been found: And whereas a skeleton without a head, and otherwise dismembered, with an axe lying alongside, has been discovered on an open piece of ground about four miles from the said gully: And whereas the said human remains are supposed to have belonged to the same individual: Notice is hereby given that a Reward of FIFTY POUNDS will be paid to any person who shall give such information as will lead to the apprehension and conviction of the person or persons who murdered the said female.

By His Excellency's Command,
WILLIAM C. HAINES.

PARTICULARS.

On Monday, 15th June, one of two miners working in an abandoned gully called "*Paddy's Gully,*" 1½ miles from Avoca, found the head of a European female at the bottom of a hole. The head was fractured in two places. It had been severed from the trunk by a sharp instrument. At the top of the forehead there is a bullet hole. The teeth are entire, except two, which are decayed. Some reddish brown hair lay beside the head. The deceased is supposed to have been about 30 years of age, and to have been dead about three months or more.

In a neighbouring hole had been previously found a tarpaulin or a canvas fly covered with blood: it appears to be a dray cover. The skeleton was found on an open piece of ground near the Four mile flat (on Mr. Bradshaw's run), it is destitute of the head, and otherwise incomplete. An American axe, rusted with blood, with a straight handle of iron bark, lay alongside the skeleton.

The murder appears to have been committed while the parties were camped for the night, and the head was carried four miles from the trunk in a direction leading up the country towards Avoca.

By Authority: JOHN FERRES, Government Printer, Melbourne.

Native Police tracking.
Courtesy La Trobe Library, Melbourne.

The 'Flashness' of the Wild Colonials

From the turbulent fifties emerged the 'Wild Colonial Boys', adventurous youths, small farm and station hands and bushmen. This was the new breed of bushrangers whose lawless deeds ranged from highway robbery to occupying a town for two or three days. A summary of the main Wild Colonial Boys and Gold Rush Bushrangers is given in Table 5 (page 19).

These bushrangers were not escaped convicts driven to crime by force of circumstances or ignorance of any other way of life. They were either sons of immigrants or colonial born with a desire for quick riches and adventure and a contempt for authority. Some, however, may well have been second or third generation descendants of original transportees and bolters and a sample of seventy-five prisoners in Pentridge in the 1860s showed that thirty-five had a convict background.

In spite of land legislation which gave settlers the right and title to some land, small settlers were at odds with the big squatters. Losing out to 'men with capital' had burnt deep and to these settlers, bushrangers like Frank Gardiner and Ben Hall were folk heroes taking as they pleased—particularly blood-stock horses from the squatter or the purse from his lady. On the run from 'the traps', a bushranger could count on help from his mates, from mountain men and small settlers.

Young bush-bred men sought prestige and approval by defying the law after the manner of legendary deer stealers of eighteenth century England and their 'flashness' was in the tradition of those young English, who 'unless he were a Hunter, as they effected to call themselves, no young person was allowed to be possessed of manhood or gallantry'. Led into cattle and horse stealing, often under the influence of small-time criminal associates and ultimately into brushes with police and mounted troopers, the inevitable use of guns led to the point of no return from outlawry and finally death or imprisonment.

Cattle duffing was a major industry of the Weddin Mountain and Monaro districts of New South Wales just as horse stealing was of Kelly country. Bushrangers such as the O'Meallys, Clarkes and Lowrys were skilled at faking brands. During the era of the Gardiner gang, blacksmiths either burnt out brands or altered the original by branding over it or adding to the initials. The 'Strathbogie gentlemen' also used iodine to burn marks into the skins of stolen animals. They would raid for a mob of horses, drive them to the hills, fake the brands and when the scars were healed drive them to market, those from the north to Melbourne, Ballarat and Geelong in the south and those from the sound to the north as far as Sydney. The Quinns' 25,000 acre (10,000 hectare) property at Glenmore often acted as a half-way area through which stolen animals passed.

Few of the 'Wild Colonials' won riches. Some gained notoriety; some, under the influence of eighteenth and nineteenth century romanticism, became folk heroes and a rich source of material for Australian romantic writers and impressionist painters. Some identified their challenge to authority with bush balladry and many of their activities were associated with grog, sly or otherwise.

A deep frustration swelled from the hardships and failures of small landholders on poorer quality land and their bitterness was taken out against the squattocracy and the representatives of law and order. Urban society was breathlessly pious and staid and insisted on protection, although some sections of the press lampooned 'the traps'.

Bushrangers attacking the mail coach, 1852.
Courtesy La Trobe Library, Melbourne.

Mail and Goods Disappear

It is ironic that the mystique of bushranging folklore centres on Victoria, as it had the smallest number of bushrangers of the three eastern colonies.

One of the main targets for bushrangers was mail coaches, and hold-ups on overland mail coaches began as early as 1840 and continued with regularity. On 2 December 1840 the Port Phillip Mail, carried by James Spittal on horseback en route from Sydney to Melbourne, was stuck up near the Murrumbidgee River and the two bushrangers treated Spittal to a billy of tea before disappearing.

The Melbourne to Sydney mail was again stuck up between Yass and Gunning in November 1845 by two bushrangers and again on 20 July 1847 at Foote's Creek, fifteen miles (twenty-four kilometres) out of Albury, but this time Edward Clark and Henry Turner were captured by Wagga police and sentenced to fifteen years at Berrima.

The Melbourne 'Overland' from Melbourne to Portland was waylaid and robbed near Bacchus Marsh on 9 October 1848, and while the mail carrier for the Belfast to Warrnambool Mail, McDermott, was spending an hour or so in the 'tap room' en route during February of 1849, his mail and goods disappeared. Three months later the Portland mail was again stuck up by bushrangers, but Peter Devlin was arrested before he got to Dandenong and Tom Jones was picked up as far away as the Snowy River. Each got a five year sentence for highway robbery. A few weeks later in June 1849, the Overland Mail to Sydney, now a coach with passengers, beat off an attempted hold-up by bushrangers on the top of Big Hill, Kilmore, but the next year, on 14 March, the Melbourne-Sydney Overland was bailed up a mile and a half (two kilometres) out of Goulburn in true gentlemanly highway robbery style, passengers being stripped of their clothes. Protests by a lady with a winning smile saved her own petticoats and a Scottish man's pants, so confusing the situation that the robbers in boisterous laughter even forgot to take the mail bag. A fortnight later the same mail was not so fortunate as all the mail and goods went and the driver and male passengers were stripped naked and lashed to the wheels with strips of green hide.

Other mails robbed were the Belfast-Melbourne and Portland-Melbourne in 1850 and the Melbourne-Geelong and Colac-Belfast in 1851. Two notorious bushrangers Owen Suffolk and Christopher Farrell who had constantly taken to the road between Geelong and Portland were caught within hours of robbing the Western Mail from Melbourne at Bruce's Creek and tying up their victims to trees. They went to gaol for ten years, the first three in irons. Suffolk effected a 'black suit of fashionable cut and wore black kid gloves' in the manner of the English highwayman cult. Farrell escaped from gaol twice, suffered a hundred lashes and was ultimately sent to the hulks. Having served his ten years, he remained incorrigible and went bushranging in New SouthWales and for armed robbery was sent to gaol for yet another sentence.

Robbery of the McIvor Gold Escort. An engraving by W. Hatherall, *Cassell's Picturesque Australia,* 1887, vol 4.

Gold Robbers, Tough and Heavily Armed

Australia's first real gold rush was at Ophir on Summer Hill Creek in New South Wales and within days hordes of men armed with pick and shovel were tramping towards Bathurst. With bagpipes playing and pistols firing into the air, parties of fifty to one hundred left Victoria to foot-slog the 500 miles (850 kilometres) to the new Eldorado. Soon, however, discoveries of gold in the Pyrenees made Victoria the 'Gold Country'. Ballarat was in its 'golden glory'. Newspaper offices added to the fever, the 'Red Rover' coach was quickly plying between Melbourne and Ballarat and a remote colony suddenly burst into world fame. The population of Victoria trebled between 1851 and 1853 placing great strain on the provision of essential services.

While finds were abundant, the diggers were optimistic and in good humour, but soon sought police protection. At first, heavily armed, they brought their gold to Melbourne and soon the government provided the first weekly armed gold escort for the gold transported from Buninyong to Geelong and thence by steamer to Melbourne. Then Ballarat became the starting point with an escort direct to Melbourne and a weekly escort from the Mount Alexander fields to Mount Macedon and thence to Melbourne was also established. Other gold escorts were organised by Alexander Tolmer, Police Commissioner in South Australia (now a colony) from the Mount Alexander fields to Adelaide for the South Australian diggers working there when the *Bullion Assay Act* made Adelaide gold prices more attractive than those in Melbourne. Some eighteen gold escorts braved bushrangers and the rugged journey till in December 1853, the Victorian Government began to ship gold from Mount Alexander for South Australia through Melbourne by sea to Adelaide.

While the goldfields were dominated by local diggers, serious crime was rare, but when in early 1852 they were invaded by what La Trobe described as 'expired prisoners from Van Diemen's Land, returned Californians and the most profligate portion of the inhabitants of this and adjacent colonies', crime increased rapidly. Gold robbers also rode the long cart tracks to the goldfields. Mostly Vandiemonians, tough and heavily armed, they were ruthless and not even the special corps of Mounted Police could check them. Pentridge Stockade was founded in 1851 and, when bluestone quarries were discovered there and convict labour was available, it became a permanent House of Correction in 1852. However, neither it nor the Melbourne Gaol and the Collingwood stockade could cope with the rise in convictions and by the end of the year, two old trading vessels the *President* and the *Success* were converted to convict hulks. Three others were soon added and prisons were established at Ballarat, Geelong and Bendigo. In order to keep ex-convicts out of the colony, a *Criminals Influx Prevention Bill* was passed in November 1852, but criminals found it easy to bypass ports and slip in overland. Evidence for the need of such measures is indicated by the fact that in January of 1853 there were 342 prisoners at Pentridge with a further 150 awaiting trial in Melbourne alone of whom 90 had been charged with capital offences. The position did not greatly improve during the next month with 118 awaiting trial in Melbourne.

In the meantime, at the beginning of 1852, on 28 January, a gang of four Vandiemonians on the Bendigo-Eaglehawk road was broken up by police, one being shot dead and the others captured. In February, mounted policeman Corporal Harvey was senselessly shot dead at Buninyong and his assailant Goldman subsequently hanged. Edward Melville gave up working as a station hand for a squatter and went highway robbing near Buninyong and

163

(Left) An official metal bullion box used for carrying gold from the goldfields.
Courtesy La Trobe Library, Melbourne.

Captain Melville's Death Mask. A specialist Highwayman of the Gold Rush, he took his own life while a prisoner at Pentridge.
Courtesy La Trobe Library, Melbourne.

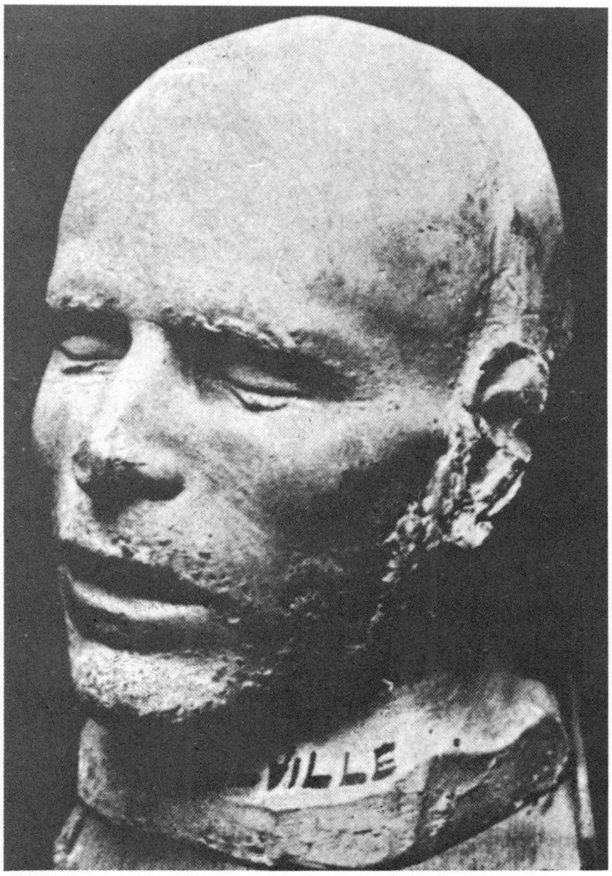

robberies soon became commonplace on the roads around Ballarat, Bendigo and Mount Alexander. In the Black Forest, on the road from Melbourne to Bendigo, an old man was wounded and his young son shot dead by bushrangers, and the Eureka gang led by John Donovan and John Finegan roamed over a wide area 'stripping' victims and stealing horses, but seldom gaining rich hauls. They were sent to gaol for twelve years and their accomplices Henry Johnston, Charles Bowe and John Baylie for six years each.

Robberies were not confined to the goldfield roads and when the ship *Nelson* arrived from London in March 1852, at the Woolpack Inn, a gang of seven or eight desperadoes from the Black Forest and the Keilor Plains concocted a scheme to steal two of Liardet's boats from the shore and board the *Nelson*. They escaped with 8,183 ounces (230 kilograms) of gold valued at £25,000 but the ship's mate was wounded. Within days John James, alias Johnson, was arrested and James Morgan and James Duncan were plucked out of bed at the Ocean Child Hotel, Williamstown. They were sentenced to fifteen years hard labour, the first three in irons. In the darkness they missed a greater haul of 120,000 ounces (3,400 kilograms) of gold on the *Madagascar* anchored nearby and it was thought this was their original objective. The *Madagascar*, however, was ill fated. On a subsequent voyage in 1853 she left Melbourne with at least 70,000 ounces (1,980 kilograms) of gold and a full complement of passengers and was never heard of again. It is believed to have been wrecked somewhere off the Victorian coast.

MELVILLE'S VIOLENT CONDUCT

Melville gained most notoriety among bushrangers of the Roaring Fifties.

Frank McCallum, a Scotsman, alias Thomas Smith, alias Captain Melville was transported to Van Diemen's Land for petty theft, and became a true highwayman with clear cut objectives of horses and gold, but his short career of freedom on the roads was ultimately terminated with three charges of highway robbery, one of which carried a sentence of twelve years and the other two ten years each — a total of thirty-two years. In December 1852, he and his associate William Roberts had raided a station near Wardy Yallock, boldly captured eighteen men, stolen two fine horses and set out on a riot of highway robbery on the Ballarat and Geelong roads. Then liquor opened the Captain's mouth in a Geelong Hotel and, in the ensuing foot-chase by police, he was captured by a civilian named Guy whose horse he was trying to steal to effect his escape. His associate Roberts, dead drunk, was easily arrested and sentenced to twelve years in prison.

Melville spent a year on the hulk *President* where he was found guilty of 'riotous and violent conduct' in trying to bite off the nose of a guard, Sergeant Kennedy. He was transferred to the hulk *Success* and for two years the public

SUCCESS
PRISON HULK "SUCCESS", AT HOBART.

The Prison Hulk *Success*.
Courtesy La Trobe Library, Melbourne.

heard little of him. Then on 22 October 1856, an escape bid was made from a launch transferring forty to fifty convicts to the hulks after breaking stones at Gellibrand Point and Melville smashed in Corporal Owen's head with a heavy stone-breaking hammer and threw him overboard. A sailor, Turner, was also murdered and a convict, Stevens, shot in the neck and lost overboard. The water police captured all the would-be escapees.

Nine of the conspirators were tried and Melville was sentenced to death, but a public meeting, chaired by the Mayor of Melbourne calling for an inquiry into the penal system and particularly into conditions on the hulks and the use of leg irons, resulted in the commutation of Melville's sentence to life imprisonment. Melville was removed to Pentridge but nine months later on 19 July 1857 he made an attack on the Governor of the Gaol, Mr Wintle, and was confined to his cell. Given to wild outbursts, he was under medical supervision but twelve days later was found dead in his cell strangled with a slip knot from his own blue and red spotted handkerchief.

Melville's trial had increased insubordination on the hulks. In a bushranger-prisoner revolt at Williamstown quarry in March 1857, during which Inspector-General of Prisons John Price was murdered, the convicts were marched back to the hulk *Success* and the harbour defence vessel *Victoria* had pulled up alongside ready to sink her in case of a general mutiny. When the coroner's inquest returned a verdict of wilful murder, fifteen prisoners were sent for trial; Thomas Maloney, Henry Smith, Thomas Williams, Richard Jones, Francis Brannigan, John Young, John Williams, John Smith, Richard Bryant, William Jones, William Brown, James Anderson, John Chesley, James Kelly and Daniel Donovan. Thomas Maloney, Henry Smith and Thomas Williams, the first to be tried, suffered a 1,500 word homily from Judge Barry on the virtues of honest labour before sentence of death was passed. Young, Smith, Anderson and Donovan were also sentenced to death and four others Chesley, Brannigan, Brown and Bryant were also hanged, but James Kelly, Richard Jones, William Jones and John Williams were acquitted.

GOLD ROBBERS SENTENCED

Captain Melville's arrest in 1853 had removed a central figure, but it did not put a stop to bushranging. Two escaped convicts in Tasmania, Connor and Brady, having captured a small vessel in 1853 and sailed to Victoria, immediately set about bushranging and murder. They senselessly shot dead an innocent farmer ploughing his field near Kilmore, without provocation. In one week, three men were murdered, several more shot at and others brutally ill-treated, the majority, it was thought, by these two who were captured by police, convicted and hanged for murder.

Even the streets of Melbourne were not safe with such gangs as the Canvas Town (South Melbourne) Mob on the prowl. A consignment of unsigned bank notes on the ship *Strathedon* with a face value of £100,000 was stolen late in 1853 but their careless passing led to the arrest of a gang of bushrangers known to frequent the bush near Melbourne. William Layworth turned Queen's Evidence and the rest of the gang, William Young, William Simpson, William Rogers and Thomas Stroud, went to gaol.

The *Geelong Advertiser* bewailed the robberies and assaults by bushrangers but the police were busy collecting licence fees at the goldfields. The great bushranging event of 1853 was the McIvor Gold Escort robbery in which the driver, Thomas Flooks, was killed, three troopers wounded and gold valued

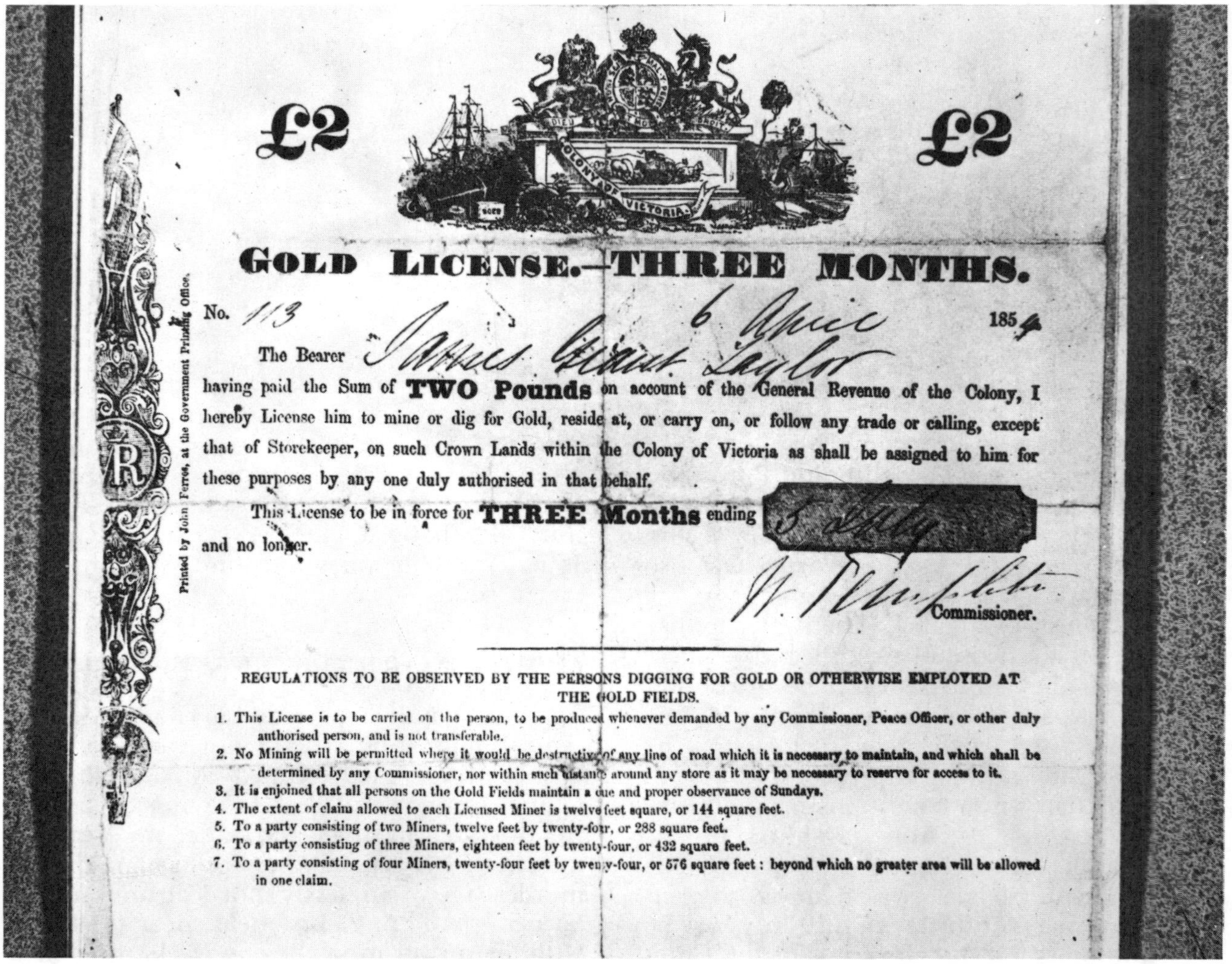

£2 £2

GOLD LICENSE.—THREE MONTHS.

No. 113 6 April 1854

The Bearer James Grant Taylor

having paid the Sum of **TWO Pounds** on account of the General Revenue of the Colony, I hereby License him to mine or dig for Gold, reside at, or carry on, or follow any trade or calling, except that of Storekeeper, on such Crown Lands within the Colony of Victoria as shall be assigned to him for these purposes by any one duly authorised in that behalf.

This License to be in force for **THREE Months** ending 5 July and no longer.

Commissioner.

Printed by John Ferres, at the Government Printing Office.

REGULATIONS TO BE OBSERVED BY THE PERSONS DIGGING FOR GOLD OR OTHERWISE EMPLOYED AT THE GOLD FIELDS.

1. This License is to be carried on the person, to be produced whenever demanded by any Commissioner, Peace Officer, or other duly authorised person, and is not transferable.
2. No Mining will be permitted where it would be destructive of any line of road which it is necessary to maintain, and which shall be determined by any Commissioner, nor within such distance around any store as it may be necessary to reserve for access to it.
3. It is enjoined that all persons on the Gold Fields maintain a due and proper observance of Sundays.
4. The extent of claim allowed to each Licensed Miner is twelve feet square, or 144 square feet.
5. To a party consisting of two Miners, twelve feet by twenty-four, or 288 square feet.
6. To a party consisting of three Miners, eighteen feet by twenty-four, or 432 square feet.
7. To a party consisting of four Miners, twenty-four feet by twenty-four, or 576 square feet: beyond which no greater area will be allowed in one claim.

A source of irritation — the Gold License — twelve square feet for a single miner.
Courtesy La Trobe Library, Melbourne.

The Eureka Uprising.
Courtesy La Trobe Library, Melbourne.

around £5,000 taken, never to be recovered. However, some months later, John Murphy was arrested on the ship *Madagascar,* turned informer and then suicided. His brother Jeremiah was arrested in Queensland and escaped punishment by informing. Their fellow desperadoes, George Wilson, George Melville and William Atkins, were hanged for the murder of the coach driver.

One of the great hauls was the hold-up of the Bank of Victoria at Bakery Hill, Ballarat, in December 1854 when, with unloaded pistols, Thomas Quinn, John Boulton, Henry Marriott and Henry Garrett stole £14,300 in cash and 350 ounces (10 kilograms) of gold. However, Boulton, Quinn and Marriott were quickly caught after being detected passing the cash and Quinn turned informer. Boulton and Marriott were sentenced to ten years gaol. Garrett escaped and took a long sea voyage to England on the *Dawstone,* but was followed by Detective Webb and extradited from London to serve ten years alongside his fellow conspirators. While in gaol, he was punished by a visiting Justice with a period of solitary confinement on bread and water for inciting fellow prisoners in the mess room 'that Almighty God had no jurisdiction beyond the Equator and consequently people in this part of the world could do as they pleased'.

THE 'EUREKA STOCKADE'

The manner in which tax gatherers Doveton, Armstrong, Captain Dana and his troopers collected licence fees from the diggers was not the most diplomatic for a delicate and inevitably unpopular task. Certainly Armstrong, an old Californian hand nicknamed 'the Monster', and his like were not the right people to be collecting the tax even if the diggers had been entirely happy about contributing any fees towards administrative costs. A tax collector 'accompanied by two troopers each with a pistol in each hand and a blackfellow going around from tent to tent, enforcing the people to take out licences whether diggers or not' was a potent irritant.

When Lieutenant Governor Sir Charles Hotham, who took over from Governor La Trobe, arrived in Victoria in June 1854, he inherited a 'financial mess'. He had been despatched from the Colonial Office to 'square the budget' but on the goldfields, a main source of the colony's wealth, he faced an inheritance of unrest centred on the monthly tax or licence fee which the diggers had to pay whether they found gold or not.

Hotham set out to find why less than half of the 77,122 male diggers paid the licence fee. When a petition to suppress the licence fee was presented to him he gave the petitioners 'to understand that they must *pay for liberty and order,* and on concluding was *loudly cheered*'[2].

He observed that the 'mass of the diggers ... are true hearted and loyal and men who if well treated may be thoroughly depended upon', and that 'this restless population must be restrained'. He noted perceptively that he 'would rather see an army of ten thousand women arrive than an equal number of soldiers ... where the soldier will fail, the interest of the wife and child will prevail'[3].

The diggers wanted roads and water for their canvas and shanty towns but objected to their fees being spent on enforcing payment rather than on improved conditions.

To defray costs, overcome the laxity of tax collectors and cope with the difficulties of wandering diggers spread in many holes over the countryside, Hotham increased the frequency of collection of licence fees from monthly to twice weekly.

The first protests came from the Bendigo fields in mid-1853, but with a strong Irish element, the Ballarat fields became the centre of

V. R.

Colonial Secretary's Office,
Melbourne, 1st September, 1853.

PUBLIC NOTICE.

His Excellency the Lieutenant Governor

Directs it to be notified that the

PROPOSED ABOLITION

OF THE

LICENSE FEE TO DIG GOLD

IN NO WAY AFFECTS

The obligation of any one to Pay

THE CURRENT LICENSE FEES,

Until a new Act may be passed by the Legislature.

In the meantime the Law must be obeyed. His Excellency relies on the good sense and loyalty of the community, and to the influence of their example in supporting order and maintaining the Law.

By His Excellency's Command,

JOHN FOSTER,

COLONIAL SECRETARY.

By Authority: JOHN FERRES, Government Printer, Melbourne.

(Left) An appeal for 'good sense' pending the passing of legislation to abolish the License Fee.

A portrait of Peter Lalor by Ludwig Becker, 1856. *Courtesy La Trobe Library, Melbourne.*

agitation. Tension deepened with the murder of a digger, Scobie, outside Eureka Hotel followed by the arrest and acquittal of its Vandiemonian ex-convict landlord, Bentley, and two associates. Angry at the acquittal, the diggers burnt down the hotel. Three alleged arsonists were convicted and Bentley and his two associates were rearrested and convicted for manslaughter.

A mass meeting of ten thousand diggers led to the appointment by Hotham of a Commission of Enquiry and he, the Colonial Secretary and the Attorney General met a three man deputation of the miners from Ballarat.

The main issues discussed[4] were whether the diggers were putting themselves above the law and overthrowing trial by jury in demanding a release of the three alleged arsonists when a retrial was under way, and whether diggers should have more privileges than other citizens by claiming a vote on payment of a fortnight's or even a three months' licence fee. They claimed that 'taxation without representation is tyranny', a licence fee being regarded as a tax. The legislation provided that anyone who followed a fixed avocation for twelve months was entitled to a vote and similarly any digger who took out a licence for a year to prove he was not a 'mere visitor' was also entitled to a vote. The diggers felt they were treated as 'wandering vagabonds' and demanded a vote on payment of any fee and the abolition of any property qualification for members of Parliament[5]. They also could not readily obtain land on which to settle since the best land was put up in the largest allotments and only men of capital could purchase it and the poorer land was 'cut up into small slices for the diggers'.

In 1854 the miners grievances eventually led to the 'Eureka Stockade', an armed clash with soldiers and some police during which about thirty men were killed. Of the original ten thousand who cheered at the mass meeting, only five hundred built the rough defensive stockade and hoisted the Southern Cross flag. Many drifted off to the pubs reducing the final number to two hundred. Not everyone supported the insurrectionists and there was a firm front in Melbourne and Geelong. Many volunteered as special constables and many squatters, bankers, merchants and landholders pledged themselves to the repression of violence and the upholding of the 'existing law'.

Thirteen stood trial for treason but only one was found guilty and even he was released after three months and a Royal Commission corrected any views that the uprising was entirely due to Irish and foreign stirrers. Most diggers wanted a 'fair go' on the goldfields and a landholding if their luck failed. The Commission recommended digger emancipation and easier access to land.

Although this rebellion has been regarded as a fight for freedom, the issues for which the diggers were fighting are clearly removed from those concerning the gold rush bushrangers. These bushrangers were anti-authoritarian like the diggers, but they were also law breaking,

Tension with the Chinese on the Bendigo Gold Fields.
Courtesy La Trobe Library, Melbourne.

(Right, top) Eureka Stockade. Original drawing 1854. Crown Prosecutor.
Courtesy Law Department Records, Public Record Office, Victoria.

(Right, bottom) Route of Eureka marchers, 1854, Eureka Stockade. Original plan for Crown Prosecutor.
Courtesy Law Department Records, Public Record Office, Victoria.

PUBLIC NOTICE.

BROTHER DIGGERS,

AS A

FALSE REPORT

Has appeared in the columns of the *Advertiser* injurious to my personal liberty, relative to the Chinese question, I call upon the Diggers throughout Bendigo to refrain from taking any steps against the Chinese on the 4th of July. A

MONSTER MEETING

Is to be called on the 8th for the purpose of Electing Prospecting Parties (of which due notice will be given), at the close of which the Chinese question will be fully discussed, and both sides will obtain a fair hearing.

I have the honour to be, brother Diggers, your most obedient Servant,

WM. D. C. DENOVAN.

N.B.—Diggers, remain quiet on the 4th July.

COOK & SHERBON, PRINTERS, BENDIGO TIMES OFFICE.

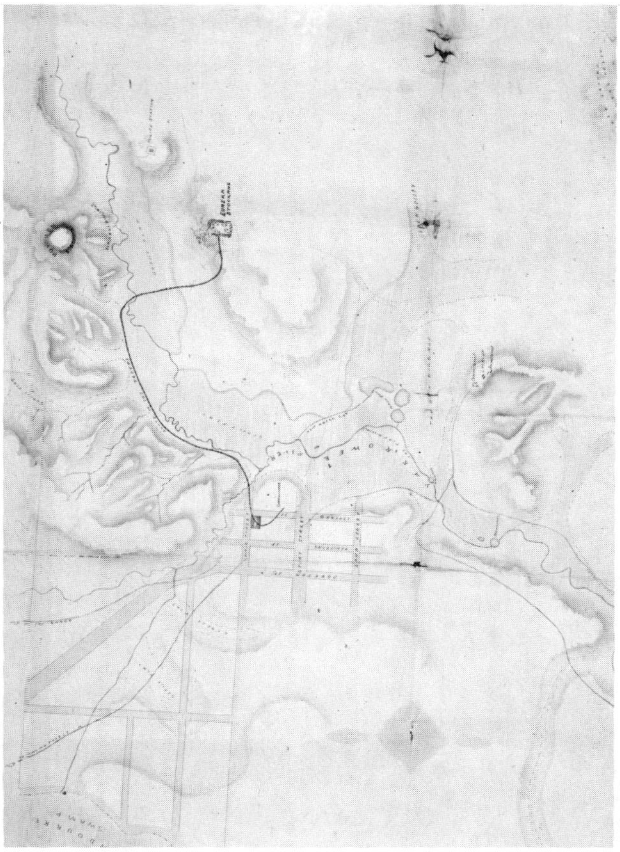

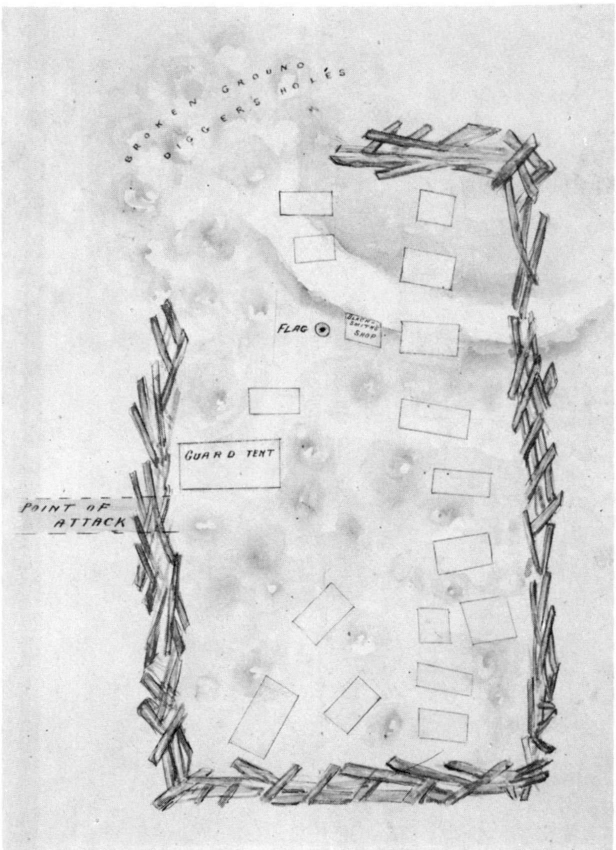

gravitating from highway looting of gold with the use of arms to cattle duffing, horse stealing, murder and so into outlawry. At the time of the Eureka Stockade bushrangers were mainly Vandiemonians or from the fringe of drifters who preyed on the diggers and their new found wealth and on the Gold Escorts. It was not until a decade later that the 'bold, free and fearless' bushrangers were regarded as fighting for freedom.

HARRY POWER AND KELLY

A central figure linking the diggings and post-Eureka bushranging was Henry Johnson, alias Harry Power. Transported to Van Diemen's Land from Ireland in 1848, he absconded to the Ballarat diggings but was unsuccessful and turned to horse trading. In March 1855 he was seen in the Maryborough district riding a valuable but suspectedly stolen horse. Challenged by police, a trooper fell wounded and Power escaped to the bush to be captured within days. He was sentenced to fourteen years gaol for 'wounding with intent to do bodily harm'. He was one of the gang from the hulk *Success* that seized the boat in Melville's rush in October 1856 in which Sergeant Owen was killed and in his later life after spending thirty years in gaol he was hired as a curiosity attraction on the *Success* when it was sold and became a tourist venue, giving lectures on life on the hulks.

In the meantime, however, he escaped from Pentridge in the gaol rubbish cart and commenced sticking up mails and robbing in the Ovens and Beechworth area in 1869. On 7 May, the Bright to Beechworth Cobb & Co coach was bailed up at One Mile Creek near Hooper's Crossing, Beechworth Road, and the Chief Commissioner of Police, Captain Standish, reported that on 28 August, the Beechworth and Buckland coach was stopped in the Bowman's Forest Gap by a man 'armed with a

Great meeting of diggers, 18 December 1851.
Courtesy La Trobe Library, Melbourne.

(Right) The Italian, Carboni, a leader of Eureka.
Courtesy La Trobe Library, Melbourne.

double barrelled gun and two revolvers . . . who boasted he was the person who robbed the Beechworth and Bright coach on 7 May last'[6].

Standish also reported that 'about Benalla and Jamieson . . . it is next to impossible for the best organised police expedition to effect his capture, owing not only to the nature of the country but to the disposition of the people to shield him and furnish him with supplies'. The *Daily Telegraph* on 3 December 1869 lamented 'it is a most disgraceful state of things that in open day the Queen's Highway should be rendered unsafe'.

Standish also complained that

> he [Power] had sympathisers and abettors in the district in which he has been mostly residing . . . it is well known to settlers and others residing near Wangaratta that there are a considerable number of cattle stealers and members of the criminal class in that part of the country (many of them being small settlers) and it is from these persons that Power receives succor and assistance[7].

Ned Kelly, as a lad aged sixteen, was arrested at Greta in May 1870, and charged with having assisted Power in robbery but he was discharged for lack of evidence. Certainly Ned rode with Power who said later, that after several shots were fired in a chase by troopers and Power's horse was grazed by a bullet, Kelly wanted to surrender.

Not everyone sympathised with bushrangers like Power. By the end of the month on 31 May 1870, a Mr Robinson wrote from the Shire Hall, Mansfield, to the Chief Secretary:

> By direction of a large number of the respectable inhabitants of this district to inform you that they are willing to tender their services to the Government as Special Mounted Constables for the purpose of assisting the Police in the capture of Power and his associates who have long infested and disturbed this district[8].

(Right) Harry Power (Henry Johnson) posing after his capture.
Courtesy Police Museum, Melbourne.

Wanted Notice for Harry Power, a transported Vandiemonian, horsestealer and highwayman, an associate of the Quinn's and the Kelly's and a formative influence on the young Edward Kelly.
Courtesy Public Records Office, Victoria.

DESCRIPTION OF THE OFFENDER.

He is described as probably English, aged 40 or 50; 5 feet 6 or 7 inches in height; with a short greyish beard, and heavy eyebrows. He wore a light-grey sac-coat of raised pattern, light trousers, blucher boots, and a light-brown felt hat.

The man described above may prove to be one Henry Power, *alias* Johnston, who escaped on the 16th of February last from Pentridge Stockade, where he had been confined under a conviction for horse-stealing at Beechworth. His description is as follows:—Native of Liverpool, aged 48, 5 feet 6¼ inches high; with sallow complexion, light-brown hair, blue eyes, scar on the forehead, scar on the cheek, two scars on the right arm, scars on the left elbow, large scar on the left shin, left third finger deformed. He suffers from stricture.

BY AUTHORITY: JOHN FERRES, GOVERNMENT PRINTER, MELBOURNE.

In the event, after the reward had been increased from £200 to £500, a search party of Superintendents Nicholson and Hare, First Class Sergeant Mountford led by Aboriginal 'tracker Donald' caught up with Power hiding out in a comfortable *gunyah* (bark shelter) on the Quinn's Glenmore property and he was taken to Beechworth with a horseback procession of civilians. Nicholson and Hare declined any pecuniary reward, but praised Sergeant Mountford and Donald who acted with 'spirit, fidelity and sagacity'. Donald received a reward of £10 and a James Quinn, Ned Kelly's grandfather, received a reward of £500. At first, the reward was held up as the police reported 'the claimant is in custody of Police on a charge of wounding with intent to kill', but later reported 'the claimant is not identical with the James Quinn as being in custody'[9]. However, Power was arrested in the King River Ranges on the Quinn family property. A suspect informer was Jack Lloyd, husband of one of the Quinn sisters, who contacted squatter Robert McBean who was set on Power's capture after Power had bailed him up on his Kilfera station near Benalla.

Described in police documents as 'the highwayman and escaped convict Henry Power alias Johnson', he was sentenced to fifteen years on four counts of highway robbery. While in prison, Julien Thomas, an *Argus* journalist who wrote under the *nom-de-plume* of 'The Vagabond' secreted himself in Pentridge during 1877 as the hospital dispenser and contributed to Old Harry's notoriety by interviewing him. A few years before his discharge two ladies known for their charitable deeds pleaded for his release and offered him a home in his old age, the rumour being that Power, who intended to stick-up their private carriage, saw they were ladies, bowed and rode away. Shortly after his release squatter Sir W.J. Clarke offered him a home on one of his stations which Old Harry thankfully accepted. Power finally fell into the River Murray when fishing and drowned in November 1891.

The Third Era

Ben Hall, Bushranger.
Illustrated Melbourne Post, 22 May 1865.

The New Breed of Bushrangers– Fearless and Free

Even before the Eureka uprising Governor Hotham had seen the need for capital to buy machinery to develop mineral resources and for land settlement for the newcomers. The two issues of capital and land became the seeds of intense struggles in the sixties and seventies between squatters and small selectors, and between organised capital and labour.

With the decline of easy goldfield pickings, the difficulties and frustrations of finding an independent living in a pastoral economy based on large squatter-occupied runs fanned a smouldering resentment against the squattocracy and the government, and anti-authoritarianism flourished.

Cattle duffing and horse stealing, particularly of the rich squatters' thoroughbreds, became almost a common trademark of young adventurous bush labourers, similar to the deer stealers of eighteenth century England. The flashness and larrikinism associated with cattle duffing and horse stealing were often the first steps to armed robbery and outlawry and to many of the growing urban population the new breed of bushrangers became romanticised as independent, bold, fearless and free.

These attitudes were all elements in a blending of European society with its economic and political institutions to a new environment.

CHINESE ATTACKED

Gold was discovered at Lambing Flat in New South Wales in 1860. With an apparent boom when there was stagnation elsewhere, 15,000 diggers soon flocked to the new field.

In the absence of police, a Miners' Vigilante Committee was formed to maintain law and order and on 12 December 1860 they first struck at the known drifters, sly-groggers and claim-jumpers and pulled down and burnt their shanties. Two were killed and ten wounded before police could be sent to restore order.

Resented on the Victorian goldfields, Chinese diggers, an alien group suspected of nameless devilries, also flocked to Lambing Flat and soon at Burrangong there were ugly scenes. A Miners' Protective League was formed with a wide ranging platform of expulsion of the Chinese, repeal of the duty on gold, unlocking the lands, protection for colonial industry and also the promulgation of the Word of God in mining districts. However, in June 1861 about one thousand enforcers narrowed these premises to expelling the Chinese and assembled at Tipperary Gully with whips and pick handles. With a brass band and 'No Chinese' banners flying they marched on the Chinese camp, increasing their numbers on the way to nearly two thousand to hunt down and whip the Orientals, plundering their gold and burning their tents to the ground and cruelly yanking out many pigtails by the roots. With the band striking up 'Rule Britannia' they then marched to the Back Creek Camp of five hundred Chinese and gave them the same treatment.

Three men were arrested for allegedly leading the riot but on 14 July, a mob of about three thousand attempted to rescue them, and when the Riot Act was read mounted troopers dispersed the mob and one man was killed and a number wounded. A detachment of the 12th Regiment, bluejackets from H.M.S. *Fawn* and an artillery party with a gun were then sent to Lambing Flat to maintain order and in November the New South Wales Government passed the *Chinese Immigration Act* to restrict immigration and settled the matter.

The Lambing Flat rioters had first attacked the criminal drifters round the diggings because Lambing Flat was notorious for robberies and hold-ups of diggers for their gold, and brutal retaliatory fights were an everyday occurrence. These drifters were the genesis of many bushrangers.

Frank Gardiner after ten years in Darlinghurst Gaol.
Illustrated Sydney News, 30 August, 1890.

Popular Heroes of some Sympathy and Adulation

Among the disreputable drifters at Lambing Flat was Frankie Gardiner, the illegitmate son of a Scottish free settler and an Irish-Aboriginal servant girl. Born Frank Christie at Goulburn in 1830, he was befriended by an old man from whom he took the name Gardiner.

A roving horse thief in his teens, he had his own gang in the rich Western district of Victoria, but caught with thirty-two stolen horses near Hamilton, he was sentenced to five years in Pentridge in 1850. Escaping after five weeks, he ended up in the Goulburn district again with stolen horses and this time a seven-year sentence of hard labour at Cockatoo Island prison. Released on a ticket of leave, he was in time for the lure of the new 'El Dorado' of Lambing Flat and ran a butcher's shop nearby as his base headquarters for robbery and as a rendezvous for many criminal drifters.

This new kind of bushranger of whom Gardiner was typical were either native born or sons of immigrant settlers and were driven by an inability to settle down and overcome the frustrations of a hard country in a robust, growing society with inherited institutions. With their dislike of authority they were easily enticed by the lure of adventure and of easy riches by theft. Summaries of the main bushrangers in New South Wales and Victoria during this final era of Australian bushrangers are given in Tables 6 and 7 (pages 26, 31).

In the rugged country of the Weddin mountains, in spite of the Robertson Land legislation which gave opportunities for settlers to take up land, small settlers were at variance with the big squatters, and to these settlers Frank Gardiner and later Ben Hall became local folk heroes; they took what they liked and they were delighted if it was the squatter's lady's purse or his bloodstock horse. On the run from the 'traps', a bushranger could rely on their help and shelter.

By the time the amiable Gardiner had staged his biggest robbery at Eugowra in 1862, he had gained a reputation for impudent flamboyance. It was said he often rode with a ragged copy of the poems of Byron, the great early nineteenth century poet of revolt, in his pocket and a pistol in his belt. The torrential force of Byron's rhetoric, of a man who had never learned self-restraint for the sake of high purposes, and, as an awakener of youth, his magnificent pictures of nature would have had strong appeal to young restless bushmen. The unhappy Byronic blend of snobbery and rebellion would also have appealed to the romantic ego of the self-styled 'Prince of Tobeymen' whose loves were a good horse, gold and pretty women.

Gardiner's first partner was flaxen-haired John Piesley, an ex-inmate of Cockatoo Island prison who after separating from Gardiner was soon captured and hanged for murder. Another intimate was Johnny Gilbert, the Canadian son of a respected Englishman who was a Freeman of the City of London. Gilbert came to Australia with his family during the gold rush. His uncle bought a hotel at Mount Waverley but was found murdered in April 1854, and young Johnny, aged seventeen, was arrested for the murder but acquitted. He then went to the bush and graduated from confidence tricks to horse stealing, for which he was sent to Cockatoo Island prison and there met Gardiner and so progressed to highway robbery.

Ben Hall, the least violent and most tragic of all bushrangers, also joined Gardiner but under different circumstances. Native born in 1837, he worked as a stockman in the Lachlan district as a youth and then took up a selection, and, in 1856, married Bridget Walsh. They had one son, Harry.

Gardiner had opened his butchering business at Lambing Flat with a man named Fogg but they closed the business and left just before

Looking out for Gardiner.
Illustrated Melbourne Post, 12 June 1862.

anti-gold robbers and anti-Chinese riots brought the police into the district. The crisis point of lawlessness and crime had been reached in New South Wales largely because the police operated in independent units and were so outnumbered that finally the military and the navy had to be called in to assist. However, the outbreak at Lambing Flat was responsible for a new order, and in 1861, the *Police Act* centralised control and divided New South Wales into police districts with an expanded force of about 800 men. After the 1850s, the quality of men entering the force had improved from the earlier ex-convict type. Leadership also improved and the police were required to perform wide duties. Although the major body that dispersed the miners at Eureka were military, police involvement was remembered more vividly long after. The romance of the bushrangers portrayed as popular heroes enjoying some sympathy and adulation was a source of antagonism to police, although most colonists were alarmed at threats to life and property posed by the bushrangers.

After the police organisation had been tightened up, Ben Hall was named as an accessory to a minor hold-up of a waggon and as an accomplice of Gardiner, by the unpopular officer in charge at Forbes, Sir Frederick Pottinger, an English baronet. Ben was held for a month before an acquittal and on his return home found that his wife had run away with an ex-policeman farmer named Jim Taylor and had taken their son with her. His home and sheds had been burned to the ground and stock had strayed. He acquired a gun and his first retaliation was to steal Sir Frederick Pottinger's fine horse. Soon his name was linked with the Gardiner gang and at sundown at Eugowra Rocks on Saturday, 14 June 1862, Hall, Gardiner, Gilbert and five others, Johnny O'Meally, Dan Charters, Harry Manns, Alec Fordyce and nineteen-year-old Jack Bow, began a vigil till dawn with tots of gin and tinned lobster provided by Gardiner from an earlier robbery. They wore Crimea shirts and red scarves and the beardless O'Meally and Bow had blackened their faces in the true tradition of the Waltham Blacks. They blocked the road with passing bullock waggons and ambushed Ford & Co's coach carrying mail and £14,000 in gold and banknotes. The driver, John Feagan, and Police Sergeant James Condell were on the box seat and armed troopers Moran, Havilland and Rafferty were seated inside. The coach was overturned, two troopers wounded and the gang rode off to their hide-out on Wheogo Mountain with bullion lashed to the unharnessed coach horses.

Dan Charters subsequently left the hide-out to check on his property but with a reward of £1,000 on the heads of the gang, Billy Dargin, a police black tracker, trailed Charters back to the hide-out to find that the gang had fled leaving some of the gold behind.

Gardiner had a narrow escape after the robbery, for when visiting Katie Brown near Wheogo, Pottinger, who had been alerted, had eight police waiting in ambush, but Gardiner raced off into the night heading for Queensland and later sent for Katie to join him at Apis Creek. The *Illustrated Melbourne Post* described the episode as 'The Australian Dick Turpin, Gardiner's Flight'.

It was suspected that John McGuire, brother-in-law of Hall's wife who shared Hall's property, and Clarke Gilbert, brother of Johnny, were in the robbery, but Harry Manns, Alec Fordyce, Jack Bow, Ben Hall and Johnny O'Meally were charged when Dan Charters turned Queen's Evidence. Manns was hanged, Fordyce and Bow, although sentenced to death, had their sentences commuted to life imprisonment and the charges against Hall and O'Meally were dropped for lack of evidence.

(Top left) Johnnie Gilbert.
Illustrated Melbourne Post, 24 June 1865.

(Bottom left) Bushrangers Hall, Gilbert and Dunn sticking up the mail at Black Springs, sketched by Police Magistrate W Rose who was at the actual stick-up.
Illustrated Melbourne Post, 25 January 1865.

Charters' reward was a job as a horse breaker for police.

Ben Hall buried his share of the gold (which has never been found) and together with Johnny Gilbert took over the leadership of the Gardiner gang. In the next three years, which are often called the 'Vintage Years', he became one of the best known but most tragic bushrangers of them all.

Gardiner was captured in Queensland at Apis Creek, inland from Rockhampton. As part owner of an inn and general store 'Mr Christie' had done so well that 'Mrs Christie', mistress Katie Brown, could not resist writing home to the Weddin mountains and Detective McGlure and two other police were quickly on the track. Charged with wounding with intent to kill Sergeant Middleton in July 1861 at Fish Creek, Gardiner, amid public acclaim, was found not guilty, but on several further counts of armed robbery and with wounding with intent to kill Constable Hosie, Middleton's companion, he was not so fortunate and was sentenced to thirty-two concurrent years in gaol. Released in the year of clemency 1874, after serving ten years, he sailed for San Francisco via China as Frank Smith and ran 'The Twilight Saloon'. He was believed to have been shot dead in a poker game in 1903.

GARDINER, GILBERT AND HALL

Johnny Gilbert, the Canadian, came to the goldfields in 1852. Cheeky and cheerful, he easily made friends as a stable boy among native bush-born larrikins around Kilmore. He became a popular hero to the Quinns and teamed up with 'Darkie' Gardiner in the Snowy Mountains in a number of raids near Wheogo in 1860 and in 1861 before gaining popular recognition, that is a price of £1,000 on his head, equal to Gardiner himself. The Gilbert gang became Gilbert and Hall and then the Ben Hall gang when Ben was joined by Michael Burke and John Vane.

After Eugowra, Gilbert and Ben Hall kept low, till Hall formed his gang with Gilbert and Johnny O'Meally and operated for almost three years along the Lachlan road and down the Southern road, robbing banks, mail coaches and the homesteads of rich squatters. They occupied the town of Canowindra for three days, where they progressively bailed up fourteen bullock teams, kept drivers as hostages in the hotel and even brought the local policeman as a prisoner to the spree and provided Ned Kelly with the bravado pattern which he later followed. After they had held up the Carcoar mail in September 1863, Hall and two of his gang captured three policemen who had chased them. They stripped them of their arms, tied them to trees and even took their uniforms for later use. The *Melbourne Punch* sarcastically lampooned the police and featured the 'gallant capture'. Again the Hall gang captured their old enemy, Assistant Gold Commissioner Henry Kneightly, Police Magistrate at Dunn's Plains near Bathurst, but not before he had fatally wounded Burke. Hall demanded and got £500 ransom for Kneightly after a sixty-mile (100 kilometre) ride by Mrs Kneightly to raise the money. Ben Hall praised her pluck.

The gang were declared outlaws and each member had £1,000 on his head and could be shot on sight. Vane, upset at the death of Burke, sought a priest and surrendered. However, freebooters James Mount, John Dunleavy and Jim Gordon became itinerant members of the gang until Mount and Dunleavy were captured. Their loss was partly made up by Johnny Dunn, a well-known jockey, who joined Hall and Gilbert. Together they raided stations such as Cliefden, Demondrille and Brubbenbong, but during the Gundagai mail coach hold-up at Black Springs

BEN HALL

(Top left) Ben Hall's capture and death, tracked down by Billy Dargin. Officially there were fifteen bullets in his body.
Courtesy La Trobe Library, Melbourne.

(Bottom left) Ben Hall's grave in 1930, restored it is rumoured either by a female admirer from Forbes or by an aging man called "Harry", perhaps Ben's son?
Courtesy La Trobe Library, Melbourne.

Ben Hall's grave at Forbes Cemetery in 1912.
Courtesy La Trobe Library, Melbourne.

near Jugiong, New South Wales, Gilbert shot Sergeant Parry dead. Gilbert was upset, 'He's the first man I've ever shot', but carrying guns created high temptation for impulsive use and there could be no excuse. In this episode they collected as many as sixty prisoners from various coaches and waggons passing by. They did much the same with the Binalong mail, this time holding thirty people. In January 1865, during a raid on Kimberley's store at Collector, Dunn shot Constable Kelly at close quarters. In March, during an attempt to rob the Araluen Escort, Constable Kelly was fatally wounded. Hall, who had never shot anyone, was shocked at the inevitable violence to which he was a party and decided to leave the country. Before leaving, he set out to make provision for his son and visited his wife and her paramour, ex-constable Taylor, and got a promise that young Harry would get Ben's property plus any money he could send. However, the *Felon's Apprehension Act* and the reward of £1,000 on his, Gilbert's and Dunn's heads, left Hall little time. 'Coobong' Michael Connolly, who vowed to carry out Ben's wishes for his son, is thought to be the one who betrayed him and, acting on information, black tracker Billy Dargin was able to lead a police party of Inspector Davidson and six police to his camp at dawn on 6 May 1865. Billy, who had known Hall all his life, tried to take him alive, but Hall went for his pistols and Billy Dargin wounded Hall, who begged Dargin to finish him, 'rather you than the traps', but the police came from cover, shooting. Either Dargin's bullet or those of the police killed him. Officially fifteen bullets were found in his body, although it was rumoured there were more than thirty. Hall was buried at Forbes cemetery on Sunday, 7 May 1865, aged twenty-seven.

'Flash Johnny' Gilbert had been shaken by his leader's death and he and young Johnny

Dunn hid out in a hut at Binalong, New South Wales, but Dunn's old grandfather, John Kelly, not only brought the police but dampened the bushrangers' cartridges and left them defenceless before four troopers. Constable Bright shot Johnny Gilbert dead, but Dunn was able to escape and headed for the Queensland border where he was later located in a stockman's camp, wounded in the foot, captured and subsequently hanged for the attempted murder of Constable Kelly at Kimberley's store. He was aged nineteen.

Between 1863 and April 1865, the Ben Hall gang had carried out twenty-one raids on various towns and homesteads, stolen twenty-three racehorses and bailed up ten mail coaches. Two constables were shot dead and one wounded. The police, whose prestige was low, were mercilessly lampooned by the press.

Taken as a continuous and coherent group, the Gardiner, Gilbert and Hall gangs show more extensive and successful enterprises and professional expertise and, in the personalities, especially those of Gardiner and Hall, more adroit and subtle leadership than was to be seen in the Kelly era. Gardiner knew when to retire and Hall set the pattern of homestead and hotel occupancy that Ned Kelly was to copy.

Lampooning the Police.
Melbourne Punch, 29 October 1863.

(Top right) Inadequate protection for the mail in New South Wales.
Sketches of Australian Life and Scenery, no. 10.

(Bottom right) Jeering at the New South Wales Police.
Melbourne Punch, 25 June 1863.

CAUGHT A TARTAR.

A 21 (N.S.W.) LEADS HALL THE BUSHRANGER IN TRIUMPH BEHIND HIM!

(Vide Sydney Telegram.)

Frederick Ward, alias Thunderbolt.
Courtesy National Library of Australia.

CHIVALROUS THUNDERBOLT

Frederick Ward was born in the Hawkesbury district in 1836. In January 1863 he was sentenced to five years imprisonment for horse stealing but on 11 September 1863 in company with Frederick Britton he escaped and swam across Sydney Harbour braving the sharks. They headed for the Hawkesbury district where they parted company, Ward to become the classical highwayman and skilled horseman in the tradition of Ben Hall, stealing racehorses and sticking up mails and stations for seven years before being chased and shot by a mounted policeman.

After his escape, Ward first stole a horse and rode to Cessnock and before Christmas of 1863 had commenced a career of highway robbery on the road between Maitland and Rutherford. He held up the Warialda mail, the first of four occasions, stole two horses from Manilla station and raided a further two stations and three hotels. At Millie Inn, a sixteen-year-old accomplice, John Thompson, was shot dead and in another hotel Constable Lang wounded. Thunderbolt crossed into Queensland in 1866 on a spree of robbery under arms but was soon back in New South Wales.

During his long career of seven years Thunderbolt gained a reputation for chivalry. He had a sad personal life, his sweetheart being committed to an asylum, he had several children by a half-caste mistress, 'Queen Yellow Long'.

In May 1870 Thunderbolt's career came to an end. With a young lad named Monckton he bailed up the Uralla Inn but police had been alerted by a hawker Ward had held up earlier in the day. Constable Mulhall pursued Monckton and Constable Walker chased Ward to Rocky River. Thunderbolt's horse was shot in the river and Ward wounded and clubbed by Walker with a revolver as he tried to climb out of the river. Left for dead while Walker went for help, Thunderbolt was not found till the next morning, alive but unconscious. He died at Uralla that day.

DARK DEEDS BY THE CLARKES

John and Thomas Clarke were of a different category. They took to the bush in October 1864, after bailing up the Queanbeyan mail and after Thomas had escaped from custody. Another brother, James, suspected of involvement with the Hall gang in the Cowra mail robbery and charged with receiving stolen property, was kept out of further mischief by a seven year gaol sentence. Sons of an ex-convict who was found guilty of the murder of a black tracker and ended his days in Goulburn gaol, and of a mother with four notorious brothers, the Clarkes were kin to a dozen reputed cattle and horse thieves, who acted for them as very effective 'bush telegraphs'.

The Clarkes shot dead five police and a

(Top) Thunderbolt's (Frederick Ward's) grave at Uralla, New England, became such a tourist attraction that the local R.S.L. erected a steel letter box.
Courtesy National Library of Australia.

(Below) Thunderbolt Rock, twenty miles from Armidale, New South Wales.
Courtesy La Trobe Library, Melbourne.

(Top) Tom Clarke on the stolen horse, Boomerang. *Courtesy Police Museum, Melbourne.*

(Below) "The surrender of the Clarke gang to Police after a gun battle and the wounding of John Clarke in the shoulder and Black Tracker 'Sir Watkin' in the arm". *Illustrated Sydney News*, 16 May 1867.

possible informer. They stole racehorses, robbed the Araluen mail, the Michelago Post Office, stores and travellers, and carried out some thirty-six hold-ups, including as many as fourteen small townships. They travelled fast, duffed cattle and planted horses and were often helped by young locals.

Joined by uncle Patrick Connell and cousin Tom Connell, and William Fletcher, a disappointed gold digger from Araluen and the Gulph, they raided the township of Nerrigundah in April 1866 robbing the hotel and store and holding about forty people hostage. The lone town policeman, Constable O'Grady, rising from his sick bed, singlehandedly and courageously sought out the bushrangers and shot William Fletcher dead before being mortally wounded by Thomas Clarke.

There were several more clashes with police, the Clarkes often being joined by their bush telegraphs, and when a posse of three warders from Darlinghurst gaol, John Carroll, Patrick Kennagh and John Phegan and an ex-policeman, Eneas McDonnell, set after them and made friends with Mrs Clarke and her two daughters, they were easily ambushed themselves. Two were killed in the fight and the other two captured but were then shot dead in cold blood by Tom Clarke. Their bodies were accidentally found by passers-by.

The Clarkes took charge of the roads, but the New South Wales government put £5,000 on their heads, taken dead or alive as a gang, or £1,000 on any one head.

Although Annie Clarke, a sister, was seen at court during the trial of four young offenders from the Clarkes' home territory, Braidwood, at the Goulburn sessions in April 1867, no link could be found between the Clarkes and the four men, Brown, Cunningham, Baldwin and Gough. Annie changed her costume including 'a hat with white feathers' four times during the trial in the manner of those English quarter sessions when all the village turned up in their best finery for the proceedings. In the meantime, Tom Clarke had shot dead a wounded member of his gang as a 'liability' and 'a possible talker', but a tall well-built tracker, 'Sir Watkin Wynne', who was described as 'handsome for a blackfellow', led a police party under Senior Constable Wright to a slab hut where the gang were sheltering and in the ensuing siege, Constable Walsh was wounded in the thigh and Sir Watkin in the arm, but the Clarkes were captured. Sir Watkin subsequently had to have his arm amputated, but was proudly promoted to Sergeant Major Sir Watkin.

When captured, the Clarkes had two revolvers, two double-barrelled guns, two revolving rifles, one single-barrelled gun and a horse pistol. They were hanged on 25 June 1867 at Darlinghurst.

In passing sentence, the Chief Justice, Sir Alfred Stephen, severely lashed out at bushrangers:

> many of them young men, capable of better things, but who died violent deaths. Piesley executed; Davis sentenced to death; Gardiner sentenced to thirty-two years hard labour; Gilbert shot dead; Hall shot dead; Bow and Fordyce sentenced to death, but their sentences commuted to imprisonment for life; Manns executed; O'Meally shot dead; Burke shot dead; Gordon sentenced to death; Dunleavy sentenced to death; Dunn executed; Lowry shot dead; Vane a long sentence; Foley a long sentence; Morgan shot dead; yourselves Thomas and John Clarke about to be sentenced to death; Fletcher shot dead; Patrick Connell shot dead; Tom Connell sentenced to death but sentence commuted to imprisonment for life; Bill Scott a companion of your own believed to have been murdered by you ... the list shows six shot dead and sixteen wounded in three

"Dan Morgan holding up a work party of Navvies and burning their tents".
Illustrated Melbourne Post, 25 January 1865.

years ... since 1863 ... and yet these bushrangers, the scum of the earth, the lowest of the low, the most wicked of the wicked are occasionally held up for admiration ... it is the old leaven of convictism not yet worked out, but brighter days are coming. You will not live to see them, but others will[1].

Although invested with the full majesty of British law and clad in imposing ermine robes and full bottomed wig, the Chief Justice's address did little to lessen the influence of the flamboyant deeds of bushrangers. Those of Gardiner, Gilbert and Hall became more infectious and soon overshadowed the uglier aspects of those of the Clarkes. The daring success against the Government Gold Escort at Eugowra attracted wide publicity, even in the English press, and the appeal of the new breed of bushrangers which was increased by the lampooning of the police by the press, was tempting to adventurous bush youths. The quiet bush life and its hardships offered no escape.

POST-EUREKA VICTORIA

In Victoria, with the exception of Power and Morgan, bushranging in the post-Eureka period survived rather than developed—desperadoes were quickly put away. In 1862, James Regent and two accomplices bailed up the Traveller's Rest Hotel at Yall-y-poora but were tracked to a hut near Mount Sturgeon in the Grampians and taken by Constables Lawler and Griffen without a shot being fired. In July 1864, there was a report that Gardiner and his gang had stuck up some people near Yea, and civilian volunteers with Constable Buck set out to investigate and instead located three bushrangers with a mob of stolen horses, shot one dead and captured the other two who went to gaol for robbery with violence.

Robert Bourke roamed south from the Murrumbidgee through Wodonga, Wangaratta and Diamond Creek (near Melbourne) robbing along the way but then wounded the young son of a homesteader who later died. Bourke was convicted for the murder of the son, Henry Hurst, and hanged in 1868.

'OUTRAGEOUS' DAN MORGAN

'Mad' Dan Morgan did however enliven the scene with a longer career. Reputedly one of the most bloodthirsty of bushrangers, he was another migrant from New South Wales into Victoria. Most active near Wagga Wagga between 1862 and 1865, his name was the most notorious in the Riverina district of New South Wales. Bushrangers such as 'Jacky Jacky' Westwood, Ben Hall and Captain Thunderbolt had some chivalrous instincts but Morgan in his later life had few and became a callous killer. Although recent research tends to treat him more kindly, nevertheless his deeds and those of the Kelly gang were the major contributing factor to the proclamation of the tough *Felon's Apprehension Act*.

Daniel Moran, alias Morgan, grandiloquently took the name of the famous pirate but is believed to be the son of widow Ann Telford, an Irish transportee, who married for the second time to William McNally, alias Moran. While still a youth, in 1850, his stepfather died and Morgan subsequently left Campbelltown for the Castlemaine goldfields in Victoria and in 1854, as John Smith, he was convicted of robbing a hawker of clothing eight miles (thirteen kilometres) out of Castlemaine, a trivial enough offence except that he carried a five-barrelled Colt revolver and the charge was that of 'armed robbery'. Caught after two weeks, he was tried as Smith, alias Sydney Hill, although he was also known as 'Billy the Native', and his occupation was given as 'jockey', that is, a dealer in horses.

Bushranger Morgan enjoying Mrs McPherson's Music.
Cassell's Picturesque Australia, vol. 1, 1877.

Sentenced to twelve years hard labour by Judge Barry, the first two in irons, Smith spent a short time in the hulk *Success* before being transferred to Pentridge later in the year, where his identity as Morgan was established. After six years, he was released on a ticket of leave, on the 23 June 1860, for good behaviour and conditional on remaining in the Ovens and Yackandandah police district. He failed to report and on 19 July 1860, he was posted as being 'at large illegally'. From a hide-out on the King River Flats he carried on with his preoccupation of horse stealing and stole a valuable horse named Grey Bobby from Thomas Evans' property. Tracked down to his cave in a hillside by Evan Evans and Edmund Bond searching for another stolen horse, he received a load of buckshot, the marks of which he carried to his dying day. He escaped to New South Wales swearing revenge.

In 1863 Morgan broke out into bushranging, raiding round the Wagga Wagga district. At Walla Walla he robbed John Manson, Maurice Branche and Robert Burton. He also held up the Police Magistrate at Wagga Wagga, Henry Bayliss, but Bayliss joined Sub-Inspector Morrow and Constable Bowen and tracked Morgan down. In the shoot-out Bayliss was wounded in the right hand, another Constable received a severe wound, but Morgan's mate and 'bush telegraph' was fatally wounded. Morgan escaped.

Morgan rode near Deniliquin to find a shepherd named Haley, whom he suspected of giving information to the police, but finding him absent, forced his wife back on to the fireplace of the hut burning her back before his rage was spent.

After a calmer period during the rest of 1863, Morgan, with two accomplices, resumed anti-social activities, stuck up the storekeeper at Corowa, stole a horse from Round Hills station and another from near Jerilderie, and then with two mates robbed the Holbrook-Tumbarumba mail near Round Hills. Morgan, alias 'Billy the Native', soon had four armed robberies to his name. In June 1864, carrying a double-barrelled gun and several revolvers, he robbed a hawker, Charles Marshall, and a young man in his employment. Eight days later, he raided Round Hills station to steal a horse and wounded the manager, Sam Watson, in the hand and a visitor, John Heriot, in the knee. The overseer, McLean, set off for Holbrook either to seek a doctor for the casualties or for assistance from the police. Assuming the latter, Morgan pursued him, shot him in the back, put him across his saddle and brought him back to Round Hills where McLean later died. Since evidence was given at the inquest that Morgan sat with the dying man for several hours, this action of bringing McLean back has been interpreted as a mercy trip and it has been suggested that Morgan unintentionally became a killer. It could be said, however, that Morgan like many compulsive killers had a sentimental streak and was not a balanced personality.

After McLean's death, the Mayor of Albury and some townsfolk became so outraged that they voluntarily formed a special posse of civilians who were sworn in as 'special constables' to hunt him down.

Eleven days later on 30 June, Sergeant McGinnerty and Constable Churchley on their way to Tumbarumba, unaware of his identity, passed Morgan and bid him good day, but Morgan recognised the unsuspecting sergeant and shot him dead and escaped with his horse, revolver and a rifle. In September, with £1,000 on his head and hearing that a police party of Sergeant Smith and Constables Cannon, Baxter and Reed was seeking him and camped for the night near Doodal station on Sydney Road, Morgan crept up to near the candlelit tent, and from the cover of the bush, shot

(Left) Morgan propped up dead at Peechelba Station.
Courtesy Police Museum, Melbourne.

Morgan's Death Mask,
Courtesy University of Melbourne.

Sergeant Smith dead and disappeared into the night. According to the police report some ten to twelve shots were fired.

Accusing him of being a spy, Morgan also shot dead one of the volunteers in the hunt for him, who was disguised as a shepherd on Wallandool station.

On 2 April 1865 he crossed the River Murray 'to take the flashness out of the Victorian people and police' and seeking revenge on Evans and Edmond Bond, Morgan stole a racehorse called Victoria at Tallangatta and stuck up another station belonging to the McKinnons at Little River, stealing a small sum of money. But time was fast running out with his career of armed bushranging. After revengefully setting fire to Evans' barns and granary, he rode up to Peechelba station. He herded up hostages for a night-long party, but a housemaid, named Alecandrina MacDonald in the police report (but named by others as Alice Keean or Alice MacDonald), was able to escape and warn a neighbour, Rutherford, who after sending a message to Wangaratta police set a dawn ambush with nine of his men. Detective Manwarring and Mounted Constables Crilley, Percy and Hall rode through thick scrub and 'a storm of thunder and lightning' and missed their way, having 'travelled 70 miles (110 kilometres) that day'. They sheltered in a deserted bullock driver's hut and at 5 a.m. set off again for Peechelba where 'Constable Evans [from Benalla police] informed them that the offender was in the house'. The rest of the story is best told from the police report:

> [The police] restrained the eagerness of the volunteers fearing that a deal of carnage would ensue ... to MacPherson and his family and other innocent persons ... [Alecandrina or Alice] the servant stole out and informed the party that the offender was nearly done breakfast and would most likely leave the house at ¼ past 8 a.m. ... the

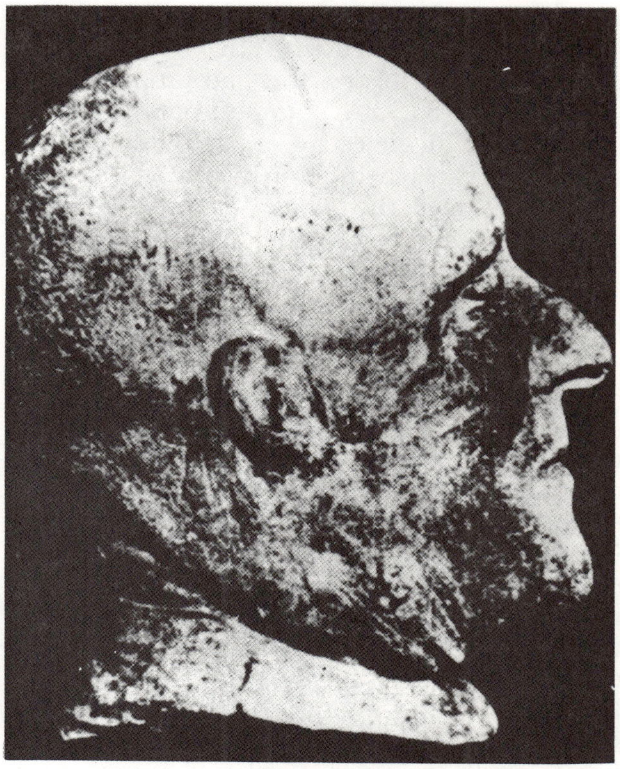

> offender left the house he had with him as prisoners Mr MacPherson, his son Gideon, Mr Telford and two men named Wenner and Maguire. They walked towards the stockyard about 250 yards [273 metres] from the house the offender carried a bridle in his hand and was quite incautious not looking around or seeming to suspect an ambush. The detective and party and Constables Evans and Leverton of the Benalla station who had arrived at 2 a.m. followed closely upon the offender at the same time warning the civilians not to rush just then and were extending to surround and challenge the offender when a man named John Windlam who is employed at Peechelba stepped from behind a tree fired and the offender fell

> wounded through the shoulder blade ... [Morgan was armed with] two of Colts large size revolvers loaded and had money to the amount of £85.5.2. ... after his removal to the woolshed, the detective spoke to him calling him Morgan when he opened his eyes ... he acknowledged the name Morgan on being spoken to and remained conscious up to the time of his death at a ¼ to 2 p.m.[2].

He was described as '6 Feet [183 centimetres], black hair very long and curly, knock kneed' and 'expression of face ferocious'.

Some say that Morgan was shot in a cowardly manner and should have been given the chance that he complained he had not been given, but he himself had not given any chance to those whom he had cold-bloodedly shot. Newspapers lampooned the police for needing so many people to catch one man, but the police report makes it clear that those he held with him as hostages were in a dangerous situation, especially if unrestrained or wild shooting had broken out. The unauthorised and irresponsible action of the Peechelba employee had unexpectedly resolved a delicate situation in which other and more innocent lives than Morgan's could almost certainly be expected to be lost.

Morgan was decapitated and a cast made of his head. As a result a Board was appointed 'to enquire into and report upon all the circumstances connected with the mutilation of the remains of the bushranger Daniel Morgan'. It concluded that it was 'of a brutal and disgusting character and an outrage upon public decency'[3].

Much has been made of the decapitation, but the medical evidence given on oath before the Board indicated that the incision at the throat was necessary for the post mortem examination ordered by the coroner and carried out by Dr Hallett of Wangaratta and Dr Henry of Benalla about 4 p.m. on Monday 10 April in the woolshed at Peechelba. It made decapitation almost complete since 'the head was merely attached by a small portion of skin and muscle'[4] and for a cast to be made, as requested by the coroner and a Justice of the Peace, after such a post mortem without finally removing the head, may well have been a difficult if not impractical task. The post mortem revealed

> two of the cervical vertebrae ... of the neck to be completely shattered by the ball. These bones were removed by Dr. Hallett for the purpose of making a preparation of them as a matter of professional interest and after Dr. Hallett had satisfied himself as to the cause of death every portion of the skin which had been divided in the course of the examination was carefully sewn up ... decently put out of hand, and the corpse sewn up in a bale, so that no portion of it was visible[5].

The Coroner's Inquest was held next day and on Tuesday 11 April the body was conveyed to Wangaratta by Superintendent Cobham and placed in the cell of the Police lock-up.

> In consequence of the numerous applications which were made by the general public, Mr Superintendent Cobham gave notice that they would be permitted to view the body for one hour; and it would also appear that the wool bagging was removed from the upper portion of the body in order that the public might view the features of the corpse dressed in the clothes worn by Morgan at the time of his death[6].

About 3 o'clock Morgan's corpse was removed to the

> end hall of the open stable. Dr Dobbyn, the Coroner of the District being under the impression that it was usual to take a cast of the head of any great criminal and Dr MacKay J.P. of Yarrawonga who was of the

opinion that it would be interesting in a scientific point of view to obtain a cast of Morgan's head, to see whether his phrenological development corresponded with his remarkable habits both made application to Mr. Superintendent Cobham to be allowed to have a cast made and permission to do so was accordingly granted by that officer ... in the presence of Mr. Superintendent Cobham, Dr Dobbyn the Coroner, and Dr MacKay J.P. of Yarrawonga and several spectators of the public the Board have ascertained that Dr Henry of Benalla fleshed the beard from the face of the corpse with a clasp knife supplied by Mr Cobham for the purpose and then severed the head from the trunk and laid it on the chest of the decapitated corpse. A barber was then employed to shave the mutilated head and it was washed with hot water. On this being completed the necessary operations for taking the cast were proceeded with and only concluded about midnight. The head was taken away by Dr Dobbyn and by his direction and with the permission of Mr Superintendent Cobham was sent to Professor Halford of the University of Melbourne. The headless trunk was then placed in a coffin and interred in the Wangaratta cemetery the following day.[7]

FLASH ALPIN McPHERSON

In Queensland the Celtic blood of Alpin McPherson was stirred by the deeds of the southern bushrangers and he endeavoured to emulate them in the now traditional activities of stealing racehorses and sticking up travellers and mail coaches. He took a number of aliases, John Bruce, Marr, Kerr, Scotia and was popularly known as 'Scotchie' or the 'Wild Scotchman', but his bushranging career lasted only eighteen months. Son of a respected Scottish migrant, apprenticed to a Brisbane stone-mason, a member of a debating class and a fluent speaker, for no apparent reason other than youthful euphoria, he ran off from his apprenticeship and, in Hall and Gilbert style, stuck up a country hotel on the Houghton River. With typical flashness, he announced his intention to fight a duel with head of police Sir Frederick Pottinger and crossed the border to New South Wales. He did in fact exchange some shots with some troopers and Sir Frederick, but was slightly wounded and returned to Queensland. His claim to have joined the Hall and Gilbert gang in robberies while in New South Wales is doubtful, but, suspected of horse stealing from Nanduran station in Queensland, he was caught by a four man civilian posse from the station and extradited to New South Wales on a charge of intent to do bodily harm. However, as the baronet's death left the Crown without their main witness, 'Scotchie' was returned to Queensland, remanded to Rockhampton but he escaped from the steamer *Diamantina* en route, still in leg irons. Recaptured, he escaped again but attempted to steal a horse from Kolongo station and was finally caught and sentenced to twenty years for highway robbery.

1872-78 BUSHRANGERS QUIET

From about June 1872 to April 1878, for almost six years, Australia was free from bushrangers. Captain 'Moonlite', the 'Reverend Gentleman', robbed the bank at Bacchus Marsh but did not recruit a gang to go bushranging till he was released from prison in 1879.

Ominously, however, during the seventies, James, the second son of 'Red' and Ellen Kelly, at fifteen years of age was sentenced to five years imprisonment on two charges of horse stealing and on his discharge in 1876, he stuck up a number of people and was sentenced to another ten years. Further, Ned himself, at the

The bearded Scott on discharge from prison. *Courtesy University of Melbourne.*

(Right) The warrant against Scott. *Courtesy University of Melbourne.*

age of fourteen, had been charged with robbery with violence but acquitted and a few months later, in 1870, he was serving a six months sentence at Beechworth for 'assault and indecent behaviour' since the family could not pay the £10 fine.

Although the Kelly gang was not formed till the Fitzpatrick affair in April 1878, the smouldering antecedents were already there in the preceding decade.

THE DEVIOUS CAPTAIN 'MOONLITE' (Andrew George Scott)

Andrew George Scott, 'Captain Moonlite', emigrated to Victoria from Northern Ireland in 1859 and fought in the Maori War in New Zealand from 1861 to 1865 and, wounded in the leg, became lame. He returned to Victoria in 1869 and became a lay reader with the Church of England at Bacchus Marsh with a view to ordination as his father, the Reverend Thomas Scott, M.A., before him.

His antecedents, influential introductions and an ability to speak fluently gained him a lay readership and his greatest friends were the Manager of the London Chartered Bank's Egerton Branch, Ludovic William Julius Brunn and a schoolmaster, James Simpson.

On 8 May 1869, Scott, masked and in a felt hat, 'feloniously and violently assaulted and robbed under arms the London Chartered Bank ... of gold and bank notes to the value of £1,195'. When subsequently arrested in Sydney, three years later, Scott said he 'knew nothing about it' and 'Brunn was charged for the offence himself and I was examined on behalf of the Crown for that offence'.

In fact Brunn and Simpson were arrested for the robbery and Scott was to be the principal witness, but 'as business called him away', the case against Brunn and Simpson collapsed.

When Scott was charged with the robbery, Brunn recounted in sworn evidence the events of that Saturday 'dark night with a Scotch mist'. Returning to the bank after tea at Simpson's house 'a man caught hold of me by the left shoulder and said be quiet or I will kill you'. Entry was forced, the safe robbed, Brunn blindfolded and taken to the schoolhouse. Testified Brunn: 'I suspected Scott by his voice ... a strong Irish accent and the peculiarity of his walk' and that at the schoolroom he said, 'you write the paper which I dictate, I hereby certify that L.W. Brunn has done everything in his power to withstand our intrusion [Scott talked repeatedly during the whole incident about a non-existent accomplice] and the taking away of the money which was done with firearms'[8]. This was written by the light of matches and signed 'Captain Moonlite. Sworn'. (The handwriting concerning the word sworn is difficult to decipher and could be interpreted as 'secret'.) Before being tied up Brunn was able to hide his penknife in his hat and so free his bonds and run to Ercildoun Mining Company to inform the manager and the police.

Scott's alibi was that the robbery was a conspiracy of Brunn and Simpson and at his

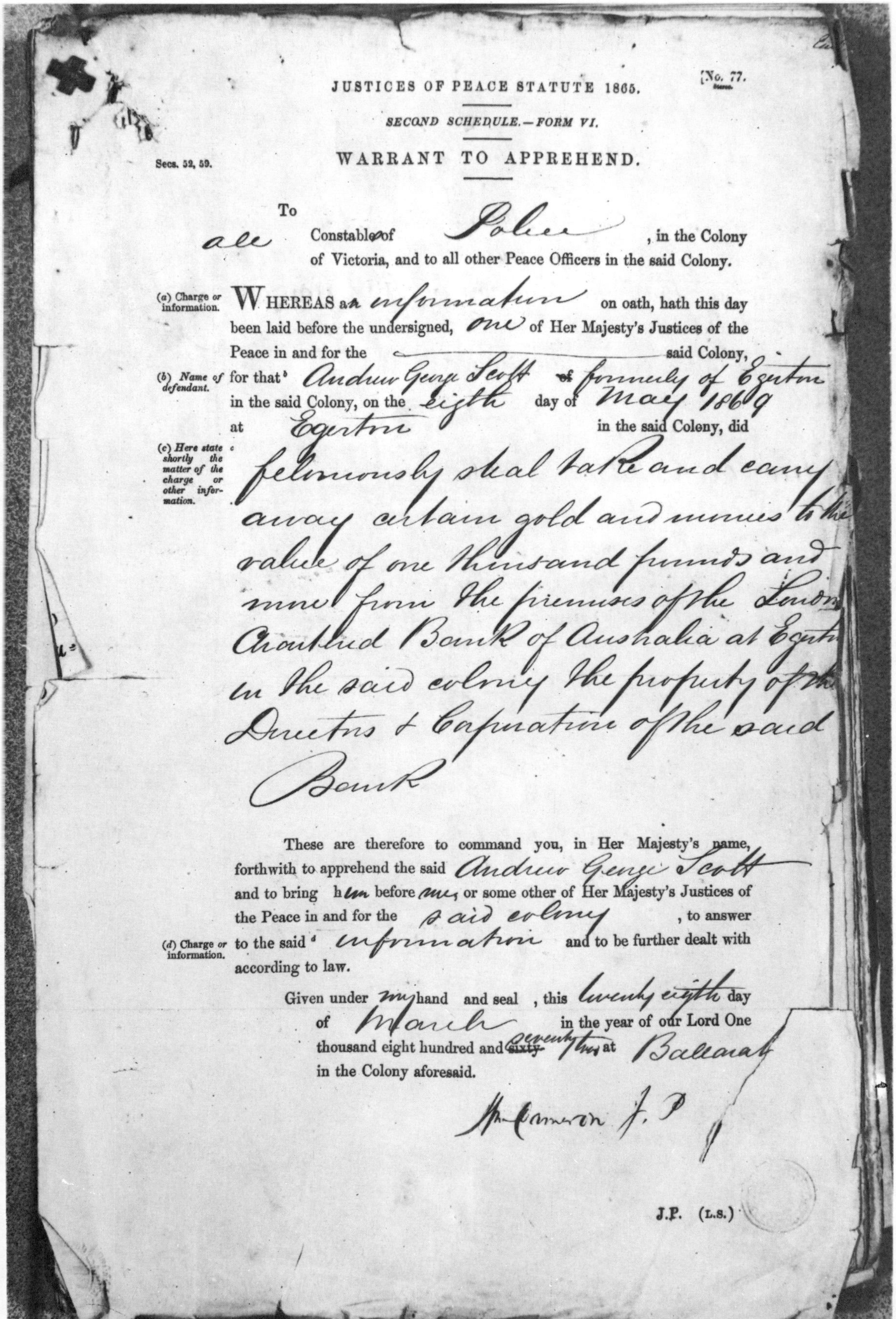

[No. 77.

JUSTICES OF PEACE STATUTE 1865.

SECOND SCHEDULE.—FORM VI.

Secs. 52, 59.

WARRANT TO APPREHEND.

To

all Constables of Police, in the Colony of Victoria, and to all other Peace Officers in the said Colony.

(a) Charge or information.

WHEREAS an information on oath, hath this day been laid before the undersigned, one of Her Majesty's Justices of the Peace in and for the ——— said Colony,

(b) Name of defendant.

for that[b] Andrew George Scott ~~of~~ formerly of Egerton in the said Colony, on the eighth day of May 1869 at Egerton in the said Colony, did

(c) Here state shortly the matter of the charge or other information.

[c] feloniously steal take and carry away certain gold and monies to the value of one thousand pounds and more from the premises of the London Chartered Bank of Australia at Egerton in the said colony the property of the Directors & Corporation of the said Bank

These are therefore to command you, in Her Majesty's name, forthwith to apprehend the said Andrew George Scott and to bring him before me, or some other of Her Majesty's Justices of the Peace in and for the said colony, to answer

(d) Charge or information.

to the said[d] information and to be further dealt with according to law.

Given under my hand and seal, this twenty eighth day of March in the year of our Lord One thousand eight hundred and ~~sixty~~ seventy two at Ballarat in the Colony aforesaid.

Wm Cameron J.P.

J.P. (L.S.)

ENGLISH SPEAKING RACES.—Above 5 ft. 7 in. to 5 ft. 9 in. inclusive.

No. 10124. **Name** Andrew G. Scott.

[Nati]ve Place	Ireland.	
[Y]ear of Birth	1845	
Arrived in Colony ...	1868.	
" per Ship ...	"Black Eagle"	
Trade ...	Civil Engineer,	
Religion ...	C. of E	
	On Arrival.	**On Discharge.**
Education—Read or Write	Both	
Height without shoes	5' 8¾	
Weight ...	10' 8"	
Colour of Hair ...	Brown.	
Colour of Eyes ...	Blue.	

Particular Marks ... Fleshy excresence top left shoulder, mole left shoulder, mole right side of abdomen, gun shot wound left breast, gun shot wounds both shins, gun shot wound right foot, which turns in walking

CONVICTIONS—

Where and when tried.	Offence.	Sentence. & under what name
Ballarat Gaol, 22. 6 72	Absconding.	12 Months. H. L. 1st 3 Mon[ths] in Irons.
Ballarat, S/C. 23 7 72.	Robbery, being armed with an offensive weapon.	10 Years. Roads. cumulative.
		Executed in New South Wales

[illegible] Bull
Governor
11/7/9

Captain Moonlite's prison record.
Courtesy Public Records Office, Victoria.

trial in July 1872, three years after the bank robbery, he said he had 'only just returned from Melbourne that Saturday night [pulled out the half of the return ticket] ... the Station Master at Buninyong could prove it'. Unfortunately the Station Master swore on oath that it was 7 May (Friday night) and not 8 May that he had seen Scott at the station and further that Scott had taken out a fresh ticket two or three days after the expiry of the return ticket and paid for it in London Chartered Bank notes. Scott also said he had walked eight miles [thirteen kilometres] from Buninyong station to Egerton, but a witness, Tanner the store keeper, testified it was a muddy road and that Scott's boots were clean. Scott's alibi also included the statement that he had had a nobbler of brandy at the Buninyong Forest Home Hotel after getting off the train at half past ten, but the publican testified that 'at half past eleven a man on horseback ... riding fast from the Egerton district ... asked for a stiff nobbler of brandy ... he had a cloak on him like a poncho ... he had a bag strapped in front of his saddle'. Another witness also testified to the hard ridden horse from Egerton to get the drink as part of the alibi of being seen to drink at the Forest Home Hotel on the night of the robbery. There was also evidence of Scott's attempt to bribe other witnesses as to his movements on 8 May[9].

The lay reader had been active in civic affairs in Bacchus Marsh and also as a civil engineer had given services as an unpaid adviser, but at his trial, evidence of some other activities were made known such as the possession of a brace of pistols, a horse pistol and a pair of duelling pistols; unclerical drinking habits; the advocacy of 'horsewhipping Brunn for scandalising him'; threats to horsewhip Tanner; borrowing money and not repaying it, paying debts by London Chartered Bank notes after the robbery, and a witness who swore that 'before the bank robbery every evening for a long time I saw Scott firing at a tree ... he was sometimes on horseback and at others on foot. Sometimes he wore a red shirt and a felt hat. I never saw Scott firing at a tree after the robbery'[10]. Scott wore a felt hat on the night of 8 May.

Further revealing evidence as to the 'Reverend's' habits was a report submitted on oath concerning Robert James Crook, traveller for Simpson's Brewery, Collingwood, who was a 'fast companion before and after the bank robbery ... they lived together at the Old Woolpack Inn, Bacchus Marsh'[11]. Crook had been arrested earlier in the year on a charge of cattle stealing, in fact he was caught in the act but 'Scott was particularly active not only in swearing an alibi himself [for Crook] but in procuring others to do the same, the result being that Crook was discharged'[12]. Another witness testified to seeing Crook and Scott on the Keilor coach and that Scott was armed with a revolver. Other evidence established the selling of stolen gold to the Sydney branch of the Royal Mint, the passing of stolen money and evidence of a handwriting expert concerning the note left at the schoolhouse.

In a period when the police were lampooned as either inefficient and flash or vindictive persecutors, the police and detective work in the Scott case was thorough, effective, fair and objective and carefully documented, particularly for a trial that took place three years after the event.

In 1872, to clear his name, Brunn wrote to a Sydney solicitor, Mr G. Sly, to get the facts of the Scott affair. The solicitor was so sympathetic to the 'deep wrong' to Brunn that he gave his services free. His documentation sheds further light on Scott's history; he sold 129 ounces (4 kg) of gold to the Sydney Branch of the Royal Mint, passed thirteen dishonoured cheques, faced five charges of obtaining money under false pretences and next day purchased

The capturers of the "Moonlite Gang".
Courtesy Police Museum, Melbourne.

the yacht *Whynot* at Wooloomooloo with a valueless cheque but was arrested before sailing when he set off 'to fetch a lady' armed with a revolver[13].

Sentenced to eighteen months hard labour in Maitland Gaol, Scott obtained easier treatment by feigning insanity and on the basis of a report that 'his insanity was delusionary and is reported to be hereditary and he fancies his food is poisonous', he was admitted to the Parramatta Criminal Lunatic Asylum on 17 February 1871. However, under observation over a period of four months, the Superintendent, Mr Wardley, reported that

> he is an unprincipled fellow without a spark of honour or honesty in him ... he does not betray any sign of insanity ... does not refrain from any particle of food ... his associates in the yard are the very lowest and hardened criminals ... a scoundrel to the core ... I never considered him insane, but an artful, designing, unprincipled criminal ready to join in any scheme of fraud or ruffianly violence that had a degree of success[14].

After his discharge and before his extradition to Victoria, Scott wrote to his father at Coromandel, Auckland, New Zealand that 'I am steady now, although I feel a little odd at liberty after 16 months in gaol I got off 3 months for good conduct'. He recounted that before his arrest he had purchased a wreck at New Caledonia, made an exchange for a small craft and went for a trading voyage round the islands, smuggled in Queensland, had a partner, a German Count Geldern who 'forged on me for nearly all I had', but that 'fortunately when I left Victoria I had left shares in a gold claim and had a share in a horse of young Crooks called Saladin who won £300 last week racing. I am therefore not badly off'. He also said that he had an offer from Victoria of a share in a craft to trade for kauri pine and concluded 'May God bless you and keep you all is the prayer of your affectionate son who has been treated badly but now triumphs'[15].

Scott, however, was unable to realise his plans and was extradited to Ballarat for trial for robbery under arms. There he led an escape with five fellow prisoners from the new solidly built gaol which was claimed to be escape-proof, using a human ladder and a rope made of blanket strips.

Four of the escapees were caught and the fifth, Deermoodie, refused to join Scott and returned to Ballarat and captivity. At this parting Scott flew into one of 'those terrible rages' that were to become frequent in his later career and alternated with remorseful piety.

Recaptured near Bendigo, Scott was sentenced to ten years and an extra year in irons for gaol-breaking. Good conduct and charming fluency earned a remission and he was released in March 1879. His gaol sentence had not, however, been without incident for in February 1877 he had the 'refractory impudence' to stick up the Chief Warder of B Division, Pentridge,

> barging into the office armed with a knife, exclaiming 'I want your watch and must have it'. He then locked himself in the bathroom with his knife shouting I intend to have satisfaction for slanderous reports that have been circulated about me, referring to an article in the *Argus* which denounced him as a scoundrel and a robber. The hospital doctor, Dr. Reed had to talk him out of it[16].

On his release in March 1879, Scott embarked on open-air lecturing and moralising, particularly on prison discipline, but perhaps influenced by his notoriety being overshadowed by the Kelly saga, at the age of thirty-seven he tragically influenced and recruited a bushranging gang of youngsters all of whom were either to die violently or be imprisoned; Augustus or Gus Wernicke, aged nineteen, Thomas Williams alias Jones, aged nineteen, James Nesbit alias Lyons, aged twenty-three, Graham Bennett aged twenty, and Thomas Rogan aged twenty-three. They all came from Victoria; Rogan although born in New South Wales had been living in Victoria.

As well as his rages and the violence followed by remorse his activities followed the traditional bushranger's pattern. He stole horses, and carried out a few small robberies, this time in Northern Victoria where there was some sympathy for any bushranger. He then carried out a typical Saturday afternoon raid at Wantabadgery on the Murrumbidgee River, herding nineteen workmen into the living room, feasting and drinking through the night with the usual rationalising or moralising on their misdemeanours before the pillaging began.

On the Sunday, Scott in a rage, threatened the manager of the station for talking to one of his youngsters fearing a lessening of his authority over the young bushrangers, and failing to master a young filly angrily put a bullet through the foal's head and was immediately remorseful. With the station owner as hostage, again a familiar pattern, he collared a buggy and went for grog, sticking up Patterson's Australian Arms Hotel, shanghaiing the hotel owner and his wife and two children and seven more men on the way back and marching them all in front of the buggy to the station living room. Again in a rage, suspecting Baynes, the station manager, of talking his men out of the hold-up, he made ready to hang him from a tree using the horse and buggy as the platform drop, but he succumbed to the pleas of the womenfolk and calmed down. With thirty-five hostages, Moonlite went scouting to an adjoining station and found another hostage, who when asked where he was going, unfortunately had replied 'to fight the bushrangers'. Moonlite took him back to the station and the highlight of the second night was a 'trial' of a hostage on a charge of 'unlawfully carrying firearms' by two bushrangers and two station hands with Moonlite as judge. The 'jury' returned a verdict of not guilty.

Again there was the pattern of relaxed vigilance as in the case of Morgan's overconfidence, and station owner MacDonald was able to slip away, ride twenty-five miles (forty kilometres) to Wagga and return with four constables for a Monday morning shoot-out. Joined by five more troopers from Gundagai sixty-five miles (one hundred and ten kilometres) away there was almost a dress rehearsal for that later early Monday Kelly gang shoot-out.

The end of Moonlite's gang at McGlede's Hut. The deaths of Gus Wernicke, Jimmy Nesbit and Constable Bowen.
Australasian Sketcher 22 November, 1874.

On this occasion, however, the hostages either escaped or were released before firing began and collected on a ridge to watch the scene below. They were joined by many other civilians who had followed the police from Wagga.

Shooting carried on for some two hours till the bushrangers rode off on some of the station's best thoroughbreds. Dallying at selector McGlede's property, some say for a brandy or two, the sergeant and nine constables caught up with them and the gun-fight began in earnest. Constable Bowen of 'Thunderbolt' fame shot Wenicke and Nesbit dead before being fatally wounded by Scott. Bennett was wounded in the arm and he and Moonlite, Williams and Rogan all surrendered.

Scott and Rogan were hanged for the murder of Constable Bowen and the death sentences of Bennett and Williams were commuted to life because of their youth and the belief that they had been led astray by Moonlite. Scott in an address to the court emotionally pleaded for their lives. The police's good behaviour in disbanding the gang so early in its life was recognised by rewards and a monument to Constable Bowen, a pension for his wife and free education for her children.

THE GOVERNOR AFFAIR

Other minor gangs of youths were infected with the 'new breed' bushranging fever. One was that of Thomas Gorman aged twenty-six, Charles Jones aged twenty and Bill Kaye aged nineteen who were joined by 'Hoppy' Bill Hobbs to leave 'warrigal' or brumby horse catching to go on the road in February 1879, but a 189 mile (312 kilometre) weekend chase by troopers in which a Constable Power was wounded, saw them all in gaol for life for 'shooting with intent to kill'.

Jack Bradshaw, self styled 'the last of the notorious bushrangers', tried to capitalise on the romantic folklore tradition by claiming to 'have known all the bushrangers' and wrote a book about it. By the 1870s, he had a reputation as a petty thief and con man with minor convictions and attempted bank robberies.

Very few Aborigines became bushrangers. Perhaps Musquito the 'Black Napoleon' who was hanged in 1825 may be classed as a bushranger, but Jimmy and Joe Governor who went berserk in 1900 near Breelong in New South Wales were straight-out murderers and together with their mate, Jacky Underwood, killed nine people and terrorised a large area.

Jimmy and Joe were half-castes and Jacky a full blood with one eye and a crippled leg. They lived in a humpy on the farm of John Mawbey with Jimmy's wife Ethel, a white girl and daughter of a miner, Underwood and other Aborigines. Bad blood soon developed between the Mawbeys and the Governors and the Governors tomahawked Mrs Mawbey, her two daughters, her son, and another woman, and wounded another. On the run, Jacky Underwood fell behind and was captured and hanged, but the Governors went on to Gulgong where Joe, while robbing for food, axed seventy-year-old Alexander MacKay to death.

Rewards for the Governors rose to £1,000, but they butchered a Mrs O'Brien and her infant son when breaking into their home for food and meeting an elderly man named Kiernan Fitzpatrick killed him on the spot and wounded Constable Richard Harris in the leg when he tried to ambush them. For 2000 miles their bush prowess allowed them to escape.

Soldiers, mounted police and volunteers hunted them down and finally caught Jimmy Governor sleeping, wounded and captured him and he was hanged at Darlinghurst on 18 January 1901. Joe, who escaped, was shot dead by farmer John Wilkinson near Singleton in New South Wales.

Theirs was a violent reaction to prejudice.

The Kelly armour.
Courtesy La Trobe Library, Melbourne.

The History of the Celebrated Ned Kelly

Edward Kelly was born at Beveridge, Victoria, in June 1855, the third child of John and Ellen Kelly. Their first child, Mary Jane, born in 1851, had died as an infant and Annie, Ned's elder sister, was born in 1853. Ned's birth was not registered as required by the Victorian Births, Deaths and Marriages legislation of 1853 but tradition has it that Ned was baptised at St Paul's, Coburg, by Father O'Dea. Five other children, Margaret or Maggie (1857), James (1859), Daniel (1861), Kate (1862) and Grace (1865) were born during Ellen Quinn's first marriage and four more during her second marriage to young George King, a wandering Californian horse thief and some nineteen years junior to the forty-two year old widow. Red Kelly paid his brother Jim's passage to Victoria from Tipperary, Ireland, and the clan was widened by the marriage of two of Ellen's sisters, Kate and Jane, to two brothers, Jack and Tom Lloyd.

Ned's father, John 'Red' Kelly, was born on 20 February 1820, at Clonbragan near May-glass in Killenanle Parish, County Tipperary. Christened Sean Ceallough, Irish for John Kelly, he was the son of Thomas Kelly, a poor farmer, and Mary Cody. One of six children, in 1840 John was a 'woodranger' or gamekeeper for Lord Ormonde when two pigs were stolen from a farmer named Quainey of Ballybo. Convicted for the offence in January 1841, John Kelly was sentenced at the Tipperary Assizes at Clonmel to transportation for seven years. After seven months in gaol, he sailed on the barque *Prince Regent* and arrived in Hobart Town, Van Diemen's Land, on 2 January 1842.

Although given two months hard labour in chains on 4 October 1842 for 'being absent from the station and misconduct in being in the potatoe [*sic*] field belonging to Mr O'Connor', his record was such that he was assigned as a convict servant to K. Murray of Morven on 15 February 1843 and two-and-a-half years later on 11 July 1845, after serving four years seven months of his seven year sentence, he won a ticket of leave and worked as a farm hand to Mrs Mary Lackay at Pontville. Although fined five shillings on 8 July 1847 for being 'drunk and disorderly', at the age of twenty-seven, on 1 January 1848, he became a 'free man'. He sailed for the Port Phillip District of the Colony of New South Wales, worked as a carpenter, went to the Bendigo goldfields and became an established horse dealer until he was able to buy a farm and build a hut at Beveridge. In the meantime, at the age of thirty-one, he had met and married Ellen Quinn, aged eighteen, at St Francis Roman Catholic Church, Lonsdale Street, Melbourne.

Ellen Quinn had arrived in Melbourne in July 1841 with her parents James and Mary Quinn from County Antrim. Ellen, then aged nine, was the eldest of six children. James Quinn, her father, cultivated a small area, first at Brunswick, then at Broadmeadows and then a 640 acre (260 hectare) selection at Wallan. It was at Wallan that Red Kelly courted Ellen and eloped with her to marry in Melbourne. The Quinns' early antipathy to her marriage to an older man and an ex-convict soon passed.

James Quinn was able to subdivide and sell his selection and by September of 1864 he acquired a run of 25,000 acres (10,100 hectares) at Glenmore on the King River Flats for £2,000. James Quinn himself had no troubles with the police and it would appear that all his troubles were through his sons and his daughters' husbands, the Lloyd brothers. He died at the age of sixty-six.

The Quinns, however, were the first of this large clan to get into trouble and Ned's maternal uncles, James Quinn junior and Patrick Quinn (who married his cousin Maggie) faced twenty charges between 1856 and 1878, eleven of which became convictions. The

(Top left) Ned Kelly's sister, Kate in the eighties.
Courtesy Police Museum, Melbourne.

(Top right) The Dapper Ned Kelly, the artist T. Carrington's impression, of short stature but with the "larrikin heel"
The Australasian Sketcher.

(Bottom left) The Kelly house at Eleven Mile Creek, Greta.
Courtesy Police Museum, Melbourne.

A contrasting, cold-eyed portrait.
Courtesy La Trobe Library, Melbourne.

close-knit clan of the Quinns, Lloyds and Kellys faced fifty-seven charges between 1856 and 1880 and the thirty-four resulting convictions, apart from sureties and fines, totalled sixty-one years four months imprisonment.

A great amount of cattle stealing was going on in the district and between 1871 and 1878, there were 842 cases of cattle stealing officially reported in the north-east district[17]. Since members of the Quinn and Lloyd families were linked with it, it was inevitable that the Kelly members of the clan were also viewed with suspicion.

Conscious that his restless relatives were an embarrassment to his convict past and that they had brought his home under police scrutiny, in 1860 Red Kelly moved his family fifty miles (eight-four kilometres) away to Avenel, where he rented forty acres (sixteen hectares) as a dairy farm on the banks of the Hughes Creek. Three years later, however, in 1863, Red's brother Jim was twice charged with cattle stealing and on a third charge sentenced to three years.

In 1868, Jim was also sentenced to fifteen years for arson, as he had set fire to Kate Lloyd's (Ellen's sister's) house after a drunken quarrel with her while her husband was in gaol.

In the same year Ned's immediate family had their first brush with the law. Their Welsh neighbours, the Morgans, who owned an adjoining 740 acres (310 hectares) suspected Red Kelly of stealing their cattle and Red was arrested, convicted and fined £25 or six months imprisonment for illegal possession of a hide. The first charge of cattle stealing was dismissed. A calf's hide with the brand cut out and some fresh and salted beef were found in his hut. The fine of £25 could not be raised for several weeks and when Red was finally released from custody he was a sick man and died the following year on 27 December 1866. A few months after his death, Mrs Kelly was arrested on a charge of using abusive and threatening language to the Morgans and was fined £2 and ordered to keep the peace. Ellen Kelly then moved her family from Avenel to a bark-roofed hut on the banks of Eleven Mile Creek between Benalla and Greta. When Assistant Commissioner of Police Nicholson inspected the Greta and Chiltern areas in October 1877 he reported 'Mrs Kelly lives on a piece of cleared and partly cultivated land, on the roadside, in an old wooden hut ... the dwelling was divided into five apartments by partitions of blanketing, rags etc ... they all appeared to be existing in poverty and squalor'[18].

The departure of the Kelly family from Avenel was a critical moment for Ned since his chances of a continuing education were curtailed, he and Grace having attended Richardson's Church of England School. He also came closer to the Quinns and their antipathy to law and order and the police. It is generally thought that Ned gained some schooling at Avenel although a school inspector for the district reported in 1860 that 'most people in the district are apathetic regarding education'. In view of his articulateness, it is thought that Ned could write, but the three letters dictated by him in prison during the eight days preceding his execution are all signed with a cross witnessed by gaol authorities 'his mark, Ned Kelly'[19].

This then was the family and clan background to the young Edward Kelly who, at the age of eleven was in the position of the eldest son and forced into adult responsibilities to help his mother on the farm. The activities and attitudes of the Quinns and the Lloyds must have had an influence on Ned and must have affected his attitude towards the police as in the opinion of the Kellys and the Quinns, his father's death had been hastened by his treatment by the police. The return of John and Tom Lloyd, husbands of his mother's two sisters Kate and Jane, from Pentridge prison after three-year sentences would not have eased the smouldering anti-authoritarian atmosphere surrounding him. Before leaving Avenel, Ned had been presented with a green sash by farmer R.J. Shelton whose life Ned had saved when he rescued him from Hughes Creek into which he had fallen. Ned was to cherish that sash.

KELLY FINED AND CONVICTED

So far Ned himself had kept out of the courts. There is some suspicion that the Quinns and others who were engaged in horse trading left their horses for agistment in widow Kelly's paddocks and that the shanty had become a rendezvous for bad characters. Two bush workers, Bricky Williamson, a bricklayer from Newcastle-upon-Tyne and later husband of Maggie Kelly, and Bill Skillion who had nearby selections, were frequent visitors and another, George King, became a semi-permanent boarder. Harry Power, who had escaped from Pentridge in February 1869 and set about robbery under arms, was back in his old haunts by September and set up camp on the Quinns' Glenmore property. Undoubtedly the fourteen-year-old Ned associated with him. Power had met Ned's uncles Tom and Jack Lloyd in Pentridge and Superintendent Hare claimed that Ned was regarded as a horse stealer from earliest boyhood and that he joined Power who had not a high opinion of his courage.

On 26 October 1867 Ned made his first appearance in court charged with 'assault and robbery'. The case concerned a Chinese poultry and pig trader named Ah Fook who had reported to Benalla police that he had been robbed of ten shillings on the road between

Constable Hall's telegraphed report of Kelly's conviction to Superintendant Nicholson.
Courtesy Public Record Office, Victoria.

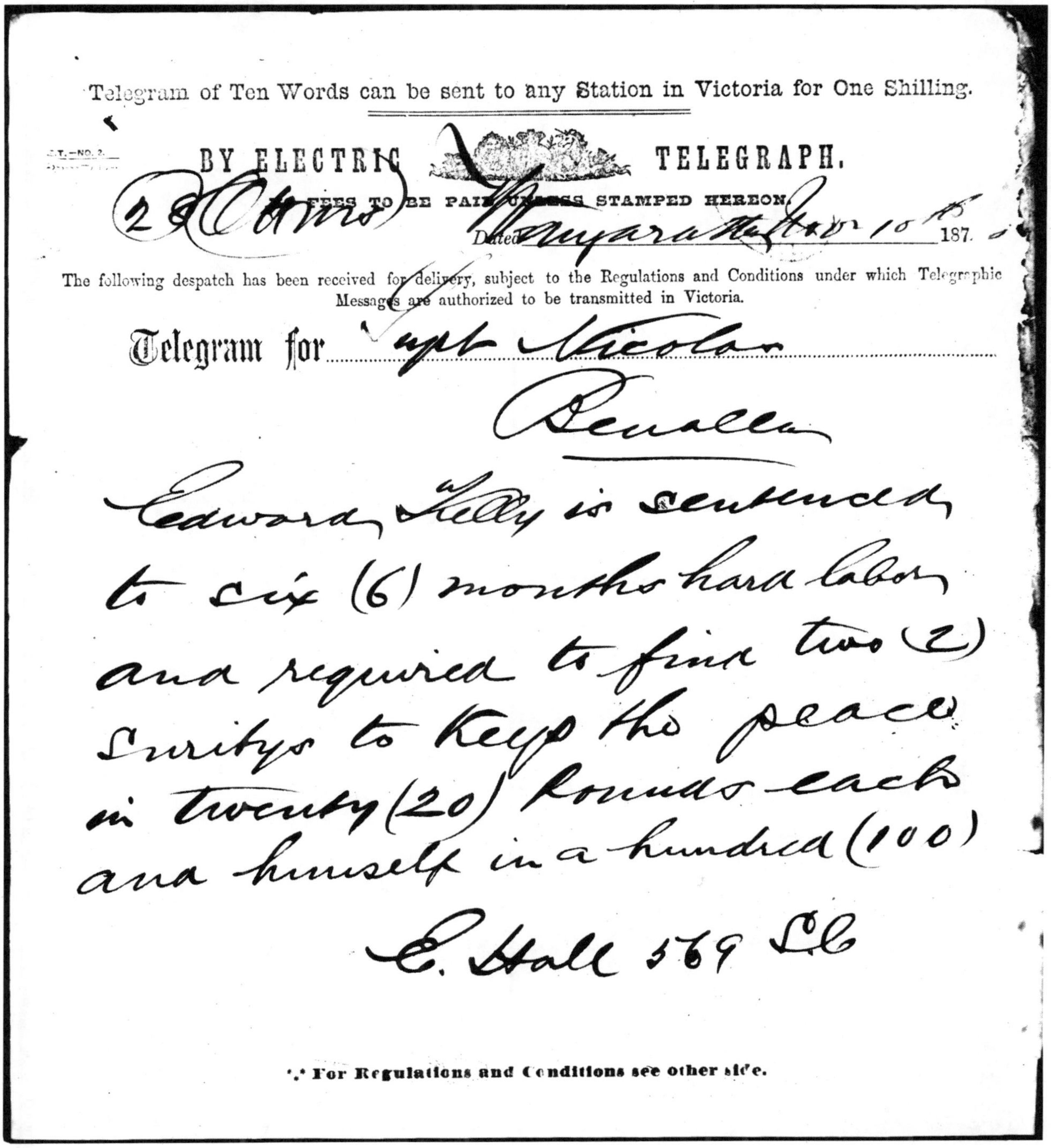

Telegram of Ten Words can be sent to any Station in Victoria for One Shilling.

BY ELECTRIC TELEGRAPH.

FEES TO BE PAID UNLESS STAMPED HEREON.

Dated Wangaratta Nov 10th 187

The following despatch has been received for delivery, subject to the Regulations and Conditions under which Telegraphic Messages are authorized to be transmitted in Victoria.

Telegram for Supt Nicolas
Benalla

Edward Kelly is sentenced to six (6) months hard labor and required to find two (2) Suritys to keep the peace in twenty (20) pounds each and himself in a hundred (100)

E. Hall 569 LC

*** For Regulations and Conditions see other side.

193

No. 10926 Name, Edward Kelly 74/1848 [No. 64 P.]

Native Place, Victoria

Year of Birth, 1856

Arrived in Colony { Ship, ——
Year, ——
Bond or free, ——

From where, ——

Religion, R. Catholic

No. 466 Date, 20 6 73

No. 925 Date, 24 1 74

	On Conviction.	On Discharge.
Education—Read or write	Both	Both
Height	5. 10	(No alteration)
Weight	11. 4	
Build	Med	
Complexion	Sallow	
Color of Hair	D. brown	

Color of Eyes, Hazel

Trade or Calling Laborer

Particular Marks, Scar top of head, 2 scars crown of do, scar front of head, eyebrows meeting, 2 natural marks between shoulder blades, 2 freckles lower left arm scar ball of left thumb, scar back of right hand, 3 scar left thumb

When and where convicted,
2nd August 1871
Genl Sessions Beechworth

Offence,
Receiving a stolen horse

Sentence,
3 Years H. L.

Remarks,
Freedom by remission
February 2nd 1874.

Criminal History and Remarks—
3 mos for assault
3 mos for obscene language
12 mos for assault in default of bail (bail found) — These convictions on same date at Wangaratta Police Ct

To be returned to Detective Office Melbourne

F. Gardiner
Superintendent
14 3 73

N.B.—Margin not to be written on.

Edward Kelly's Gaol Record.
Courtesy Public Records Office, Victoria.

Winton and Greta and had been beaten with a stick. From the description he had given Ned was arrested and charged on 16 October. After ten days in gaol and two remands because of difficulties in obtaining Chinese interpreters the charge had not been sustained since Ah Fook had been carrying £25 and was only robbed of ten shillings. Ned's story was that Ah Fook had stopped for a drink of water. When sister Annie gave him a glass of water from the creek instead of the house, Ah Fook became angry and waved a stick and Ned came to the rescue and gave him a hit or two on the leg with his own stick. Bill Skillion, William Gray and Annie gave the story supporting evidence.

When Harry Power held up Kilfera station near Benalla on 16 March 1870, he was accompanied by a youth and two months later, on 12 May, Ned was charged with robbery in company. He was discharged because of lack of positive identification. A second charge of robbery under arms near Benalla also failed through lack of witnesses and again on a third charge of robbery under arms near Kyneton after several remands, the police could not produce adequate evidence of association with Power. Power ceased to have any influence on Ned when he was convicted on four charges of highway robbery and sentenced in October 1870 to fifteen years imprisonment. Power was officially betrayed to the police by Jacky Lloyd but he always maintained it was Ned that betrayed him and Superintendent Hare agreed that Ned was probably implicated in the circumstances of Power's arrest. However, Superintendent Sadlier said it was Jack Lloyd who collected the reward.

Four months after he was acquitted on charges of having abetted Harry Power, Ned was arrested again and this time there was enough evidence for him to be convicted. In October 1870, the carts and waggons of two rival hawkers, Jeremiah McCormack and Ben Gould, had become bogged. According to Ned, Gould waited at the Kelly house for the road to improve, but McCormack camped beside his bogged waggon four miles (seven kilometres) from the Kelly hut. One of his horses became loose and Gould before returning it used it to pull his waggon free. McCormack was suspicious and accused Gould of 'working the horse'. Ned recorded:

> I pleaded Gould's innocence and Mr McCormack turned on me and accused me of bringing the horse from Greta to Gould's waggon to pull him out of the bog ... the same day me and my uncle was cutting calves Gould wrapped up a note and a pair of calves testicles and gave them to me to give to Mrs McCormack. I did not see her when she would come instead of giving it to her husband consequently McCormack said he would summons me[20].

> Ned then stated that he was dismounting when Mrs McCormack struck my horse in the flank with a bullock's shin it jumped forward and my fist came in collision with Mr McCormack's nose and cause him to lose his equilibrium and fall prostrate I tied up my horse to finish the battle but Mr McCormack got up and ran to the Police camp[21].

Afraid to take proceedings against Kelly, McCormack swore an information against him 'stating that he was in grevious bodily fear of his life' and thus three charges were laid, 'violent assault on Jeremiah McCormick', [*sic*] 'insulting behaviour in a Public Place to Margaret McCormick [*sic*]' and 'profane, indecent and obscene language to Margaret McCormick' [*sic*][22]. Kelly was convicted on the first two charges. He was also bound over to keep the peace for twelve months, in default £100. The third charge was withdrawn at the suggestion of the court.

The youthful Edward Kelly at his imprisonment.
Courtesy Public Records Office, Victoria.

The boy whom Kelly asserted delivered the package and the note to Mrs McCormack was his cousin Tom Lloyd who is reputed to have said 'Ned Kelly gave me this package for you'. Ben Gould admitted he wrote the indecent note to the childless Mrs McCormack. Presumably Ned could not write, but his own words recorded almost nine years later in his Jerilderie letter reveal at least complicity in the nasty incident[23]. He also gave a similar account of the incident with slight variations in his letter to Donald Cameron, M.P., three months earlier in December 1878[24].

In his report on the McCormack case, it is significant that Senior Constable Hall also added that 'from information received a few days ago Kelly was trying to get some firearms in place of some another offender stole from him' and also that Kelly was expecting Allen Lowry, alias Davis alias Cook 'in this locality in a short time and who was an old friend of Kelly's family when residing at Avenel and that he intended if he could get him to join him it was his intention to take to the bush during the summer months'[25].

There can be no doubt that Ned Kelly's first six months sentence to Beechworth Gaol had a hardening effect on the fifteen-year-old youth even though he was released after five months, but if Senior Constable Hall's report is accepted it would appear he was already on the way to the use of guns. If there had been any hope of breaking free of the attitudes of his family and relatives, imprisonment hardened the mould and further confrontation with the then society and its law and order became inevitable as guns led to outlawry and its consequences.

KELLY, HORSE STEALER

When Ned returned home 'Wild' Wright was lodging with Mrs Kelly on the introduction of his droving associate Alex Gunn, Mrs Kelly's son-in-law. He had with him a mare he had stolen from Maindample Station. Ned, either aware or unaware that the horse was stolen, unfortunately rode her to Wangaratta and Greta where Senior Constable Hall recognised the horse as one described in the *Police Gazette* as stolen. Ned recalled Wright

> lost his mare both him and me looked all day for her and could not get her, Wright who was a stranger to me was in a hurry to get back to Mansfield and I gave him another mare and he told me if I found her to keep her until he brought mine back[26].

He told how he rode the horse to Wangaratta, and that 'the horse was the property of a telegraph master in Mansfield'. At Greta, where Hall recognised the horse, Ned claimed he made the pretext he 'wanted me to sign some papers that I did not sign at Beechworth concerning my bail bonds ... I had no idea he wanted to arrest me or I would have quietly rode away'[27]. He continued:

> Hall caught hold of me and thought to throw me but made a mistake and came on the broad of his back ... I tried to catch the mare. Hall got up and snapped three caps or four caps at me and would have shot me but the colts patent refused ... I kept throwing him in the dust ... I threw the big cowardly Hall on his belly I straddled him and rooted both spurs into his thighs he roared like a big calf attacked by dogs ... he called for assistance to a man named Cohen and Burnett, Lewis, Thompson, Jewitt looking on ... they got ropes tied my hands and feet and Hall beat me over the head with his six chambered colts revolver nine stitches were put in some of the cuts by Dr Hastings[28].

Ned was charged at Wangaratta Court on 21 April 1871 on a charge of 'receiving a horse' and after three months in custody was sentenced at Beechworth to three years imprisonment with hard labour. In the meantime, on 11

May Wild Wright received eighteen months for stealing the horse and at the same time Alex Gunn was sentenced to three years for stealing a horse from a schoolmaster named Adair.

This horse-stealing incident is often used to illustrate the view that the Kellys were persecuted by the police for Ned was not actually in possession of the horse, and it was a common practice to use other people's horses without an intent to steal. However, Ned was charged with 'receiving' not 'stealing' and it was the Bench and not the police that handed down the sentence. In his Jerilderie letter Ned had a few words to say about Constable Hall's character, that as a perjurer he had bribed James Murdoch, a sympathiser, with £20 to give false evidence and that Murdoch had been in gaol with Ned who had allegedly tried to persuade him to go horse stealing with him.

The seventeen-year-old Ned spent a year and a half in Beechworth gaol and in early 1873 was transferred to Pentridge and thence successively to the hulks *Sacramento* and *Battery* off Point Gellibrand. Although Ned was able to claim 'I can say I was never convicted of horse or cattle stealing' he also boasted that 'me and my stepfather taking their horses [Whitty and Burns] their brands altered by me, two were sold to Kennedy and the rest to Baumgarten ... they paid me full value for the horses and could not have known they were stolen'[29].

While Ned was serving his three-year sentence his young brothers Jim, aged twelve, and Dan, aged ten, were charged with illegally using a horse and the charge was dismissed, but a year and a half later Jim, then almost fourteen, was charged at Beechworth with an older youth Tom Williams, aged seventeen, with stealing two of George Chandler's heifers and two heifers from James Cook. Jim was handed down two two-and-a-half year sentences to be served cumulatively. In later life Jim was to keep out of trouble, although at the age of twenty-seven, Constable Hoslabt was to report to Sergeant Mountford at Benalla in 1866 that

> he is of very restless disposition and is continually looking for new life. His mother is very anxious to keep him straight and she will not allow him to go away from the place unless he is accompanied by his sister Grace. He is very friendly to police.

Constable Timothy Kane also reported that James Kelly in conversing with other camarades at his mother's residence at Greta about a fortnight ago ... that it was his intention to take to the bush and if he did not get plenty of work he would make it warm for some of the police in the district[30].

Earning a remission of six months for good behaviour, on his release Ned would not have been happy to find his younger brother in gaol together with a number of other relatives, James Quinn serving three-and-a-half years from 1872 on a conviction for 'bodily harm', Patrick Quinn 'bodily harm' (1870) four years, James Kelly 'arson' (1863) fifteen years and John Lloyd 'maliciously killing a horse' (1873) four years. Two weeks after his return, his mother married George King. Nearing twenty years of age he made his way to Mansfield to stay in regular employment for almost three years.

NED'S REFORM WEAKENED

During a period of reform, Ned worked at felling trees for timber mills; first, one owned by Saunders & Rule and then one owned by Heach & Dockendorf and after about a year back to Glenrowan where he found employment in quarrying and carting granite for the building of a house by a settler. He then returned to Saunders & Rule as overseer of the timber mill they had acquired closer to Greta to cut railway sleepers for the Wangaratta-

Beechworth line. When that work was completed, the mill moved to the Gippsland area to cut sleepers but Ned decided to go gold mining with his brother Dan.

Two factors apparently weakened Ned's reform. First, according to Ned in his Cameron letter, rumours were circulating about him stealing cattle possibly from a local squatter named Whitty and his son-in-law Farrell. One concerned stealing a mob of calves from Whitty and Farrell and another a wild bull which Ned chanced upon 'when I was on the King River and gave to a farmer named Lydicher who in turn sold it to a local butcher Carr'[32]. In his own words Ned used these rumours as an excuse for turning from honest labour to more lucrative and easier pickings, 'I began to think they wanted me to give them something to talk about. Therefore I started wholesale and retail horse and cattle dealing ... no one had anything to do with the stealing and selling of the horses but me and George King. He gave as an excuse that wealthy squatters Whitty and Burns 'impounded every beast they could get, even off government roads... I have known over sixty heads of horses impounded in one day by Whitty and Burns all belonging to poor farmers'[31]. However, Ned overlooked the fact that his stealing and selling did not get the horses back to the 'poor farmers'.

Second, Superintendent Nicholson inspected north-eastern Victoria in 1873, and visited not only Greta police station but also 'the notorious Mrs Kelly's house at Eleven Mile Creek'. His observations regarding the Kellys and their relatives resulted in a much-quoted memorandum:

> I expressed my opinion to the officer in charge of the district that, without oppressing the people or worrying them in any way, he should endeavour, when they had committed any crime, to bring them to justice and send them to Pentridge even on a paltry sentence, the object being to take their prestige away from them ... their flashness helps to keep them together, and that is a very good way of taking the flashness out of them[33].

Certainly in little more than a year Kelly and his 'mates' stole nearly two hundred horses, altered the brands and sold them in Victoria 'in Benalla, Melbourne and other places' and in New South Wales. As a result twenty-seven graziers formed themselves into the North Eastern Stock Protection Society after a meeting at Moyhu and began offering rewards for information that would lead to arrests and ease their losses.

In October 1876 young Dan Kelly, after being discharged earlier on a charge of stealing a saddle, was sentenced to three months gaol for 'wilful damage', that is housebreaking. Next year, while Ned was in New South Wales, or so he said, having 'left the colony and become a rambling gambler soon after I left there was a warrant for me and the Police searched the place and watched day and night for two or three weeks and when they could not snare me they got a warrant signed against my brother Dan and on the 15th April Fitzpatrick came to the eleven mile creek to arrest him'[34].

In November 1880, eight days before his execution, Ned was to qualify his statement about this warrant against him in a letter to the Marquis of Normandy: 'it was merely a warrant for my apprehension on suspicion of horse stealing, had I been apprehended they could not possibly have secured a conviction', although he had earlier boasted of his horse-stealing activities.

When Ned returned from being a 'rambling gambler' he was involved in a fracas with police. He rode his horse across a footpath when drunk at Benalla and was arrested and charged on 18 September 1877 for being 'drunk and assaulting police' and fined

£3 1s 0d or three months imprisonment. After a night in the cell, the four police who were escorting him to court decided on handcuffs. Ned resisted, escaped to King's the bootmakers across the road and in the struggle with Sergeant Whelan and Constables Fitzpatrick, Lonigan and O'Dea, according to Ned his trousers were torn off and Lonigan grabbed him by the genitals. Ned shouted 'I've never killed a man yet Lonigan, but if I ever do so help me God, you'll be the first'. He was either prophetic or kept his threat for Lonigan was the first man he killed and he was hanged for it. A local Justice of the Peace, William McInnes, was finally able to peaceably handcuff Ned.

THE FITZPATRICK AFFAIR AND THE FORMATION OF THE KELLY GANG

The formation of the four-man gang was the direct outcome of the Fitzpatrick affair and the events of 15 April 1878 can be seen as the point of no return.

According to Chief Commissioner of Police Standish the 'wholesale system of cattle duffing was carried out extensively. This appears to have culminated in the disturbance at Greta when Constable Fitzpatrick went out to serve a warrant on Dan Kelly for horse stealing'. The events which followed had far reaching effects, some tragic, on many lives, and although Fitzpatrick survived even he was to lament that his 'character had been greatly injured in the country ... by being mixed up with the Kellys'[35]. There are a number of accounts of what actually happened but Fitzpatrick's version was the one accepted in court.

Although there was a local instruction that no policeman should go to the Kelly house alone and that a policeman should always take a colleague as a witness. Fitzpatrick went there alone to execute a month-old warrant for the arrest of Dan Kelly for alleged horse stealing. At the Royal Commission into the affair he later said that he was unaware of the regulation that no single person should go to arrest 'characters such as Dan Kelly'[36]. He declared he had 'seen in the *Police Gazette* that there was a warrant issued by the Chiltern Bench for the arrest of Dan Kelly and John Lloyd'[37] and had proceeded on that basis. Fitzpatrick had much to gain from a spectacular single-handed arrest in view of retrenchments in the Police Force in January 1878 and rumours of his friendship with the Kelly family. Although Ned later recorded 'he said we were very good friends but he was the biggest enemy I had in the country except Lonigan'[38].

Stationed at Benalla but temporarily in charge at Greta, on his way to the Kelly house Fitzpatrick had a lemonade and brandy at Linton's Hotel, Winton, and when he arrived at

The Kelly Gang, a postcard from a series of the 1880, but of doubtful authenticity.
Courtesy Police Museum, Melbourne.

the Kelly's house arrested Dan in the presence of Mrs Kelly and her daughters.

His account of what then happened was as follows. He told Dan:

> I wanted to arrest him as there was a warrant issued for his arrest on a charge of horse stealing ... he said I suppose you'll wait a little while and let me have something to eat I've been out riding all day. I allowed him to wait and he went inside and I followed him in... Ned Kelly then came to the doorway and fired a shot at me ... the shot did not strike me a second or two afterwards Mrs Kelly rushed at me with a shovel she struck me with the shovel. I was in uniform had my helmet. She struck me on the helmet... Ned Kelly fired at me again and the ball lodged in my left wrist... Skillion was present all the time he was armed with a revolver ... Williamson came out from the bedroom ... he was armed with a revolver or pistol ... Ned Kelly said to Skillion you buggar why did you not tell me who was here he said if I had known it was Fitzpatrick I would not have fired ... my wound was bleeding and I fainted. When I came round ... I got up Ned Kelly said to me I'm sorry that this happened it will get me into trouble I will get it pretty heavy[39].

Fitzpatrick then went on to describe how he took the bullet out and Mrs Kelly bandaged his arm.

> [Ned] followed me outside he said now I spared you you spare me how will we manage to say that you were shot. I said I would not mention who shot me. He said you had better say you went up to arrest Dan he was in company with Williamson and I was putting the handcuffs on him and I had my revolver out and it went off and shot me... He asked me did I know Whitlow. I said no he said say this [*sic*] two men rushed from behind a tree as you were arresting Dan describe them as two big men one of them like me and they'll think it my brother Jim and the other Whitlow ... he gave as a reason for naming these men that they were miles away ... he made me make an entry in my book[40].

Fitzpatrick then stated that Ned and Dan went part of the way back with him and

> when I got about two and a half miles [four kilometres] from Kelly's I saw Williamson and Skillion coming up. I spurred on to Winton to David Lindsay's and got off but could not stand up. Richard and David Lindsay helped me in and gave me some brandy. Richard Lindsay accompanied me to Benalla ... have been to Mrs Kelly's since and looked for a bullet mark but found two sheets of bark removed from place where I had previously noticed the bullet mark[41].

It was a remarkable story which resulted in Ellen Kelly, William Williamson and William Skillion being arrested on a charge of aiding and abetting the attempted murder of Fitzpatrick. They were convicted on the basis of a statement sworn by Fitzpatrick on 17 May 1878. The only person who could strongly support Fitzpatrick's evidence was Dr Nicholson who stated on oath:

> I examined the left wrist there appeared to be a bullet wound, the bullet had apparently entered at the outside of the wrist ... at the exit end there was a clean incision a little more than half an inch [thirteen millimetres] in length ... it could not have been caused by the first bullet produced the second one could have caused it[42].

When cross-examined, Nicholson said he 'could not swear it was a bullet wound but it had all the appearance of one'.

David Lindsay also gave sworn evidence that when Fitzpatrick stopped at his place

> he appeared faint and weak he sat down beside the house he had his hand bandaged I

Sergeant Steele in charge of Wangaratta Police Station since 1876. Issued the warrant for Ned's arrest for horsestealing which led to the Fitzpatrick affair, arrested Mrs. Kelly, led search parties for the Kelly's and attempted to shoot Ned dead immediately he was captured at Glenrowan.
Courtesy Police Museum, Melbourne.

> undid it and wet the clothes and bandaged it up it was bleeding then gave him some drink he could not take it at first. He was quite sober[43].

Ned was later in his letter to Cameron to describe David Lindsay as 'a shanty keeper having no licence ... keeps a book of information for the police and his character needs no comment'[44].

Unexpected evidence supporting Fitzpatrick's statement came three years later from Bricky Williamson in a letter dated 6 August 1881 to the Inspector General of Penal Establishments asking for a remission of sentence. Standish said he was 'decidedly of the opinion that his [Williamson's] account of the occurrence when ex-Constable Fitzpatrick was wounded in the wrist is correct'[45]. Williamson's story was

> I heard Fitzpatrick say something about a warrant and Dan said he would have something to eat before he went ... soon after Ned Kelly rushed round the corner of the house and fired two shots at Fitzpatrick ... a man named King passed me with a revolver in his hand[46].

Bricky then described how he was sent to bring horses. When he returned 'King was for taking him [Fitzpatrick] with them and Dan was for letting him go. Skillion and I were told to take the horses up on the hill and wait there till they came'. Williamson then corroborated Fitzpatrick's account of Ned Kelly's proposed alibi concerning the wounding of Fitzpatrick:

> we met Ned Kelly who said he had been seeing Fitzpatrick on the road and he [Ned] had made it all right with him ... if there was any noise about it I was to say that Fitzpatrick was standing talking to me when he saw two men on the next range and started away to try to arrest one of them when the other man fired from behind a tree at him, that there were two or three shots fired... Fitzpatrick was to be said to have then gone in the direction of the Kelly's one of the men to be described as being like the herdsman and the other like Whitlow the poundkeeper and Kelly's mother would state how she dressed the wound in his wrist. I told Kelly I should never be able to think of that story and had better say that I knew nothing about it. Ned Kelly said very well mind you stick to that. He then left and went in the direction of the other two namely King and Dan Kelly. I never saw any of them after[47].

Williamson also stated that King 'wanted the Kelly's not to let Fitzpatrick get away alive and said that in place of being shot in the arm he should be shot through the heart'[48]. He also said that when in his cell 'at Beechworth he spoke to Mrs Kelly who was in the yard after they were sentenced when she said "they would play up now", that there would be murder now'[49]. An intuition of the future murders at Stringybark Creek or a mother's knowledge of her son's intentions?

The account of the Fitzpatrick affair from the Kelly point of view is somewhat different. Mrs Kelly claimed that she asked to see the warrant but Fitzpatrick could only produce a telegram. When Dan refused to go with him Fitzpatrick drew his revolver and threatened Mrs Kelly and she caught hold of the fire shovel and menaced the policeman. In the ensuing struggle, the revolver went off accidentally, Fitzpatrick fell, cutting his wrist on the door latch and denting his helmet. After his arm was bandaged Fitzpatrick agreed to leave, advising Dan to clear out for his own good. Any thought that Ned was involved was imaginary since Ned was miles away across the New South Wales border, a story Ned persistently reiterated in the Jerilderie and Cameron letters. Also in a letter written on 3 November 1880 from Pentridge he claimed that

ARNES,
PHOT

(Top left) Steve Hart, a local lad from Wangaratta, and according to Mrs Jones "a very good boy" was eighteen when he joined the Kelly gang. A portrait drawn by Carrington for the *Australasian Sketcher.*

(Top right) Joe Byrne, son of a gold miner from Woolshed diggings near Beechworth. A friend of Aaron Sherritt.
Courtesy La Trobe Library, Melbourne.

(Bottom left) Aaron Sherritt, a fringe member of the gang or a double agent.
Courtesy La Trobe Library, Melbourne.

(Bottom right) Dan Kelly.
Courtesy La Trobe Library, Melbourne.

> my mother William Skillion and William Williamson could not be guilty of aiding and abetting. Nine respectable witnesses can prove that Wm. Skillion was not within miles of the place at the time ... I had witnesses to show that I was a great many miles from the place at the time but as I was not tried on that charge I could not call my witnesses and show the illegality of the charge[50].

There are similar claims in the letter written on the eve of his execution. But at Ned's final trial Senior Constable John Kelly testified that when he had asked Ned in the lock-up on 29 June 1880, in the presence of Constable Ryan. whether Fitzpatrick's statement was correct, Ned had replied 'Yes. I fired at him'.

Whatever were the facts of the situation, Fitzpatrick's version was accepted and was later presented to the Royal Commission into Police and the Kelly outbreak by both Fitzpatrick and the Chief Commissioner of Police. The incident precipitated the formation of the Kelly gang and the chain of events that led to the Stringybark killings, the robberies at Euroa and Jerilderie and finally Glenrowan.

After Fitzpatrick returned, Sergeant Steele and Constable Brown from Wangaratta arrested first Williamson and then, in company with Constable Strahan, Skillion and Mrs Kelly. Her husband George King disappeared for ever from Mrs Kelly's life and Ned and Dan could not be found. They had presumably 'gone bush', or alternatively Dan had gone bush and Ned was still in New South Wales if his story is accepted. Williamson, Skillion and Mrs Kelly accompanied by her newly born babe were placed in Beechworth gaol pending trial, but Mrs Kelly and her child were returned home after seven weeks on compassionate grounds, after being released on £200 bail, while the others remained in custody till the trial on 8 October 1878. Williamson and Skillion were sentenced to six years and Mrs Kelly three years.

Although her husband George King, father of four of her children, did not stand by Mrs Kelly, the Police Magistrate at Benalla, Alfred Wyatt, was informed verbally through Pat Quinn and 'Wild' Wright that Ned and Dan would surrender if their mother was released, but there was no bargaining. Fitzpatrick was transferred to the Police Depot and thence to Lancefield for nine months before he was discharged on the basis of a report by Senior Constable Mayes.

Much has been made of Fitzpatrick's unreliability and dismissal from the Police Force, but he pointed out to the Royal Commission that he was dismissed on the single report of Senior Constable Mayes of Lancefield which stated 'that I was not fit to be in the police force as I had associated with the lowest persons in Lancefield and could not be trusted out of sight and never did my duty'; that he was not given any opportunity of reply; and that there were 'petitions of two hundred respectable citizens of Mansfield and Romsey and nine justices of the peace asking for my reinstatement'[51]. The petition from Lancefield citizens was 'that we came into contact with him every day ... he was ... zealous, diligent, obliging and universally liked'[52].

Later Ned was to add his usual few insults to his so-called 'natural enemies the police' and to dictate in the Jerilderie letter:

> I have heard from a trooper that he never knew Fitzpatrick to be one night sober and that he sold his sister to a chinaman but he looks a young strapping rather genteel more fit to be a starcher to a laundress than a policeman for to a keen observer he has the wrong appearance for a manly heart the deceit and cowardice is too plain to be seen in the puny cabbage hearted looking face[53].

This was reiterated in his Cameron letter.

BRAY
PHOTO

(Top) Steve Hart, son of a farmer near Wangaratta and a leading member of the Greta Mob of larrikins. Prided himself on the distinguishing "larrikin heel", a high-heeled shoe. The photograph was taken in Wangaratta before he joined the gang.
Courtesy La Trobe Library, Melbourne.

(Below) The clearing at Stringybark Creek in the Wombat Ranges where the three police troopers were murdered.
Courtesy La Trobe Library, Melbourne.

When Steve Hart and Joe Byrne joined Ned and Dan in their hide-out in the Wombat ranges the Kelly gang came into existence. Ned was twenty-three, Dan seventeen and Steve Hart, a local lad from Wangaratta, almost eighteen. Steve, a close friend of Dan, had already served twelve months in Beechworth gaol for horse stealing. Joe Byrne, aged twenty-one, was also a local lad whose father had died when he was a child and whose mother struggled to bring up her seven children in Woolshed Valley.

Aaron Sherritt, a schoolmate of Joe Byrne, was only loosely associated with the gang. He often warned them of police movements but became a double agent listed on the police pay sheet — a dangerous game which ended in his death, blasted by Joe on the eve of the events at Glenrowan after having been found out by Mrs Byrne as aiding police. It is doubtful if Sherritt was of any real value in helping police break up the gang.

The Kelly mountain hide-out in the Wombat ranges was later described by a newspaper reporter as a

> perfect selection within half a dozen miles [ten kilometres] of relations ... twenty acres [eight hectares] round the hut had been cleared ... in the creek to the North there had been gold-digging mainly by sluicing ... the workings were of the extent that four men must have worked for several months.

This description is close to that given by Ned:

> We had a house two miles [three kilometres] of fencing twenty acres [eight hectares] of ground cleared for the purposes of growing mangle worsels and barley for the purpose of distilling whisky. We were also digging for gold we had tools and sluice boxes and everything requisite for the work. We had a place excavated close to the House for the purpose of erecting a small distill. So if any one informed on us they would not get the most valuable or main distill that was further down the creek with the sugar and other requisites[54].

During this period Ned claims to have intended to work 'a still to make whisky as it was the quickest means to obtain money to procure a new trial for my mother ... it never crossed my mind for revenge'[55].

KELLY GANG WELL ARMED

By August 1878, only a few months after the incident, Superintendent Sadlier of the Benalla Police District was planning to arrest the Kelly brothers, unaware that there was now a gang of four. On 25 October a party from Mansfield and one from Benalla set out to form a base depot at Stringybark from which to search the Wombat ranges; Senior Constables Strahan and Shoobridge and Constables Thom and Regan from Benalla and Sergeant Kennedy and Constables Lonigan, Scanlon and McIntyre from Mansfield. Ned believed 'John Martin a wild dog poisoner and Boundary rider in the employ of Mr Johnson station owner at the Wombat gave information to the Police of me and my brother's presence in the Stringybark'[56].

Kennedy's party were dressed as diggers on a prospecting tour, a fact which Ned ridiculed, no doubt preferring an easier uniformed target, and he implied that they were 'ashamed to wear their uniforms'. They made twenty miles (thirty-two kilometres) by 2 p.m. on the first day and camped at Stringybark. The following day Sergeant Kennedy and Constables Lonigan and Scanlon were killed by Ned and Dan Kelly and two others who at that time were unidentified. Constable McIntyre escaped. Ned later wrote that he was aware of the presence of the police party. In his account of what happened he wrote:

> on 25 October I came on the tracks of police horses between Table Top and the boys ...

(Below) Police diagram of the four bushrangers advancing on Constables McIntyre and Lonigan.
Courtesy Public Record Office, Victoria.

(Opposite Left) Constable Thomas Lonigan, the first to be shot by Ned Kelly and for whose murder Ned hanged. Aged thirty seven, he left a wife and four children.
Courtesy La Trobe Library, Melbourne.

(Opposite Right) Sergeant Kennedy.
Courtesy Police Museum, Melbourne.

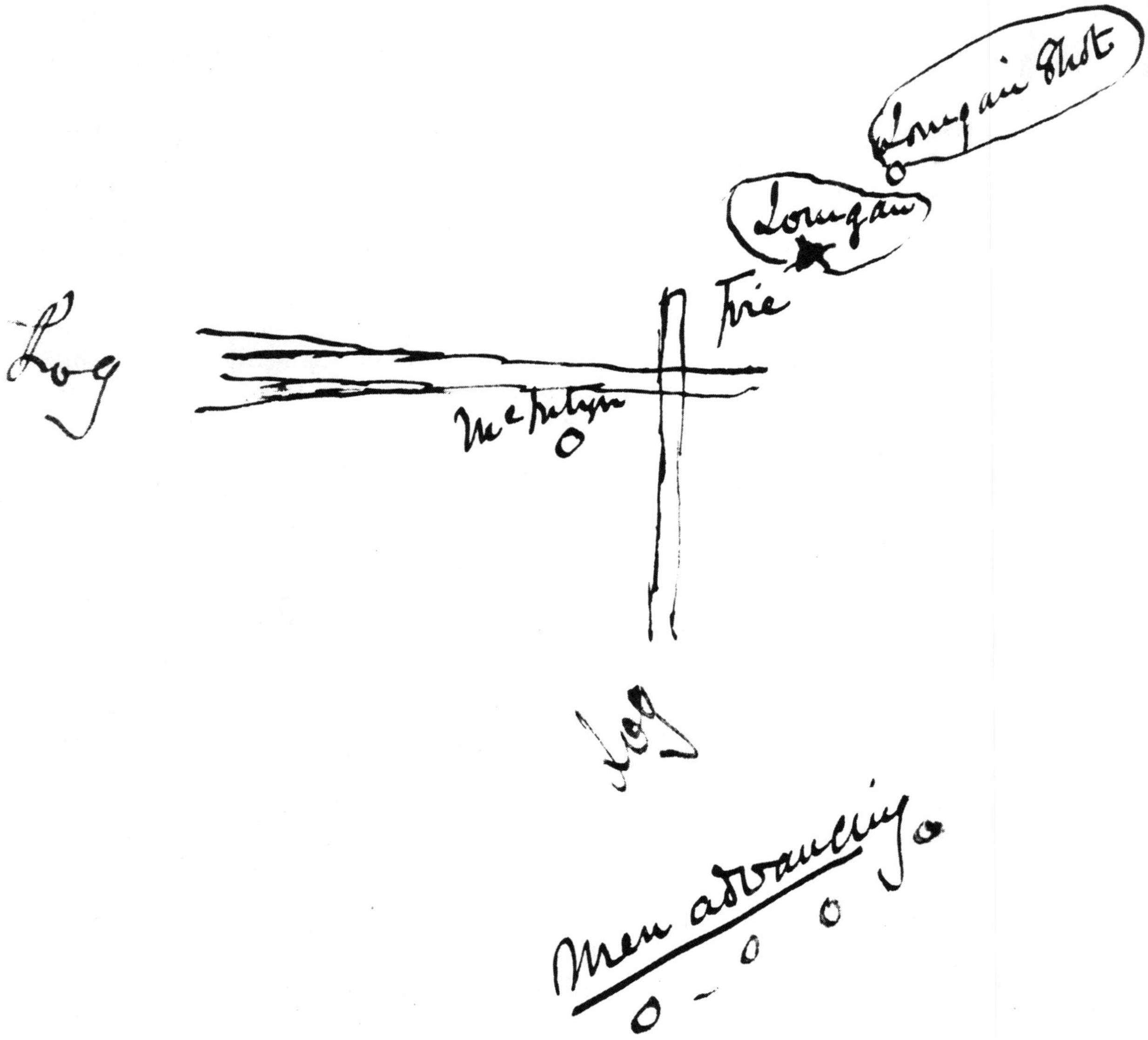

me and my brother went out next morning and found police camped at Shingle hut with long fire arms and we came to the conclusion our doom was sealed unless we could take their firearms as we had nothing but a gun and rifle[57].

On another occasion he added: 'I knew ... if they came on us in our camp they would shoot us down like dogs at our work as we only had two guns we thought it best to try and bail them up'[58].

Evidence was given, however, that they had more than two guns. McIntyre, the sole surviving Crown witness swore:

I saw the prisoner and three other men armed with guns the guns were pointed and presented in the direction where Lonigan and I stood. The men were about thirty yards [twenty-seven metres] from me ... I heard Lonigan then fall ... [the] accused immediately after firing threw his gun from left to right and drew his revolver the four men came up to me they covered me with their weapons[59].

Later on McIntyre stated 'all the four had possession of their guns the whole time', and at the City Court, Melbourne: 'I turned quickly round and saw four men each armed with a gun'[60].

Another account which points to the outlaws being well armed and supplied with ammunition was that of the reporter who later visited their hide-out: 'we saw trees which were marked with bullets from five to fifty having been fired into each at ranges varying from twenty to four hundred yards [eighteen to three hundred and seventy metres'.

Early in the morning of the 26th, Kennedy

and Scanlon had ridden out on mounted patrol while Lonigan and McIntyre carried out camp chores. At about midday McIntyre, hearing a noise, went down the creek and fired at two parrots, shots which the gang naturally heard, since their camp was only a mile away, and at four that afternoon Lonigan and McIntyre made a fire to guide the patrol in, but towards five o'clock the four-man gang approached, spread out through the spear grass.

Just what happened is difficult to ascertain but it is an important legal point. McIntyre's version was that 'Kelly fired ... I remembered standing I saw Lonigan fallen down'. This statement at the Beechworth preliminary trial was repeated at the City Court:

> I was unarmed ... I saw the man on the right of the party move his rifle from the line of my chest and shoot Lonigan who had no time to get under cover or draw his revolver ... the prisoner Edward Kelly is the man who fired the shot which killed Lonigan[61].

Ned's version was that 'Lonigan got behind some logs and pointed his revolver at me'. In his Jerilderie letter he wrote 'Lonigan ran some six or seven yards [six or seven metres] to a battery of logs instead of dropping behind the one he was sitting on, he ... put his head up to take aim when I shot him that instant or he would have shot me'[62]. Ned went on to add 'as I took him for Strahan the man who said he would not ask me to stand he would shoot me like a dog'[63]. Kelly also told a similar story to George Stephens in December when he held up Younghusband's station and also went through the whole affair with Frank Beecroft, an employee of James Gloster, a draper; 'he talked of the murders of his own accord and freely' and both Stephens and Gloster became Crown witnesses at his final trial. Naturally Ned claimed that he fired in self defence and that 'McIntyre was a rascal'. In the letter on the eve of his execution he also claimed, 'if it was any intention to take life I should have shot McIntyre when I had him first covered'[64].

If Kelly shot Lonigan as he stood still or ran for cover it was clearly murder. If, as Kelly said, he put his head up from the battery of logs so he could shoot then the verdict could possibly be self defence. However, McIntyre was the only Crown witness at the scene and the other witnesses, the remaining three members of the gang, were dead at the time of the trial.

The police occurrence book of the Mansfield Police Station for the 28 October 1878 states: 'Lonigan suffered four wounds ... a bullet wound on the right temple, on the left arm, on the outside of the left thigh and one on inner side of right eyeball'. Dr Samuel Reynolds, a Crown witness at the trial, also testified he had examined Lonigan's body which had been struck by *four* bullets. If McIntyre said only one shot was fired at Lonigan by Kelly, and Kelly in conversation with Crown witness Stephens said he 'fired at Lonigan grazing him along the temple' as well as 'I shot him through the head', there remains the question of the other two wounds.

When Scanlon and Kennedy returned to the camp Scanlon was first to die. A bachelor aged thirty-six, he was a fine shot and an expert bushman. According to McIntyre

> Scanlon was in the act of dismounting when Kennedy was fired at, he became flurried and fell on his knees ... then it was the accused [Ned] fired ... Scanlon never took the rifle in his hands and did not fire. The rifle was strapped on his shoulder[65].

Kelly's version of the same events were

> Scanlon who carried the rifle slewed his horse around to gallop away but the horse would not go and as quick as thought fired at me with the rifle without unslinging it and was in the act of firing again when I had to shoot and he fell from his horse[66].

McIntyre, cross-examined by Kelly's defence

The charge against Kelly for an indictable offence.
Courtesy Public Record Office, Melbourne.

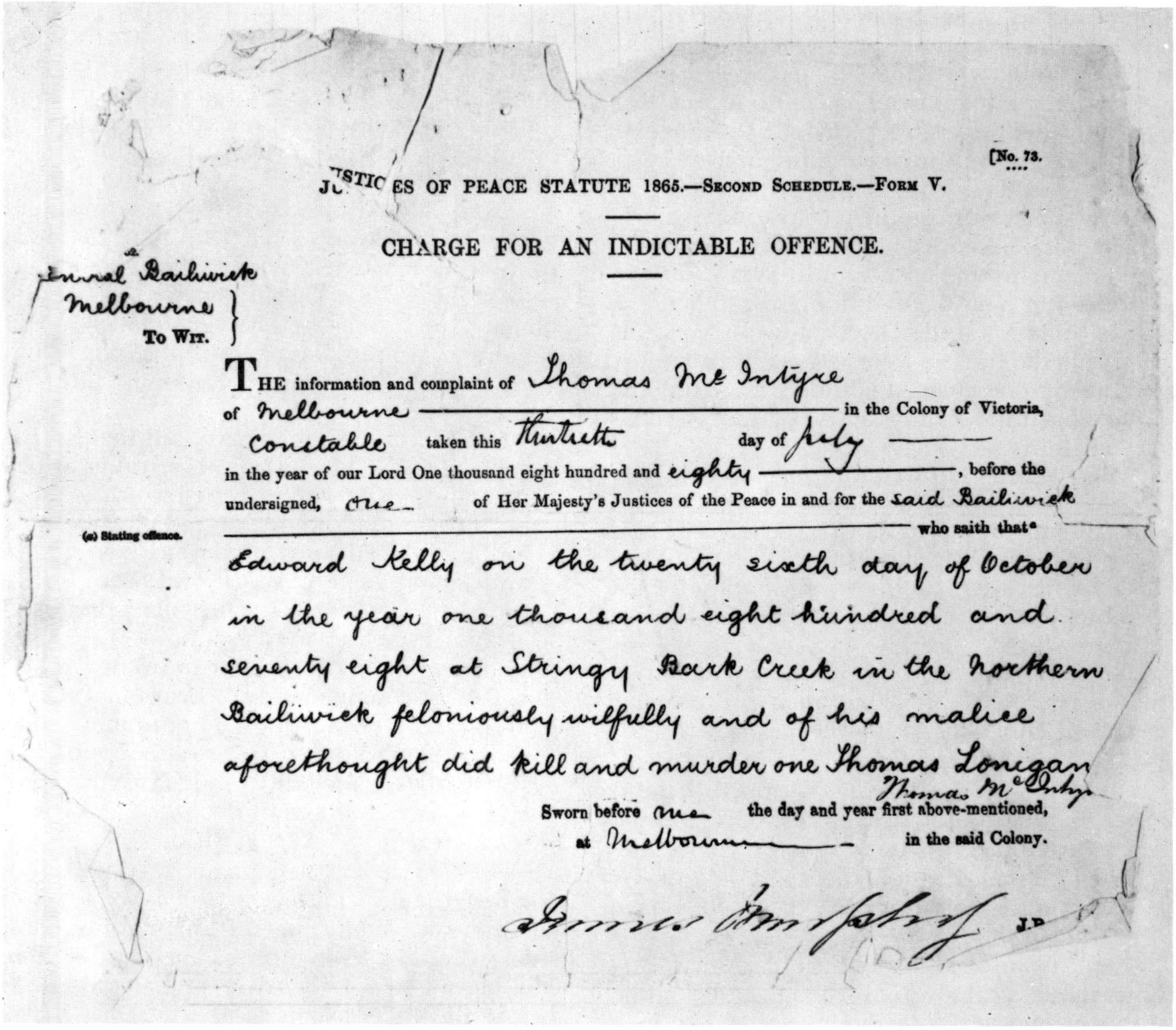

[No. 73.

JUSTICES OF PEACE STATUTE 1865.—SECOND SCHEDULE.—FORM V.

CHARGE FOR AN INDICTABLE OFFENCE.

Central Bailiwick
Melbourne } To Wit.

THE information and complaint of Thomas Mc Intyre of Melbourne in the Colony of Victoria, Constable taken this thirtieth day of July in the year of our Lord One thousand eight hundred and eighty, before the undersigned, One of Her Majesty's Justices of the Peace in and for the said Bailiwick who saith that(a) Edward Kelly on the twenty sixth day of October in the year one thousand eight hundred and seventy eight at Stringy Bark Creek in the Northern Bailiwick feloniously wilfully and of his malice aforethought did kill and murder one Thomas Lonigan

(a) Stating offence.

Thomas McIntyre

Sworn before me the day and year first above-mentioned, at Melbourne in the said Colony.

[illegible] J.P.

lawyer at the trial, repeated: 'Scanlon did not fire before he was shot, I do not believe he could have fired afterwards'[67].

> Continuing his statement McIntyre recalled: while this was going on the other men advanced into the open and fired I heard two other shots beside the prisoners and immediately afterwards another, before these shots were fired Kennedy had thrown himself along the horses back with his head on the horses neck and got off on the offside. I caught hold of the horse after some little trouble the horse was restive with the firing. I rode off and escaped while I was getting on the horse and riding away I heard several other shots[68].

Kelly wrote 'I allowed him to go as I did not like to shoot him after he surrendered'[69], but subsequently at Faithfuls Creek Station he told Crown witness William Fitzgerald 'I sent Hart and Byrne after McIntyre they came back without him. I was vexed with them for not catching him'.

The only evidence on Kennedy's death is that of Ned Kelly, since the others in his gang died at Glenrowan. In his letter Ned wrote:

> Dan advanced and Kennedy kept firing and ran I followed him he stopped behind another tree and fired again I shot him in the armpit and he dropped his revolver the bullet passed through the right side of his chest and he could not live or I would have let him go.

There is an almost identical account in his Cameron letter. However, when recounting the story on another occasion he said: 'Kennedy asked him to let him live he said he could not leave him in a dying state so he put his gun to him and shot him. He said he covered him up then'[70]. Ned's justification for shooting a wounded man through the heart at close range was that it was humane to put him out of his agony. Judge Barry's Notes of Evidence at the trial records Ned's words as 'seeing he could not live from his wounds to end his misery I shot him'[71] and James Gloster gave evidence that Kelly told him 'as we were going to leave the place I did not wish to leave him to be torn by wild beasts while dying. I thought it more humane to shoot him'[72].

In classical Romantic style of the innocent hero who knows no other truth than his own, in two of his letters written from Pentridge shortly before his execution, Ned illogically blamed McIntyre for both Kennedy's and Scanlon's deaths. Later, in his letter from Pentridge on 3 November, Ned, wise after the event, wrote:

> what McIntyre should have said that he was covered by Ned Kelly and three other armed men and not to move or they would be shot as Lonigan had been shot and have pointed to the fact then his companions would have understood their position and would have pleased themselves whether they galloped away or whether they fought[73].

On the eve of his execution he went further:

> both for Kennedy and Scanlon's death McIntyre is the man most accountable ... [he should have told them] if you attempt to fight you will be shot but if you surrender your arms you won't be shot then the men would have known the exact position[74].

However, Ned had had plenty of time before Kennedy and Scanlon returned to instruct McIntyre on what to say if he had thought of it then instead of seven months later, and if there had been time for McIntyre to make a speech before the shots began.

Dr Reynolds testified that

> Scanlon received four wounds one on the right hip, one on the right shoulder, one on top of the breast bone one on the right side of the body under the arm ... that wound proved fatal from internal haemorrhage and injury to the vital lungs.

The discovery of the body of Sergeant Kennedy five days after Stringybard.
Courtesy Public Record Office, Melbourne.

Superintendent Hare.
Courtesy Police Museum, Melbourne.

In another reply, to Mr Gaunson, Kelly's defence lawyer, he said, 'I saw one of Kennedy's ears were off ... I thought it might have been gnawed off by native cats. The body was much decomposed'.

Constable McIntyre reached Mansfield police station at 4 p.m. on Sunday 27 October and reported that he had had to abandon the horse after a couple of miles (three kilometres) 'as he supposed it was shot'. He had hidden in a wombat hole till dark and walked through the night till he reached a station belonging to a settler, McColl, and from there got a lift to Mansfield in McColl's buggy. He reported:

> Sergeant Kennedy, Constables Scanlon, Lonigan and myself were fired at by Edward and Daniel Kelly and two others, names unknown at 6 p.m. on 26th instant Constables Lonigan and Scanlon were shot dead. Sergeant Kennedy cannot be accounted for[75].

Sub-Inspector Pewtriss and McIntyre together with three constables and five Mansfield civilian volunteers left within two hours for the scene of the murders in search of the dead bodies. By midnight they reached Stringybark Creek and returned the next day at 1 p.m. with the bodies of Scanlon and Lonigan wrapped in hessian and tied to a packhorse. Their cold and stiff bodies were found lying on their backs apparently where they fell, their pockets turned inside out and rifled of their contents. Everything of value but the clothes had been taken by the Kelly gang and the tent and the blankets burnt. No trace of Kennedy could be found.

The next day, 29 October, a Magisterial Inquiry at 10 a.m. returned a finding of wilful murder against Daniel Kelly, Edward Kelly and two other men, names unknown. At the same time Sub-Inspector Pewtriss and a party of six police and eleven civilians started for Wombat and Stringybark Creek in search of Sergeant Kennedy and searched till sundown without finding any trace. Superintendent Sadlier arrived at 10 p.m. that evening having ridden from Dookie, where the news reached him, to Benalla, his headquarters, and thence to Mansfield, a total of sixty-five miles (one hundred kilometres) in one day. He returned to Benalla the next day at 9 a.m. after calling on Sergeant Kennedy's wife. The two murdered constables were buried in Mansfield cemetery after a Roman Catholic service.

The next day Sub-Inspector Pewtriss returned to Wombat with a large search party of civilians and stayed at Monk's sawmill overnight and on the fifth day after the murders found Kennedy's body about 8.30 a.m. about half a mile (one kilometre) from the camp where the first attack had taken place. Despite later protestations that he had no intent to kill except in self defence Ned had hunted down Kennedy for a good half mile (one kilometre). All valuables had been taken from the body amongst which was a gold watch and locket. Kennedy's body was brought back to Monk's sawmill and thence by spring cart to Mansfield. En route to Monk's, a party of eight constables searched for the murderers up to the head of Rowes River.

On the Friday morning there was another magisterial inquiry and a return of a finding of wilful murder against some person or persons unknown, and in the afternoon some two hundred people attended Kennedy's funeral service.

At ten o'clock that night, Sergeant Steele and a party of nine police returned having searched the King and Rowes River districts and locating a hut 'about four miles [seven kilometres[from the tragedy in the direction of Greta in which they found twelve rounds of Snider ammunition and provisions'[76].

On 1 November 1878 the Victorian Berry Government had passed the *Felon's Apprehension Act* which gave police the power to arrest on suspicion of harbouring or assisting out-

(Top) Sub-Inspector O'Connor in charge of the Queensland Black Trackers.
Courtesy Police Museum, Melbourne.

(Below) Queensland Black trackers whom Ned Kelly feared so much.
Courtesy Police Museum, Melbourne.

One of Ned's "post offices" while on the run?
Courtesy Police Museum, Melbourne.

laws. It also provided that 'whenever after information made on oath before a justice of the peace and a warrant thereupon duly issued charging any person . . . with the commission of a felony punishable by death' a judge could cause the accused to be summoned. If he failed to appear he could be declared an outlaw and could be captured dead or alive without anyone being accountable for his death, that is, shot on sight by anyone.

Chief Justice Stawell granted an application for the surrender by 12 November of Ned and Dan Kelly and two other members of the gang then specified as Charles Brown and William King. The reward of £100 for Ned and Dan was increased to £500 each and extended to other members of the gang.

THE GANG'S NARROW ESCAPES

In the meantime, after looting the Stringybark camp the Kelly Gang had set out for Dan's hut at Bullock Creek. There they met Tom Lloyd who had kept the hut supplied with food and after an overnight stay at the Greta house set off for New South Wales via the Beechworth ranges. Finding the Murray River in flood and the punt sunk they returned through Wangaratta at 4 a.m. on the morning of 3 November heading for the Warby ranges.

They had two narrow escapes. Detective D.S. Kennedy and Sergeant Harkin just missed them at the farmhouse of a convicted horse stealer near the Murray. His wife had no liking for Ned Kelly blaming him for her husband's conviction since the Kelly's had been involved in the offence. Again, when four young men on horseback with two packhorses were sighted passing through Wangaratta, Inspector Brooke Smith was slow off the mark, delaying for two days before following the tracks and finding Sergeant Michael Kennedy's stolen packhorse. Both Detective Kennedy and Brooke Smith were severely criticised by the Royal Commission on the Police Force in Victoria for missing these opportunities.

The Kellys paid another visit to the Greta house before disappearing into the mountain ranges with plenty of sympathisers in their home territory to keep them appraised of police movements. The hunt was to last twenty months and cost approximately £50,000. The Kelly Gang had the advantages of bush telegraphs and sympathisers and wide areas to manoeuvre in if necessary. The police were hampered by unreliable and often false information, a division of opinion on strategy as to whether to use search and watch parties or secret agents or a combination of both, and a problem of personal jealousies at high level in the force between Captain Standish and Superintendent Hare, suspected of being in

Superintendant Hare's search party in the Wombat Ranges.
Courtesy La Trobe Library, Melbourne.

collusion against Superintendent Nicholson.

In December 1878 Nicholson was replaced by Hare and then Nicholson replaced Hare in July 1878 when Hare's health broke down. Hare was subsequently sent back to replace Nicholson in June 1880 at the direction of the Chief Secretary. There were also complications arising from the differing opinions of Hare and Inspector O'Connor of the Queensland police on the strategy of the use of his Aboriginal trackers. Even the Royal Commission on the Police Force in Victoria, which was critical of many of the police involved, the only unqualified favourable reports being on Senior Constables Kelly and Johnston, and Constable Bracken, was divided over the relative performances of senior officers and the Kelly Reward Board divided the rewards in some contrast to the opinions of the Royal Commission.

A cumbersome operation was mounted by police. Aware of Kelly's friendship with Joe Byrne and Aaron Sherritt and that the telegraph lines to Beechworth had been cut by sympathisers, Standish accepted an alcoholic splitter's story of a sighting of the gang at Beechworth and with Nicholson, nine troopers and a tracker went by special train to Beechworth there to be joined by further police and civilians to make a posse of nearly thirty armed men and an additional black tracker to raid Sherritt's hut in the early dawn. A cordon was placed round the hut and Nicholson and six troopers charged down the hill into what was found to be a deserted hut. In breaking into the hut a trooper's rifle was accidentally discharged, which, mistaken for a signal, brought the rest of the posse to chaotically join in confused jostling. Although this was a clumsy operation confused by an accidental discharge of a rifle, Ned himself was later guilty of the same fault. When handling a captured platelayer's gun at Glenrowan he accidentally discharged it, wounding a railway employee.

A Branch Bank Manager armed and on the alert.
Australasian Sketcher, 15 March 1879.

Once the Sherritt house was discovered as deserted the posse moved over the next hill to the Byrne house, but Mrs Byrne was unresponsive. When the posse settled down for breakfast in a nearby paddock, locals gathered including old John Sherritt and his son Aaron. It was at this stage that Aaron, in the presence of other constables, was engaged by Standish as an informer or police spy. There were others, some of whom while outwardly friends of the Kellys were prepared to betray them to the police for money. A list of the code names and payment of secret agents in police records reveals that at one time there were twenty-five agents paid either by Standish, Hare or Detective Ward. Some were suspected double agents like Aaron Sherritt and Wallace. The Sherritt's code names were Moses and Jones, and Wallace's Bruce, and there was a special secret service fund.

CAPTIVE AUDIENCE AT EUROA

It was not long before the outlaws faced the problem of continued sustenance. After he had been outlawed, Ned no doubt concluded that sympathiser support would not last for ever and that funds were necessary to keep them going.

On 11 December 1878, the gang invaded a station property near Euroa, twenty-seven miles (forty-five kilometres) west of Benalla. The manager of Younghusband and Lyle's property, Macauley, was away from the 11,000 acre (4,500 hectare) property when a horseman approached during lunch and then returned with three others. As station hands came into lunch they were bailed up, locked in a storeroom and guarded by Joe Byrne. When Macauley returned he found the station taken over by the gang.

The outlaws also waylaid a hawker named Gloster from Seymour, his assistant Frank Beecroft, and a passing selector and his son. Some sixteen persons spent the night in captivity and Ned with his captive audience began lecturing them on his career, the first of many self-revealing accounts.

Two years later, some of his audience were to directly quote Ned in supporting evidence for the Crown, and Redmond Barry, Senior Puisine Judge of the Colony of Victoria concluded:

> The history of the prisoner during the last two years and the numerous criminal acts which he admitted on several occasions to different people he was connected with are sufficiently well known to render it unnecessary for me to say more than that the case was amply proved[77].

Next evening the gang collected more prisoners from a passing kangaroo-shooting party including Casement, a local farmer, and Dudley, an employee of the Government Printing Office on holiday, and four railway employees who had come to investigate the cutting of telegraph wires and the felling of six poles. After lunch, leaving Byrne to guard the prisoners, Ned drove into Euroa in the commandeered hawker's cart with Dan in Casement's cart and Steve Hart riding ahead. The outlaws were dressed in new clothes stolen from Gloster's stock.

Euroa had a population of about three hundred with an unpretentious National Bank. At about four o'clock in the afternoon, Ned entered the front door of the bank, Dan the rear and Steve Hart the kitchen door. Steve was recognised by one of the maids, a fellow school pupil at Wangaratta; until then there had been no definite indication that Hart was a member of the gang. The three outlaws left the Bank with about £2,400, Dan with the captured bank clerks and a female servant of the bank manager in the hawker's waggon, Mrs Scott with her mother and seven children in the Scott's buggy and Ned in Casement's cart with bank manager Scott and another servant. The Scotts and the new hostages joined the prisoners at Younghusband's and before the gang left with Macauley as a temporary hostage to ensure a three hour wait for the prisoners and headed for the Strathbogie ranges, Mrs Scott soon had Ned on his favourite topic, his career, and particularly the Fitzpatrick and Stringybark affairs. (Robert Scott and others were later also to be Crown witnesses at Ned's trial.)

The daring acts of swooping down on a township, cutting off communications with Melbourne, holding hostages, robbing a bank and providing their captive audience with a display of exhibitionism by trick horse riding before returning to their haunts in Victoria marks the episode as one of the most extraordinary in the whole career of the outlaws. It could, however, also be viewed as an unnecessary way of robbing a bank to support outlawry as it provided so many eyewitnesses and needless possible complications. The coolness and daring of the whole operation is indisputable but there may have been simpler, more direct and less open and time-consuming methods of robbing a bank. The pattern of holding up stations and townships and using hostages followed that of earlier bushrangers. The larrikin, romantic and even theatrical aspects of the operation which gained admiration and lessened the impact of the cold-blooded murders at Stringybark, as well as increasing their funds, may well have been too subtle to plan. Although the pattern succeeded again at Jerilderie, and then at Glenrowan, it eventually led the gang to its destruction. It would almost seem that unwittingly self destruction may be a possible key to the demise of the gang rather than the effectiveness of the police, with their difficulties of planning a strategy with a large organisation in the closely knit north-eastern district.

The Euroa robbery had three results. First, the government increased the rewards on the heads of each of the Kelly gang to £1,000 and contingents of the Defence Corps were sent to Euroa, Seymour, Avenel, Wodonga, Violet Town, Chiltern and Wangaratta on 15 December 1878 and subsequently to Beechworth a fortnight later on 3 January 1879 and to Shepparton on 8 March. As well as increasing security the use of the Defence Corps released police to pursue the outlaws.

Secondly, Superintendent Hare replaced Nicholson in charge of the hunt. Hare was diffident at first and protested 'since Mr Nicholson and Mr Mountford had reaped the benefit for the capture of Power ... I who was directed to organize the whole affair am still in the same position ... did not see any advantage to be gained in this special duty'[78], but he took up the duty when the Chief Secretary Mr Ramsay informed him:

> this Kelly business has been discussed by the cabinet and it is their unanimous decision that you should be sent up to take charge of affairs. I give you carte blanche to do whatever you think proper and I leave you entirely untrammelled. The Government have such confidence in you[79].

Thirdly, the *Felon's Apprehension Act* introduced in 1878 was used to arrest sympathisers. Hare was convinced that sympathisers kept the Kelly Gang well informed and supplied with food and ammunition and were effective in helping them hide. In January 1879, Steve Hart's brother Jack, Jack Lloyd (Ned's cousin), 'Wild' Wright (an early associate of Ned), a Wangaratta publican, Henry Perkins, Bob Miller and Danny Delaney were the first to be arrested followed by Jim Quinn and Tom Lloyd (Ned's uncles), Frank Harty (who gave evidence for Mrs Kelly over the Fitzpatrick affair) and two neighbours of the Kellys, McElroy and McMonigle. Also arrested

The Kelly Gang Captures Senior Constable Devine and Constable Richards at Jerilderie Police Station.
Illustrated Australian News, 21 February 1879.

Edward Richard Living — states

I am a Clerk in the bank of New South Wales, Melbourne. In 1879 I was a teller in the banks branch at Jerilderie N.S.Wales. About noon on the 10th February the bank was stuck up & robbed by the prisoner and three other men. I & a number of others were made prisoners and confined for some time in a room in Cox's hotel. I heard Kelly haranguing the crowd in the bar — mostly about the Police. I remember his saying the gun he shot the police with was an old one he had for some

Statement of Edward Living, bank teller at Jerilderie.
Courtesy Public Record Office, Victoria.

were the two Clancys and Hannan (friends of Hart), Jack Quinn (another uncle) Strickland, Woods, Ryan (a pro-Mrs Kelly witness) and Walter and Jack Stewart. Aaron Sherritt was a notable omission; also Wallace, about whom the police were to launch a special inquiry as a suspected double agent.

After twelve days in gaol, six were released and another four after a seven-day remand but the others languished on remand for longer periods. There is also some evidence that on the recommendation of police, suspected sympathisers were possibly rejected in their applications for land selections.

GANG IN POLICE DISGUISE

A month later on 10 February there was more action. The gang crossed the Murray River into New South Wales and headed for the Bank of New South Wales at Jerilderie. It was a Saturday night and they captured the two local police Constables Devine and Richards, handcuffed them and locked them in a cell. Next day, Sunday, they dressed themselves in police uniforms and Byrne and Hart appeared in the town with Constable Richards as a blind, disguised as his 'reinforcements'. On the Monday, Ned and Dan on foot and Byrne and Hart on horseback rounded up over sixty townspeople and drinkers in the Royal Hotel dining room. At 12.10 p.m. Joe Byrne bailed up Living, the clerk at the Bank of New South Wales, and his junior clerk Mackin. The manager Tarleton was found having a bath after a long horse ride and Hart supervised his dressing while Ned made Living hand over £691 out of the teller's cash drawer and another £1,490 from a locked drawer after a key was forced from Tarleton. Two customers, Elliott, a schoolmaster, and Rankin, a merchant who was also a Justice of the Peace, were forced to join the prisoners, but Gill the newspaper editor escaped. Ned set off to Gill's house with an 8,300-word letter which he wanted published but Mrs Gill refused to accept it. Gill's escape forced the gang to cut the telegraph wires and force the postmaster and his assistant to join Constable Devine in his cell. They also locked up Richards again. The four man gang then left Jerilderie by different routes and by dawn had crossed back into Victoria. By 8 p.m. the previous night the telegraph wire had been repaired and the alarm given.

Although the New South Wales Government also passed a *Felon's Apprehension Act* and offered a reward of £4,000 which the Victorian Government matched so that there was a total price of £8,000 on the gang's capture, the gang remained at large, though in hiding, for another sixteen months and the Victorian police received reports of fifty-three sightings of the gang, very often of single members particularly of Dan Kelly and Joe Byrne. Reports came from many differing places, Rutherglen, Barnawartha, Wodonga, near Peechelba, Sebastopol, Corowa, and during the first six months of 1880 the sightings were mainly round the Kelly country. Twenty-three reports were stated to be untrue or unreliable, others were too stale, some needed only inquiries but in thirteen cases practical steps were taken without result. Many people sent the police various plans of how to capture the outlaws and many volunteered to help. The press were highly critical of police failures to bring the outlaws to book.

In the meantime, Ned's letter which he had failed to get printed at Jerilderie and then handed to Living, was forwarded to the government where it was copied by the Law Department and on 14 December 1879, Ned forwarded another letter to Donald Cameron, M.P., who had spoken in Parliament against the *Felon's Apprehension Act*.

In June 1879 Joe Byrne, who if rumours were

Aaron Sherritt's "execution" by the "friend" of his youth and fellow ex-convict, Joe Byrne.
Illustrated Sydney News, 30 August 1890 (reprint).

to be believed, often visited his family, had written to his closest friend Aaron Sherritt 'a few stolen lines to let you know I am still living' and suggesting he join the gang wrote, 'it is best for you to join us Aaron. A short life and a jolly one'[80].

Immediately after the Jerilderie hold-up Superintendent Hare sent for Sherritt and together with Detective Ward they watched Mrs Byrne's place through the night in case the outlaws had returned there, and subsequently set up a police watch led by himself for twenty-five days and bitterly cold nights. Aaron spent most of the evenings at Mrs Byrne's house with his 'young woman', Kate Byrne, to whom he was engaged, joining the police watch towards midnight, but Mrs Byrne became suspicious of Aaron after finding traces of another watch or 'cave' party higher up in the hills and on one Sunday morning found Aaron asleep in the police camp. Kate's engagement to Aaron was broken off and in retaliation Aaron stole her horse which he had given her previously and sold it for £3 to Maggie Skillion, Ned Kelly's sister. Mrs Skillion charged Sherritt with selling a stolen horse but nothing came of these particular charges.

Five days after Jerilderie, the Victorian Government sent for Queensland black trackers and on 1 March 1879 Inspector S. O'Connor and six trackers joined the Victorian Police and were based at Benalla. Despite the ability of the trackers, problems soon arose. Hare wanted to split them up and attach them to various towns, but O'Connor wished to retain full control and the Queensland Government supported him. A personal factor also intruded. O'Connor was married to a sister of Superintendent Nicholson whom he met at Benalla, and both Standish and Hare had crossed swords with Nicholson. Although Hare thought the trackers very useful, Captain Standish, his superior, disagreed. In July, Hare was recalled for health reasons after his twenty-five days in the bush and Nicholson resumed charge of the hunt. He discontinued the use of search parties at random and the investigation of all rumours as expensive and unsatisfactory and favoured the use of secret agents to gain reliable information on what action could be taken. The use of trackers declined.

Chief Secretary Berry objected to secret service expenditure except in 'exceptional circumstances' and asked Nicholson for his views. Nicholson referred to it as 'Special Detective Assistance' and replied that the

> expensive and unsatisfactory practice of despatching search parties must again be resorted to if information upon which the police can act is not obtained . . . information from an agent . . . is much more likely to be successful and costs little in comparison with the sending out of police at random into the mountain country[81].

Nicholson also pointed to the results:

> the sympathy with which the outlaws were regarded through their successful outrages at Euroa and Jerilderie has almost died out excepting among their own class . . . they are afraid to trust even their best friends beyond a limited extent and are mere skulkers among the mountains . . . the entire extinction of wholesale horse and cattle stealing which prevailed between New South Wales and the North East district . . . the disappearance of the insolence and defiance after the murders[82].

He said that

> to relax in the steps taken for the capture of the four miserable though cunning and bloodthirsty fugitives would be to throw away all that has been gained and to invite the criminal class to emerge and renew their attacks upon life and property[83].

Superintendent Sadlier supported Nicholson and said:

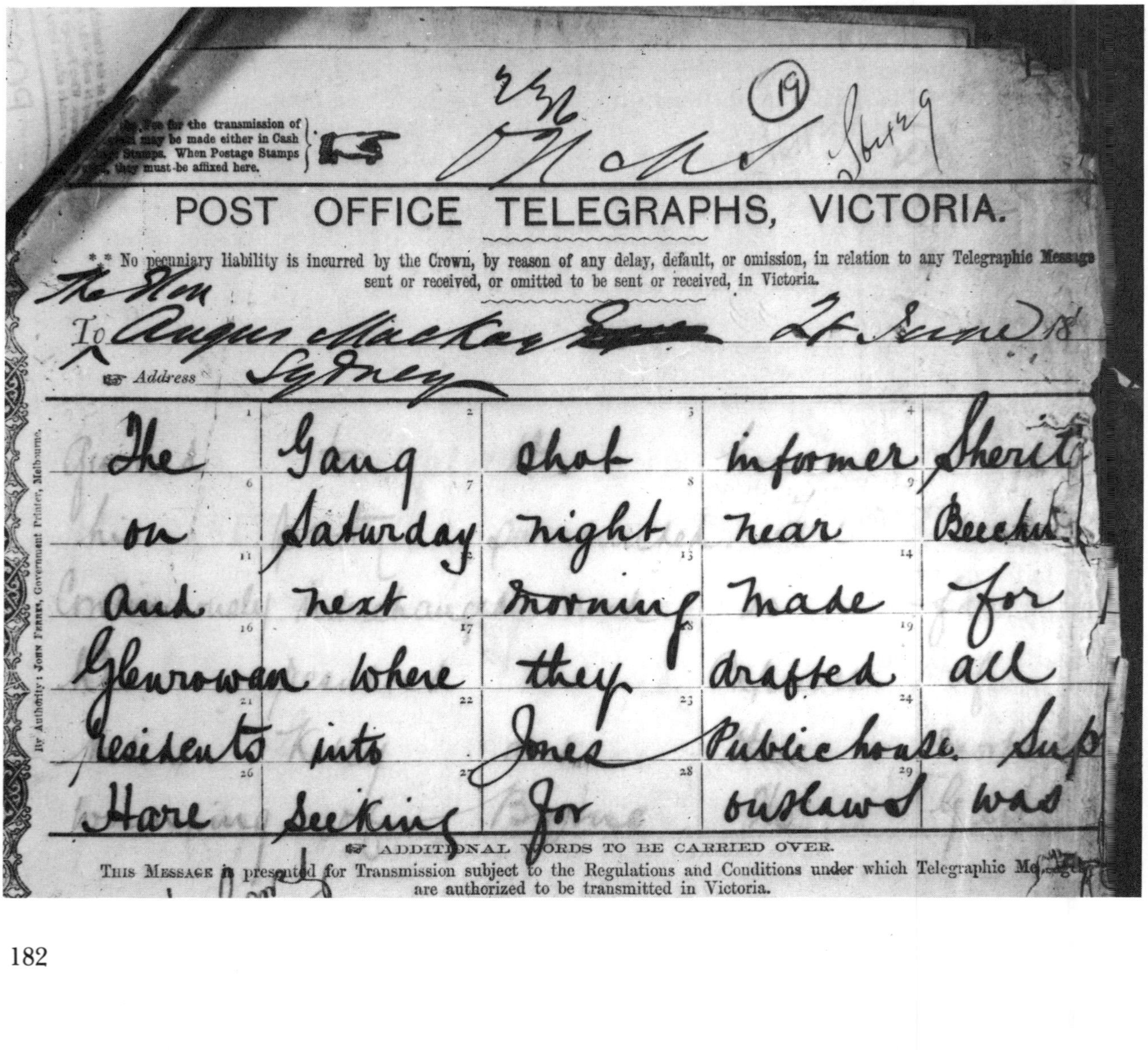

... the Fee for the transmission of ... may be made either in Cash ... Stamps. When Postage Stamps ... they must be affixed here.

POST OFFICE TELEGRAPHS, VICTORIA.

** No pecuniary liability is incurred by the Crown, by reason of any delay, default, or omission, in relation to any Telegraphic Message sent or received, or omitted to be sent or received, in Victoria.

To The Hon Angus Mackay 28 June 18

Address Sydney

The Gang shot informer Sherif on Saturday night near Beechw and next morning made for Glenrowan where they drafted all residents into Jones Publichouse. Sup Hare seeking for outlaws was

ADDITIONAL WORDS TO BE CARRIED OVER.

This Message is presented for Transmission subject to the Regulations and Conditions under which Telegraphic Messages are authorized to be transmitted in Victoria.

By Authority: John Ferres, Government Printer, Melbourne.

(Top left) Drawing of Sherritt's house by T. Carrington for *Australasian Sketcher,* 1880.

(Bottom left) Chief Secretary Robert Ramsay informs the New South Wales Government of Sherritt's murder by telegram.
Courtesy Public Records Office, Melbourne.

Ground plan of Sherritt's hut, by T. Carrington for *Australasian Sketcher,* 1880.

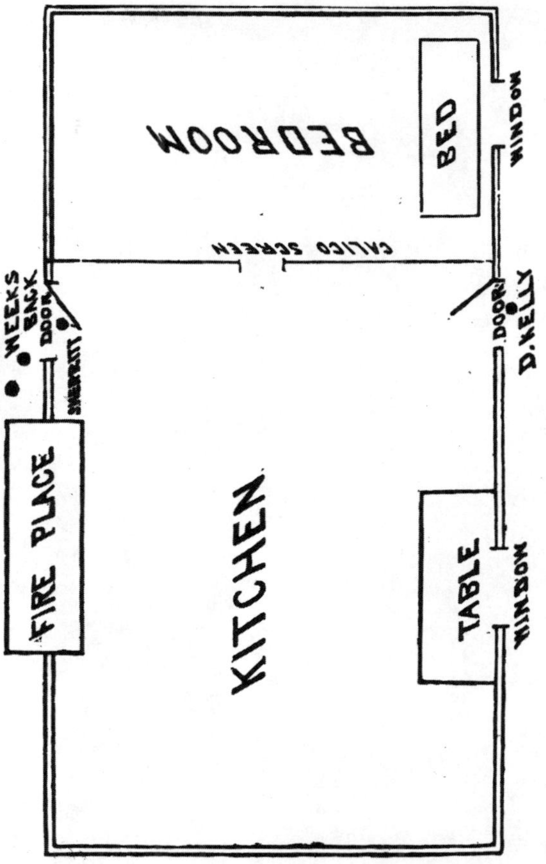

> had a hundred pounds or so judiciously been spent in this manner before the Kelly outbreak, the fifty thousand pounds said to have been spent in consequence, not to speak of the loss of life might all have been saved... through the secret service ... I have been able to effect large reductions in general expenditure[84].

From February 1880 on, a new kind of theft had been reported by farmers round Oxley and Greta—ploughshares. Some twenty mouldboards from ploughshares were reported missing and in May, Nicholson received a report from his agent 'Diseased Stock' that 'jackets were being worked'. Just exactly who made the Kelly gang's armour has never been satisfactorily established. Two months after Glenrowan Detective Wilson had to report that he had visited Kilfera's Station (Henricks), Mason and West's Station, Greta township, Oxley, Millawah, Wangaratta, Glenrowan, Winto, Benalla, Beechworth and farms where sympathisers and other friends of the gang were located and that

> suspicion rested on Pat Delaney, blacksmith of Greta and Chas. Culph, blacksmith of Oxley, the former because he was an intimate friend and could be relied upon by Ned Kelly and the latter because he was away from his place of business a short time before the gang were exterminated and captured[85].

Meade, 'a special', reported to Sadlier in December, six months after Glenrowan:

> Jack Kean of Benalla, a well-known sympathiser of the Kelly crowd or Pat Delaney was not the man but a man named John O'Brien a selector farmer also a bush blacksmith residing at Yarrawonga is the man that made it.

Mountford had three suspects, Delaney, Jim Brien of Wanganderry and Culph. He stated:

> some say Kelly himself is a blacksmith and could have done it with Byrne's assistance. However Brien is the main suspect, very fly and bought a complete set of tools and lives in a secluded place and could have built a steamer without being seen. He is a clever smith[86].

A man suspected of making Byrne's armour was 'a blacksmith named Strunghan who was particularly intimate with Byrne and with whom James Wallace was very thick'[87].

A couple of weeks after Nicholson got his written report on 20 May 1880 from his agent 'Diseased Stock' about the jackets being made, Hare replaced Nicholson on 2 June and although Nicholson sent a telegram to the Senior Constable at Beechworth 'to pay off all the agents he had employed', Hare instructed Detective Ward 'to carry on as usual'. He went about the district and sent out parties into the country for information and set up watch parties at certain points as the outlaws' agents and sympathisers were particularly active. He was of the opinion that the 'outlaws were afraid to show out because of the trackers' and that

> the sooner Mr O'Connor and the men were removed the better because should the gang make a raid there would be a probability of

(Top) Inside the press carriage en route for Glenrowan. *The Australasian Sketcher,* 1880.

(Below) The Glenrowan Station before the hotel was burned down. Two at least of the citizens are armed. *Courtesy La Trobe Library, Melbourne.*

capturing them but as long as they remained in the mountains we had little chance of finding them. Mr Ramsay agreed with me in this opinion . . . the trackers were removed on the 25th June, the outlaws believing they had left for Queensland shewed out on the 26th, on the 28th the gang was destroyed and its leader captured[88].

KELLY FEELS A MIXTURE OF GLOOM AND PERSECUTION

On Saturday 26 June 1880, the Kelly gang dramatically emerged from their hiding place. Two of them, Dan Kelly and Joe Byrne, were to cut down Aaron Sherritt as a police informer and as a bait to draw police to the Glenrowan railway line, and Ned and Steve Hart were to ride across country to Glenrowan with the heavy personal armour to break the railway line. They were then to join up, put the police, who they assumed must come by special train out of the way by derailing the train, and rob nearby banks for more funds. It has even been proposed that they would have gone on to lead a selector rebellion.

That Saturday night, Aaron Sherritt was sitting by the fire with his young wife, formerly Miss Barry, and her mother, in his selector's hut near Sebastopol. With them were four policemen, the watch posted there to protect Sherritt but also to keep a watch on the nearby house of Joe Byrne's mother.

At pistol point and handcuffed, Joe Byrne and Dan Kelly brought Anton Wicks, a nearby German settler, to call unsuspecting Sherritt to the doorway and Joe Byrne blasted a bullet into Aaron's chest at point blank range and then put another bullet into the fallen man to make sure that he was dead. The four police refused to come out as they were standing targets. Instead they took Mrs Barry and Mrs Sherritt as protective hostages into a bedroom and hid. Having wasted precious time in threats Dan Kelly and Byrne kept Anton Wicks for nearly three hours before releasing him and did not ride till nearly nine o'clock. The gang had estimated that news of Aaron's murder would reach police at Beechworth early Sunday morning and bring the special police train quickly to the chosen point of derailment. The police in Sherritt's hut, however, thought the outlaws' departure a ruse and did not emerge till daylight. Even then Armstrong, the leader of the police watch, tried unsuccessfully to get a Chinese digger and then a schoolteacher, O'Donoghue, to take a message to Beechworth and finally walked the eight miles (13 kilometres) himself arriving at 1 p.m. Sunday. The news did not reach Hare till 2.30 p.m. some thirteen-and-a-half hours later than Ned had expected. Ned and Steve Hart had been at Glenrowan since 1 a.m. that Sunday morning and had roused Mrs Jones at her hotel and taken her to where they were 'taking tools out to go up the line' and were already at work trying unsuccessfully to remove sections of the rails with spanners, their packhorses and armour close by. The timing of the plan was already going astray, even before Joe Byrne and Dan Kelly rejoined Ned and Steve Hart.

In contrast to the cool and successful, if needlessly lengthy, raids on Euroa and Jerilderie, this plan was strangely impractical. In previous raids no one was injured, the gang scored points on the police and fired people's imaginations with their daring and Captain Moonlite and his youngsters offered to join Ned's gang. The Glenrowan strategy suggests Ned's power to tactically maintain his war against authority was being impaired by the arduous strain and restrictions of being on the run for twenty months. He had not been leading the 'bold, fearless and free life', his own words. Nicholson thought the gang threatened 'to

(Top) Ned lying wounded on a bunk in the Station Master's house.
The Australasian Sketcher, 1880.

(Below) Jones Hotel before being set alight to smoke the outlaws out at 3 p.m.
Courtesy La Trobe Library, Melbourne.

expose themselves more and more to the danger of betrayal' and that 'they conceal themselves during the day and move out at night on foot'. Although it is difficult to analyse Ned's mind, platelayer Reardon gave evidence that at the gate house to the station before going up to breakfast at Jones' hotel and in the presence of Neil McHugh and MacDonald, 'Ned Kelly was talking about how he was tired of his life and was fighting his battle and came there to fight it out, they were hunting him like a dog'[89]. This appears to indicate he felt a mixture of gloom and persecution.

The gang were certainly known to be in regular contact with their families and friends but it was inevitable that Ned and the gang had grown gloomier about their prospects of survival. Ned's careful plan depended upon timing, and he had made no allowance for delays caused by changing circumstances. The plan miscarried and brought about a situation of disaster and the total destruction of the gang.

Many different motives for the final break-out have been suggested: a break-out borne of the frustrations of outlawry and adventureless activity in the bush; the decimation of police so that they would be freer to rob nearby banks; to capture the police as hostages in return for Mrs Kelly's freedom; or to lead a selector rebellion. Whatever the motive, two civilians and three outlaws lost their lives and one outlaw was hanged.

Although there was discontent among selectors, Irish and others alike during the period, and Ned had threatened 'to show some colonial strategem which will open the eyes not only of the Victoria police and its inhabitants but also the whole British Army',[90] there seems no real evidence to show that an organised selector army existed. It has been suggested that Ned left the hotel during the siege to meet some of the 'selector army' since at that stage there were only sixteen police surrounding the hotel and a small band of sympathisers could feasibly have overcome the police, rescued the outlaws and then gone on to an uprising.

Another hint that the gang had grandiose ideas on the eve of Glenrowan came from Superintendent Hare when he reported 'I was privately informed [thought to be by Mrs Byrne] that the outlaws were about to commence some outrage which would not only astonish Australia but the whole world'[91].

The gang had to emerge from hiding some time or else split up and merge into society, always beset by thoughts of betrayal. The railway line at Glenrowan was a logical setting in which to easily ambush police and a psychological stage close to home where their leader could redeem his waning prestige amongst sympathisers.

These elements together with their hatred of authority and their 'natural enemies' the police, the need for funds and the need to cut down informer Sherritt which would also create an example to possible reward seekers, all seem reasonable aspects in a rationale for the Glenrowan offensive that led to the final debacle.

When his first attempt to break the line was unsuccessful, Ned decided that they needed expert help and roused Reardon and Sullivan, railway platelayers, from their beds and then herded them with Reardon's wife and eight children and Larkin, a lodger at Reardon's, to Station Master Stanistreet's house, where Hart was standing guard over the captive family with three loaded guns. They took the platelayer's tools from a box at the station and finally the two lengths of rail were taken up with the assistance of the platelayers. Jane Jones, aged fifteen, was with them. She later testified 'Hart ordered me up the line' and told me 'to sit down on the line and he rested his head on my knee and said he was sick'[92].

GLENROWAN INN
1
2
3

(Top) Schoolmaster Curnow stopping the pilot engine.
Courtesy La Trobe Library, Melbourne.

(Below) The broken railway line near Glenrowan repaired after the destruction of the Kelly gang.
Courtesy Police Museum, Melbourne.

The outlaws and their captives returned to the station master's house bringing in a contractor named Puizzi. Constable Eason later reported that Puizzi attempted to use his gun when Kelly fired at him and very nearly shot Ned. He also reported that later in the day

> when Metcalfe was bailed up outside the Station Master's house, Kelly was fiddling with this gun of Puizzi's when it exploded striking Metcalfe in the face ... Kelly said 'I did not mean to fire it went off accidentally'[98].

At this stage Ned had twenty people bailed up at Stanistreet's and at breakfast time Mrs Jones came from the hotel and asked 'the boys' to come up to breakfast. Mrs Jones said she had been ordered by Dan Kelly to provide breakfast at the hotel but Reardon later testified that she had invited Ned to 'come on up and have a wash and your breakfast and it will do you good after the night'[94] to which Ned had replied 'let ye all walk up here to Mrs Jones'. Dennis Sullivan testified that he had seen 'Ned and Mrs Jones in the bedroom and Ned Kelly having a towel in his hand and after wiping his face'[95]. The two Kellys went to the hotel and as Joe Byrne and Jane Jones had brought a half-full bottle of brandy to Stanistreet's and it was necessary to keep a watch there, there was a bacon and brandy breakfast there for the rest around 5 or 6 a.m.

As the gang's schedule had gone astray, they had to stay on longer than expected at Glenrowan, before they could halt the special train. As they had to prevent news of the break in the line reaching Benalla and Wangaratta, it was essential that no one leave the township. Ned commandeered the Glenrowan Inn in similar fashion to the hotel at Jerilderie. He had probably thought of the hotel earlier as a similar base headquarters.

As the morning advanced, more Glenrowan residents were made captive and brought to the inn until there were sixty-two. Arms, ammunition and armour were locked in Mrs Jones' best room. Schoolmaster Curnow on a Sunday morning buggy drive with his wife and child with David Mortimer, his brother-in-law, on horseback, were stopped at the railway level crossing by the armed Ned Kelly on horseback with Joe Byrne also armed standing nearby. At the same time a wild outburst by Ned against Pat Delaney to whom he had been talking before Curnow arrived, threatening him with a revolver and with accusations of wanting to be a policeman, caused consternation to the group till Kelly calmed down and forced them all to join the Stanistreets as prisoners. The Curnows' horse and buggy were taken to Mrs Jones' backyard and the Curnow family joined the prisoners in the hotel. All except the Stanistreet family were now there and Mrs Stanistreet was able to secure 'two leather bags of ammunition, a valise with bullet moulds and a pair of police handcuffs which Steve Hart dropped several times when fooling about'[96]. While at Stanistreets, Ned Kelly once again spoke of 'his shooting the police at Mansfield'[97]. Hart and Byrne kept watch until the Stanistreets were marched up to the hotel, where Mr and Mrs Stanistreet and Curnow 'consulted together whenever an opportunity offered of checkmating the outlaws'.

Superintendent Hare had heard nothing positive about the movements of the outlaws but having heard privately that something was on, he was at the Benalla telegraph office at 10 a.m. on Sunday morning receiving telegrams from all his stations that all was quiet, but making an appointment with the telegraph master for 9 p.m. in the evening. At 2.30 p.m., however, he received the message that 'Aaron Sherritt in whose house I had a watch party had been shot the previous evening at six o'clock'.

By 8 p.m. a special train from Melbourne

A Strange Apparition — Ned Kelly just before capture. *Illustrated Australian News,* 19 July 1880.

had been organised for O'Connor and his boys to track the outlaws from Sherritt's house and a pilot engine made ready at Wangaratta to go to Beechworth with the train at approximately 1.30 a.m. (that line requiring particular engines). Trucks were also organised for the horses and Hare gathered a party of six police under Senior Constable Kelly. The special train consisting of an engine, single carriage and brake van brought four members of the press: Thomas Carrington, artist for the *Australian Sketcher* who was to record many of the now familiar illustrations, John McWhirter of the *Age*, Tom Allen of the *Daily Telegraph* and Joseph Melvin of the *Argus*. At Essendon, the train picked up Sub-Inspector O'Connor and his five trackers and also his wife and sister who hoped to spend a few days holiday at Beechworth. The train crashed the gates at Craigieburn and the engine's brake was torn away and the train had to rely on the brake in the guard's van. At Benalla, trucks carrying horses were attached, and when the engine driver refused to continue with Constable Barry tied to the front of the engine as a look-out, he was taken off and the damaged engine replaced by the good engine at Benalla. With Rawlings, a Winton man who had a free railway pass, the engine driver, stoker and guard together with Hare and his seven troopers and others, a complement of twenty-four, left Benalla at two o'clock in the morning. Thirty-five minutes out from Benalla they were stopped by the waving red lamp of Guard Bell and heard the whistle of the pilot engine as it slowed down after it had been alerted by Schoolmaster Curnow. Curnow had gained the confidence of Ned and had been allowed to go home with his family, but having heard the train coming, ran down the line to warn it by lighting a candle in a buggy lamp behind a red scarf.

At the inn there had been convivial, if forced, activity. Jane Jones had played the concertina, 'some were dancing, some playing cards and some were jumping with them'[98]. Curnow had earlier been forced to dance with Dan Kelly. Mrs Jones later complained 'they were all drinking. I objected to drinks because the outlaws were filling out drinks for the men behind the bar at my expense'[99]. Also:

> Ned Kelly had asked the people all about to sing and one young man sang two songs and then he looked at me and said, are you not going to sing? I said I could not and he said try and I said I had a little boy who could sing a little bit but he was delicate and I called the boy and he sang 'The Wild Colonial Boy' and 'Colleen das Cruitha na mo' [the pretty girl milking the cow][100].

On Sunday evening, Ned and Joe Byrne, escorting a number of prisoners, had knocked up Constable Bracken who was in his night-shirt ill in bed, unaware of events. An hour or so later, Curnow and his family had been allowed to go home to bed having pleased Ned by telling him that Stanistreet had a loaded revolver in his possession and it ought to be taken. Ned also told

> Dan Kelly to tell Mrs Reardon they could all go home with the children but the husband and boys could remain; but to let them go with a caution that they must be kept at home and the women objected to go lest their husbands got drunk and said they would rather see it out[101].

Mrs Jones had two dances during the night and Mrs Reardon gave evidence that 'she seemed quite pleased and merry and said she would kiss Ned Kelly. She said she did'[102], and a labourer, Edward Reynolds, said he saw that in the 'backyard Mrs Jones had her arm around Ned Kelly's neck' and it 'was moonlight'[103]. Jane Jones also guarded the prisoners saying Dan Kelly 'gave me a revolver and told me to take charge of the room for a short time'[104]

By 2 a.m. both outlaws and prisoners were

(Top) The Wangaratta police reinforcements at Glenrowan.
Courtesy La Trobe Library, Melbourne.

(Below) Joe Byrne's body being photographed propped up against the cell door at Benalla police station.
Courtesy La Trobe Library, Melbourne.

showing signs of strain and Ned had begun his usual lecture, but was interrupted by the train whistle. It was the special train. Both Mr and Mrs Reardon testified that the outlaws ordered 'all stop here and they turned into Mrs Jones room'. Reardon added, 'I could hear the armour rattle'. All the lights and the fires were doused not only because Dan Kelly ordered it but as Mrs Jones later said 'I did it through fear as everybody else did . . . throughout the night I was afraid the large fires may burn the house down'. Later when her son was wounded, according to Mrs Reardon, Mrs Jones remonstrated with Ned 'why did you not do as you promised me to go out and fight like men'[105].

Despite his family's reluctance, it was Curnow who warned the approaching troopers on the train. Under Hare's instructions the horses were untrucked and saddled in case of a chase and the police fanned out on foot to surround the hotel. Hare approached to within twenty yards (eighteen metres) of the hotel and the battle began as three armoured outlaws fired together from the verandah. Hare was badly wounded in the wrist but used his right hand till he could no longer reload. Bullets also hit Ned in one foot and an arm and Joe Byrne received a leg wound. There was a state of terror in the hotel as the prisoners sought the safety of the floor, ordered there by Constable Bracken. 'Only for him we would have all been shot'[106] said Mrs Reardon later.

Hare, out of the battle, returned to Benalla to send Sadlier up with reinforcements. Neither Sadlier nor Nicholson allowed Hare to return to Glenrowan and both set off in a special train with eleven police, two trackers, and Jesse Dowsett, a railway guard, rode the footplate beside Driver Burch and Fireman Hollow. Dr Nicholson accompanied them. In the meantime Senior Constable Kelly held the fort at Glenrowan, Sub-Inspector O'Connor voluntarily kept in the background, an action for which he later suffered some criticism. Ned had escaped from the hotel and was in the bush encumbered in his own armour. With more police, the cordon was tight and the other three outlaws were leaderless in the hotel. The police cordon was further reinforced when Constable Bracken, who had also escaped from the hotel and ridden to warn any further trains of the break in the rails, joined Sergeant Steele and four other mounted troopers who were helping the police besiege the outlaws. Two other police arrived by train, as well as Marsden, the Clerk of Courts at Wangaratta, who came as an onlooker. Not even reporting to Sadlier, Sergeant Steele firing away enthusiastically soon had a mistaken target. In escaping with her baby Mrs Reardon screamed when a bullet from Steele passed through the baby's shawl, and following her, her son, outlined in the doorway, was hit in the shoulder from one of his bullets. Soon after, young Jack Jones, the singer of the Wild Colonial Boy, was shot in the left hip, the bullet slanting upwards to emerge from the right ribs. He died next day in the Wangaratta Hospital.

With dawn approaching, Joe Byrne while going to the bar for a whisky took a fatal shot in the groin through a chink in his armour and was dead within minutes. Martin Cherry, an old man, was shot while sitting on the floor. Prior to Byrne's death McHugh had escaped carrying the wounded Jones boy on his back. Constable Phillips later wrote that McHugh said:

> Dan Kelly and Steve Hart and Joe Byrne were in the hotel with a suit of armour on but that Ned had not returned to the hotel after shooting at us [he] also warned me that the remaining three intended coming out at daybreak to shoot us all[107].

Phillips also described how Senior Constable Kelly found a revolving rifle smeared with blood at the back of the house and placed Constables Phillips and Arthur at the rear.

(Top left) The hotel beginning to burn.
Courtesy La Trobe Library, Melbourne.

(Bottom left) The hotel well alight.
Courtesy La Trobe Library, Melbourne.

Only the sign post remained.
Courtesy La Trobe Library, Melbourne.

THE
GLENROWAN INN
ANN JONES

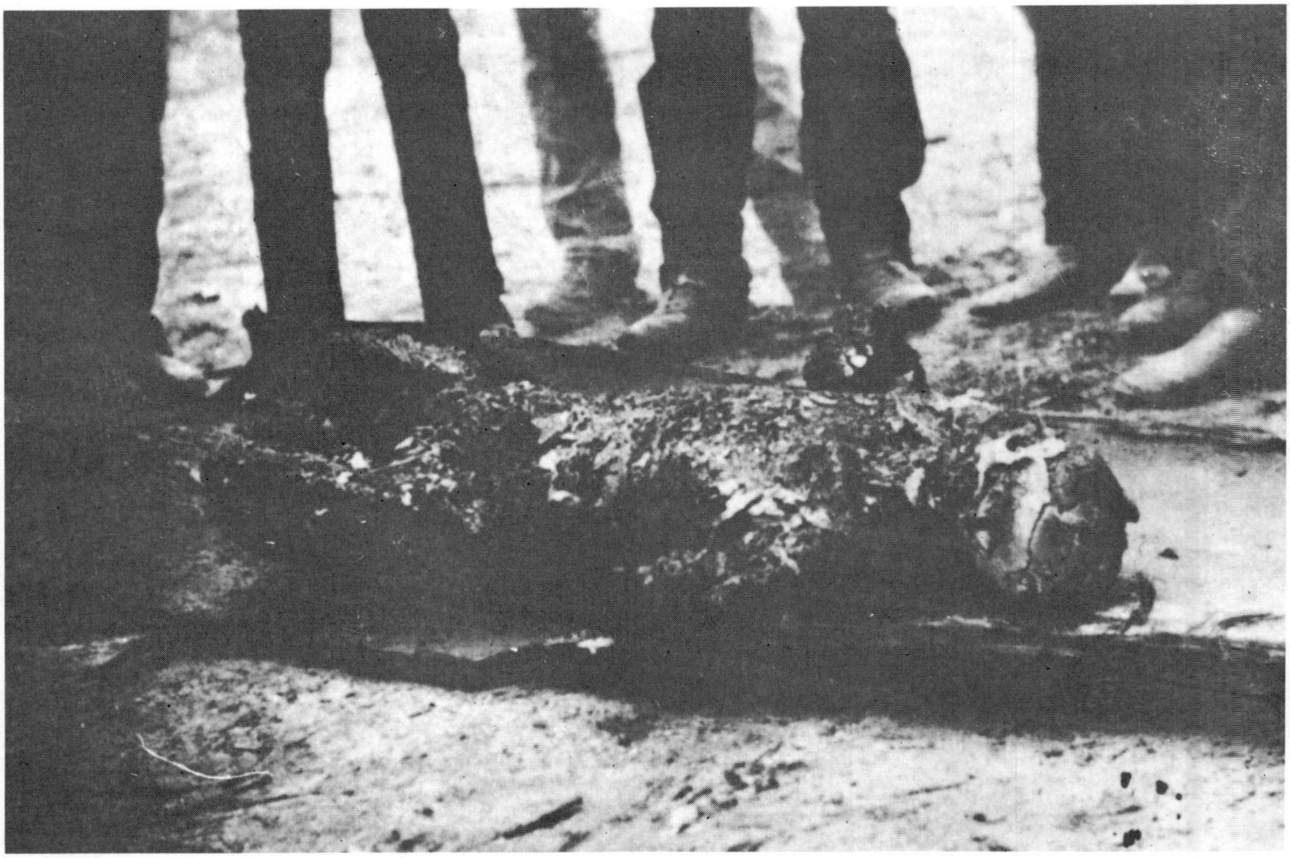

(*Left*) A burnt body taken from the hotel and lying on a sheet of bark.
Courtesy La Trobe Library, Melbourne.

The log where Ned Kelly finally fell and was captured.
Courtesy La Trobe Library, Melbourne.

About 7 a.m. the police were attacked from the rear by the armour-clad Ned wearing a long grey overcoat and an iron mask. Kelly moved from tree to tree receiving police fire and returning it. Three men went after him, Sergeant Steele, Senior Constable Kelly and Dowsett, the railway guard, firing persistently as Ned's shots went wide. Ned was brought down by Steele's shot in the leg and was prevented from shooting him dead by Dowsett and Senior Constable Kelly. This seems a critical few seconds for had Steele succeeded the course of the Kelly myth may well have been altered. Ned was carried to the station master's office and although no bullet had pierced the armour, he had two wounds in the left leg and wounds in the left and right arms and two in the groin. Some accounts list the wounds as twenty-eight, but Ned had complained that the police used buckshot as well as bullets.

In his report Constable Phillips complained: 'the public and the press appear to believe that the capture of Ned Kelly is in all honour due to Sergeant Steele alone. That I utterly refute ... others and I can claim as meritorious a part'. In his version, he went on to say:

> Constable James Arthur cried Phillips look behind you Ned Kelly revolver in hand coming out of the bushes about thirty yards [twenty-seven metres] distance. Arthur and I fired simultaneously but without any effect. We discharged our rifles again with the same result. Ned exclaimed, 'Good shot, boys... Fire away you b...s you cannot hurt me. He kept walking slowly towards us and discharged three or four shots at us without injuring any of us. Constable Healy then rushed within ten yards [nine metres] of him and discharged both barrels as did Constable Monteford [Mountford] but Ned only laughed ... Ned took a rest on the limb of a tree took a deliberate aim at Constable Healy but with no effect. The bullets at this time

Telegraph reporting Ned's three wounds.
Courtesy La Trobe Library, Melbourne.

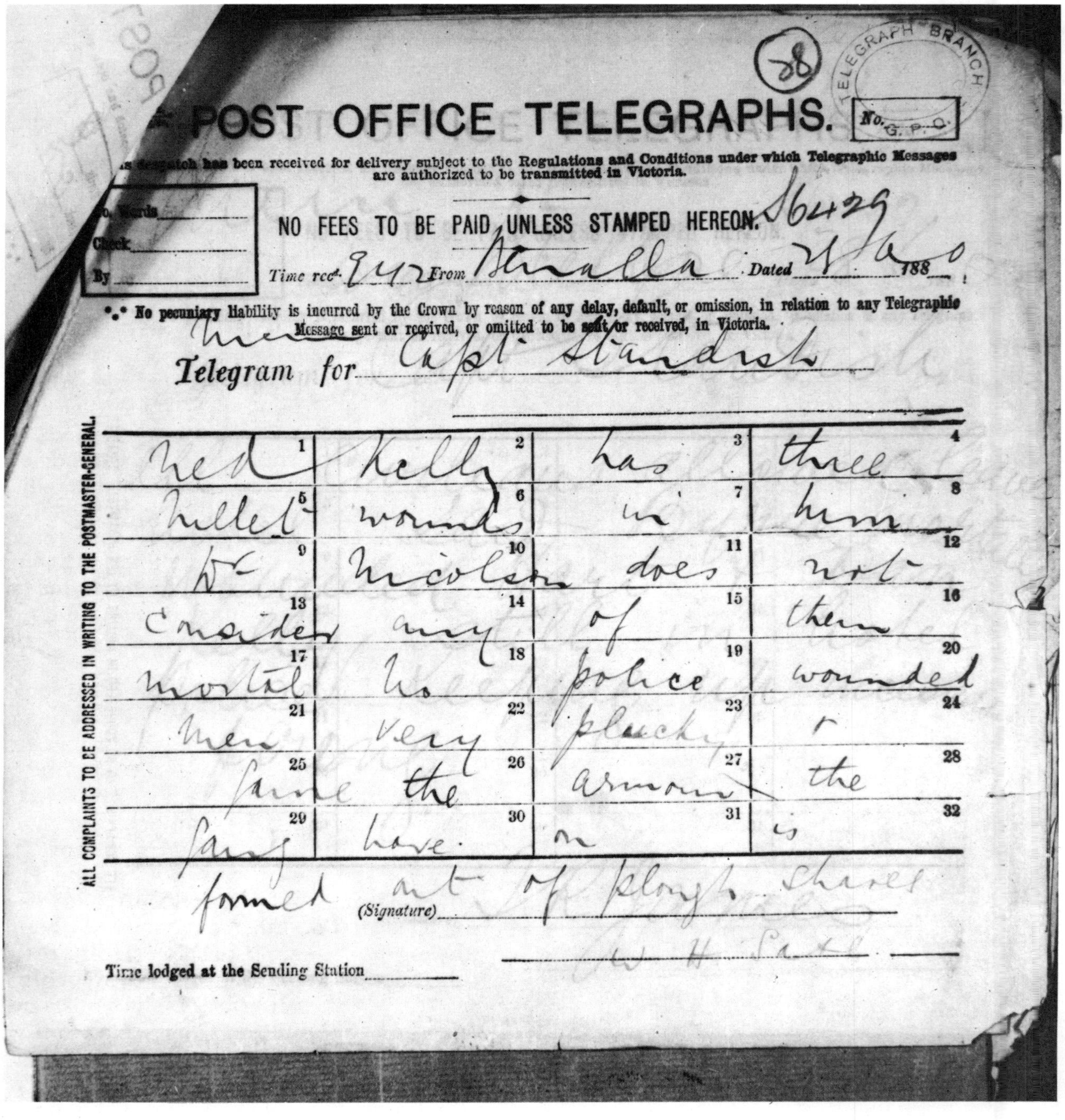

TELEGRAPH BRANCH G.P.O.

(28)

POST OFFICE TELEGRAPHS. No. G.P.O.

...s despatch has been received for delivery subject to the Regulations and Conditions under which Telegraphic Messages are authorized to be transmitted in Victoria.

NO FEES TO BE PAID UNLESS STAMPED HEREON. S6429

No. Words .... Check .... By ....

Time recd. 9.42 From Benalla Dated 28 ... 188...

*** No pecuniary liability is incurred by the Crown by reason of any delay, default, or omission, in relation to any Telegraphic Message sent or received, or omitted to be sent or received, in Victoria.

Telegram for Capt Standish

Ned	Kelly	has	three
bullet	wounds	in	him
Dr	Nicolson	does	not
Consider	any	of	them
mortal	Us	police	wounded
men	very	plucky	&
same	the	armour	the
gang	have	on	is

formed out of plough shares

(Signature) W H Saxe

Time lodged at the Sending Station ....

ALL COMPLAINTS TO BE ADDRESSED IN WRITING TO THE POSTMASTER-GENERAL.

were whistling past our heads from our comrades so we had to retreat about forty yards [thirty-six metres] to be avoid being shot ... I retreated to a large tree where Constable Moore was and then discharged four shots at the outlaw. We saw Ned Kelly rise and walk about twenty-five yeards [twenty-three metres] and fall. I immediately rushed forward and saw Sergeant Steele, Senior Constable Kelly and several others rush on him[108].

Sadlier, however, although reporting 'my only difficulty was in restraining a few too eager spirits' found 'that Sergeant Steele, Senior Constable Kelly, Constables Bracken, Dwyer and Mountford were the men concerned. I find also that Constables Arthur and Healy were all more or less directly assisting the arrest of Ned Kelly'. He especially called

attention to the conduct of Mr Jesse Dowsett ... who armed with a revolver only stood manfully to his ground in the capture. His conduct has been specially commended to me by the members of the Force who witnessed it[109].

Nevertheless Phillips' eyewitness account captures some of the excitement and confusion of Ned's last stand on that early Monday morning.

The siege continued and about 10 a.m. Sadlier 'called on the prisoners to make their escape and allowed ten minutes grace before recommencing firing'. There was a general rush and no shots were fired while the outlaws' hostages were ordered to lie on the ground, individually examined, and passed through the police cordon. The two brothers McAuliffe were picked out as sympathisers and arrested. Sadlier refused the requests of several police to rush the building in order to avoid a needless sacrifice of life in view of the certainty of capture, the long narrow passage in the house favouring an enfilading fire by the outlaws.

Finally about 3 p.m. under cover of fire, Senior Constable Johnson set fire to a bundle of straw to smoke the outlaws out just as Mrs Skillion, with an almost perfect timing and sense of gallery, dramatically rode up 'dressed in a black riding habit with a red underskirt and a white Gainsborough hat' presumably with the object of persuading the remaining outlaws to surrender and became 'a prominent object at the scene'[110].

With the hotel ablaze, Dean Matthew Gibbney, a Catholic priest in Victoria from Perth, despite remonstrances from police and Sadlier who rushed to stop him, heroically went into the building to find Joe Byrne's body and touch both Dan Kelly and Steve Hart's bodies lying side by side and decide they were dead before being forced back by the flames. The move to stop Gibbney going into the blazing hotel turned into a general rush of police to bring the wounded Cherry out and then Joe Byrne's body. A Webley revolver fell from Byrne's clothes as he was dragged from the fire and a Roman Catholic prayer book was later taken off his body. Sadlier concluded 'it was impossible to say whether they [Dan Kelly and Steve Hart] had been killed by our last volley or had shortly before taken their own lives'[111].

Martin Cherry, a sixty-year-old Irish bachelor died minutes after his removal from the building, shot either by a police bullet or, according to Sadlier, 'shot by Ned Kelly early in the day because he would not hold aside one of the window blinds'[112]. Subsequent police questioning of hostages Delaney and Mortimer revealed that 'as far as they knew he was shot by police' and Larkins who went to Cherry's aid said 'he was shot from the westward of the kitchen by the police'. Larkins also said that 'he never saw Ned Kelly after the first volley that was between the outlaws and the police at 3 a.m.' which indicated that Ned Kelly left his

The wake at Maggie Skillion's hut on Seven Mile Creek, Greta.
The Australasian Sketcher, 1880

fellow outlaws leaderless. This was verified by others and also Ned's revolving rifle was found outside and at the back of the hotel 'between 3½ a.m. and 4 a.m'.

When the fire eased, the charred bodies of Steve Hart and Dan Kelly were recovered from beside the armour. Burnt beyond recognition they were given to relatives. There was no inquest since on the application of their friends, Sadlier procured an order for burial, for which they 'expressed their acknowledgements for the consideration shown to them'[113]. The body of Martin Cherry was handed to his sister and that of Byrne buried at four o'clock on the Tuesday afternoon in the Benalla cemetery, unclaimed. Three of the outlaws' horses which were wounded were shot by police and Joe Byrne's fine horse captured.

Maggie Skillion, Kate Kelly, Dick Hart, 'Wild' Wright and his brother Tom arrived at the scene and Ned's three sisters and Tom Wright were allowed to see and talk with the wounded outlaw before he was taken on a stretcher to Benalla and guarded overnight before being transferred to Melbourne Gaol.

Friends and relatives first took the remains of Dan Kelly and Steve Hart wrapped in blankets to McDonnell's Hotel and then left that night for Maggie Skillion's hut at Seven Mile Creek. With the charred bodies laid side by side on a table a wake began, but the crush of two hundred people annoyed Maggie who brandished a gun and only allowed three at a time to view the remains. The *Argus* newspaper gave a full account of the wake and the *Melbourne Herald* said 'the scene at Greta was indescribable' and that Tom Lloyd was inspired to swear an oath to avenge their deaths, but this did not eventuate. The wake continued with additional supplies from O'Brien's Hotel in Greta.

Wisely, the Greta sympathisers were left alone at their wake and no recovery of the bodies was sought for the normal procedures of an inquest and magisterial enquiry as to the cause of death but, in the case of Joe Byrne, in a calmer atmosphere his body was photographed propped up against a door outside Benalla Police Station and there was a magisterial enquiry but no inquest before interment.

'A COWARD AND A HYPOCRITE'

Detrained at North Melbourne to avoid the sightseers at the Spencer Street Railway station, when Ned Kelly reached Melbourne Gaol, according to the prison doctor he was 'suffering from mental depression'. Elsewhere however, there was elation.

Congratulatory official telegrams from other Colonial Governments and also from Downing Street, London, poured into the Chief Secretary's Office. On 1 July the *Melbourne Punch* declared that 'the complete extermination of this band of cowardly murderers . . . is a matter of sincere congratulations among all classes' and described the depressed Ned as 'a liar, a bully, a coward and a hypocrite as well as a murderer'. A fortnight later the *Australian Sketcher* devoted many illustrations to the affair — the scene, the hotel, the dancing before the fighting and even Ned Kelly's 'grey mare' and gave a full written description by reporters who were eyewitnesses[114].

Some six weeks later the *Illustrated London News* of 11 August supported the establishment:

> after a career of crime unprecedented in colonial annals, the Kelly gang of bushrangers whose murderous deeds created almost a reign of terror . . . has already been announced by telegram from Melbourne being conquered by the representatives of the law, three of the offenders having been killed and the principal, the notorious Ned Kelly captured.

SKETCHER

o. 102.—VOL. VIII. MELBOURNE, SATURDAY, JULY 17, 1880. PRICE 6d.

TRIAL: THE TWO DAY DRAMA

In view of Kelly's wounds, a court was held in the kitchen of the hospital at the Melbourne Gaol on Saturday 31 July by Police Magistrate Call. Kelly was identified as one of the men who took part in the murders and remanded to Beechworth on a charge of wilful murder. Next morning he was provided with a serge suit and under guard of Sergeant Steele and three troopers, Constables McIntyre, Bracken and Faulkner, was taken to Newmarket station and entrained for Beechworth with two railway officers and another three police.

Kelly was committed for trial on 14 October at Beechworth but was taken back to Melbourne on 10 August to finally face trial on Thursday 28 October after two postponements, one to allow friends and relatives access to the prisoner and the other to allow Kelly's counsel to read depositions and other documents.

Sir Redmond Barry, K.C.M.G., presided over the two-day drama. The Crown had two cases, the first one for the murder of Constable Lonigan for which Ned Kelly was convicted and the second for the murder of Constable Scanlon for which as the Crown Solicitor noted 'not tried as no object could be attained by a second trial'[115].

Prosecutor for the Queen was C. A. Smyth assisted by A. W. Chomley. H. M. Bindon appeared for Kelly.

Constable McIntyre was the main witness for the Crown and its case was supported by George Stephens, William Fitzgerald, Henry Dudley, James Gloster and Frank Beecroft, all of whom gave evidence of Ned's freely spoken statements at Faithful's Creek. Similar witnesses from Jerilderie were Robert Scott, Edward Living and John Tarlton of the Bank of New South Wales, and Constable Richards. Evidence as to Ned's conversation about Stringybark in the Glenrowan lock-up was given by Sergeant Steele. Dr S. Reynolds gave medical evidence that Lonigan received four bullet wounds one of which killed him.

Bindon claimed that all hearsay evidence other than that of an actual witness to Lonigan's death was extraneous and also objected to evidence concerning the deaths of Kennedy and Scanlon being admissible since Kelly was only being tried for the murder of Lonigan. Barry, however, admitted evidence as to the deaths of Kennedy and Scanlon on the grounds that it was relevant to the motive for the shooting of Lonigan as deliberate, accidental or in self defence, and also admitted as evidence the testimony of the Crown witnesses on Kelly's conversation with them concerning the shootings. Some cast doubts about these rulings from the Bench.

Bindon called no evidence on Kelly's behalf. It was in effect McIntyre's word versus Kelly's and Bindon attempted to denigrate McIntyre's credibility as a witness on the grounds that in a flurry at the time of the shooting he could not recall the events so clearly and in such detail as he had given in evidence and also that since other shots were fired at the time it was not possible to identify who fired the fatal bullet. However, in his charge to the jury Sir Redmond said it was not necessary for McIntyre's evidence to be corroborated. Bindon also pointed out that Kelly could not speak in sworn testimony lest he possibly incriminate himself, but Kelly could have made an unsworn statement to the court if he had so wished but he made no attempt to do this.

Barry in his charge to the jury ruled out manslaughter since even if it could have been proved that Kelly acted in self defence, that is if he was hunted, the unintentional killing of a policeman carrying out a lawful arrest was murder. Whether they were in plain clothes or not, the police were in pursuit of normal duty.

Telegraph advising the removal of Ned Kelly from Benalla to gaol via North Melbourne station.
Courtesy Public Records Office, Melbourne.

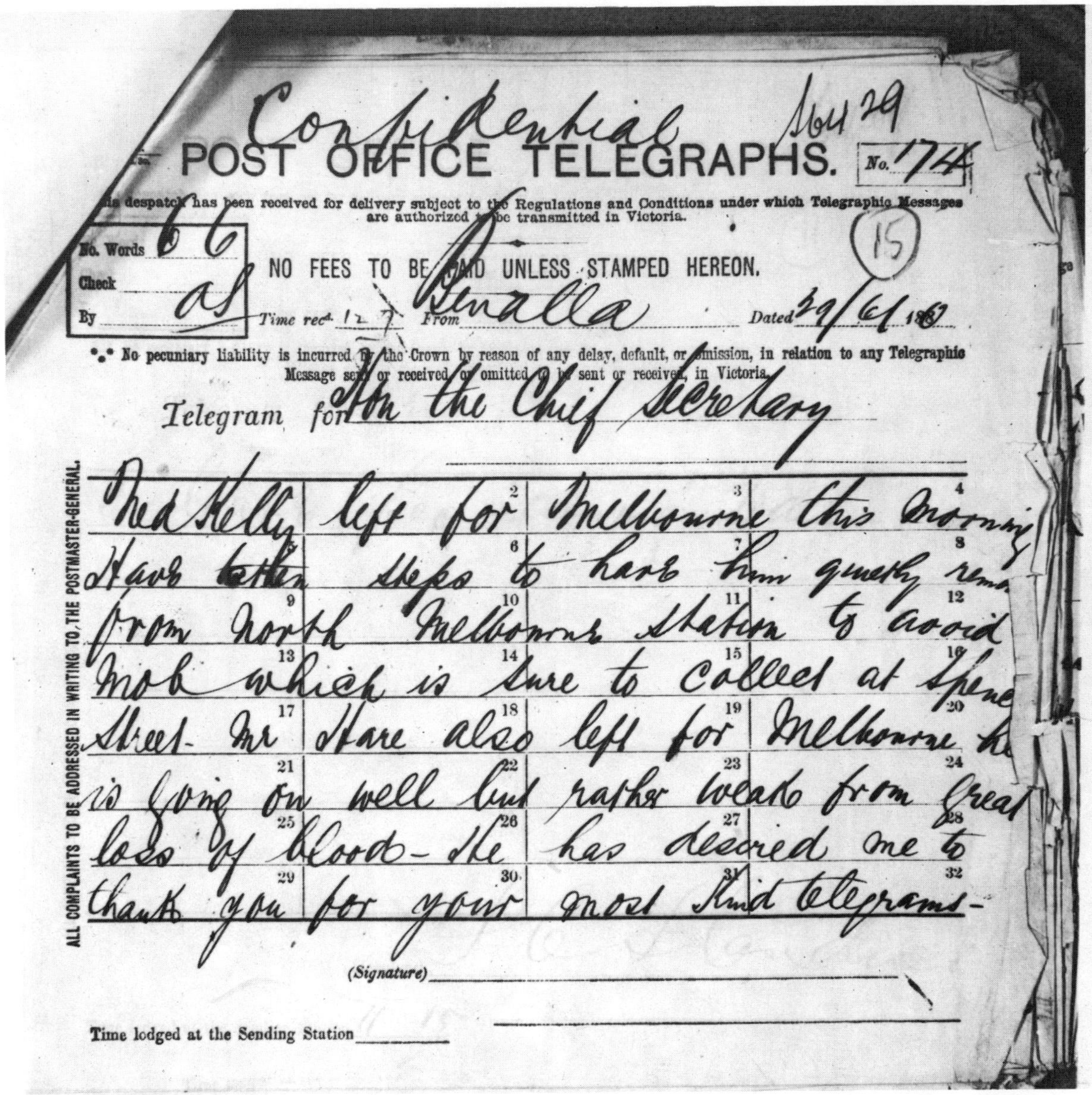

Confidential

POST OFFICE TELEGRAPHS. No. 174

This despatch has been received for delivery subject to the Regulations and Conditions under which Telegraphic Messages are authorized to be transmitted in Victoria.

No. Words 66
Check
By as

NO FEES TO BE PAID UNLESS STAMPED HEREON.

Time recd. 12 7 From Benalla Dated 29/6/80

*No pecuniary liability is incurred by the Crown by reason of any delay, default, or omission, in relation to any Telegraphic Message sent or received, or omitted to be sent or received, in Victoria.

Telegram for Hon the Chief Secretary

Ned Kelly left for Melbourne this morning Have taken steps to have him quietly removed from North Melbourne Station to avoid mob which is sure to collect at Spencer Street- Mr Hare also left for Melbourne he is going on well but rather weak from great loss of blood- He has desired me to thank you for your most kind telegrams-

(Signature)

Time lodged at the Sending Station 11 15

ALL COMPLAINTS TO BE ADDRESSED IN WRITING TO THE POSTMASTER-GENERAL.

SKETCHER

No. [illegible] VOL. VIII. MELBOURNE, SATURDAY, AUGUST [illegible]. PRICE 6[illegible]

Mr CALL Mr CASTIEAU KELLY CONSTABLE M'INTYRE

Examination and remand of Edward Kelly in the hospital kitchen in Melbourne Gaol.
The Australasian Sketcher, 1880.

The question of lawful arrest raises the warrant issue and although two of the outlaws including Ned had been gazetted as persons against whom a warrant had been issued, Ned, in dictating his last letters before his execution, took up the issue of the lawfulness of the warrant and also the issue of self defence. It has been suggested that manslaughter, not murder could have been a possible verdict and that Barry was incorrect in ruling it out as a possibility. The jury took thirty minutes to bring in a verdict of guilty of murder.

Ned entered into dialogue with Judge Barry in reply to the usual practice in a conviction of felony of 'what have you to say why the Court should not pass sentence upon you' and this was fully reported in the *Argus* of 30 October and elsewhere. Naturally Kelly argued 'no one understands my case as I do ... before you and my God that my mind is easy and clear as it possibly can be' which Barry thought blasphemous but it was quite in keeping with a view that a Romantic hero could do no wrong. Ned continued: 'I dare say the day will come when we shall all have to go to a higher court than this. Then we shall see who is right and who is wrong', and in reply to 'May the Lord have mercy on your soul' came the defiant 'Yes, I will meet you there'.

In his debating dialogue with Kelly, Barry alluded to the costs of the acts of which Kelly and his party had been guilty, approximately £50,000, and to the previous examples of Clarke, Gardiner, Melville, Morgan and Scott who had all met 'ignominious deaths' and said that some steps must be taken to protect society, especially a new one.

Efforts by Gaunson and the Society for the Abolition of Capital Punishment to gain a reprieve by a public meeting and petitions failed. Some 2,500 people attended a meeting in the Hippodrome in Melbourne on 5 November and it was estimated that there was double the number outside. A motion was passed for a reprieve of the death sentence on Kelly and the meeting sent a deputation of A. S. Hamilton, President of the Society, David and William Gaunson and Kate Kelly to the Governor, but His Excellency said he could not enter into argument on the merits of the Kelly case and that his only power was to forward the resolution and petition to the Executive Council, which rejected them. Gaunson declared that over 30,000 people signed the petition but it appears to have been organised by a few people. The number of signatures in Law Department files total only 12,246, but this does not necessarily mean that all the signatures to the petition reached the Law Department and if they did that they all survived. Many are difficult to decipher and do not list an exact address merely giving a town or a suburb.

Kelly went to the gallows at 10 a.m. on 11 November 1880 with the last words 'Ah well, I suppose it had to come to this'. The execution was witnessed by the Sheriff and Deputy Sheriff, the Governor of the Gaol, a Superintendent of Police, a Justice of the Peace, three doctors, six warders, eight journalists and the clerk at the Melbourne Gaol. One of the doctors, Andrew Shields, testified at the Prothonotary's Office that 'Edward Kelly was in pursuance of the Central Criminal Court hanged by the neck until his body was dead'.

Two weeks later Sir Redmond Barry died from congestion of the left lung and there was a large public funeral for this distinguished citizen, who apart from the fame of being involved in the Kelly affair had given much public service to the community and was one of the colony's earliest settlers in 1839.

The Kelly story was not yet finished. The Government appointed a Reward Board. Its three members took evidence from the Chief Secretary, the Hon R. Ramsay, M.L.A., three

(Left) The scene in court at the Kelly trial.

(Top right) The Crown v. Kelly, the Recognizance to give evidence, the Crown Law Brief, the Jerilderie Letter. *Courtesy Public Records Office, Melbourne.*

(Bottom right) "The charge against Ned Kelly". *Courtesy Public Record Office, Melbourne.*

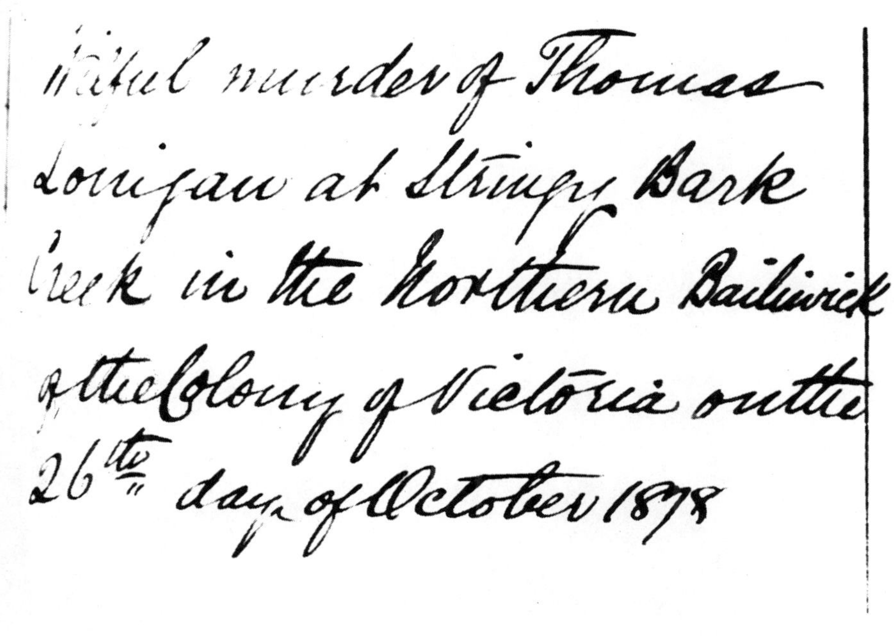
Wilful murder of Thomas
Lonigan at Stringy Bark
Creek in the Northern Bailiwick
of the Colony of Victoria on the
26th day of October 1878

Sir Redmond Barry (1813-1880) in full scholarly regalia.
Courtesy La Trobe Library, Melbourne.

The Official Verdict at the Central Criminal Court, Melbourne.
Courtesy Public Record Office, Melbourne.

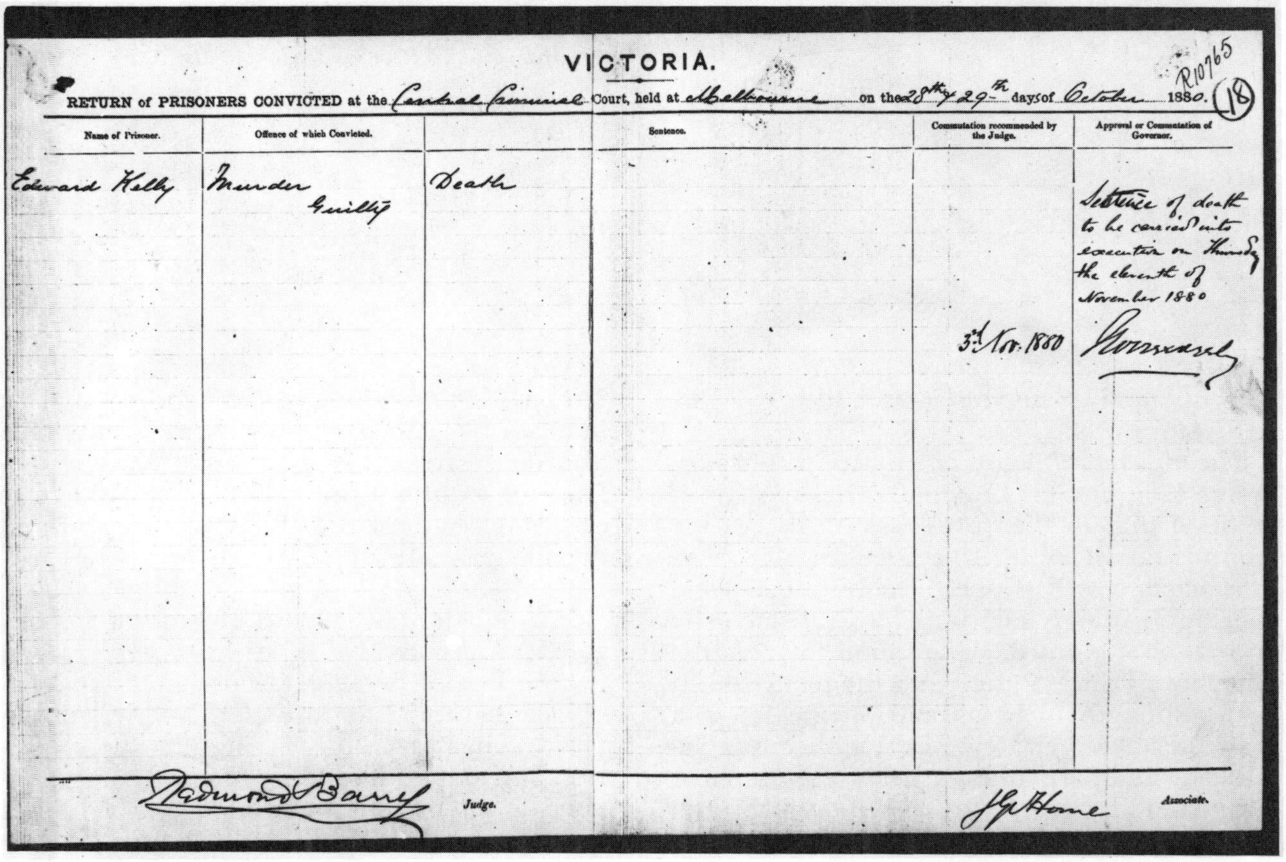

VICTORIA.

R10765 (18)

RETURN of PRISONERS CONVICTED at the Central Criminal Court, held at Melbourne on the 28th & 29th days of October 1880.

Name of Prisoner.	Offence of which Convicted.		Sentence.	Commutation recommended by the Judge.	Approval or Commutation of Governor.
Edward Kelly	Murder Guilty	Death		3rd Nov. 1880	Sentence of death to be carried into execution on Thursday the eleventh of November 1880 Normanby

Redmond Barry Judge.

Associate.

newspaper reporters and a farmer from near Glenrowan, and distributed £8,000 among sixty-six people, mostly members of the Police Force, after rejecting the claims of twenty-four people.

Within days of the destruction of the Kelly gang and a common enemy out of the way, dissension at senior level in the Police Force had come out into the open. Nicholson forwarded to Standish, for transmission to the Chief Secretary, a request 'for an inquiry into Police administration in the North Eastern district since the Kelly outbreak in October 1878 and particularly into the circumstances of my recent withdrawal from that district'[116]. Standish sent Nicholson's request on the next day and three weeks later on 24 July, wrote to the Chief Secretary that

> ever since the perpetration in October 1878 of what is known as the Mansfield murders remarks have been made in the public papers and elsewhere in which reflections have been thrown on the character of the Police Force and its proceedings generally in connection with the search of the outlaws and now that the gang has been destroyed these remarks have taken a more specific and definite character. I have long felt the injustice of these reflections and I think the time has arrived when I can properly ask to have it ascertained whether they are deserved or not. I have the honour therefore to request that an enquiry may be instituted into the whole proceedings of the management of the Police Force from the perpetration of the murders to the present date[117].

Six weeks later, Sub-Inspector O'Connor complained of 'his treatment by the police officers during service in pursuit of the Kelly gang' and requested an inquiry[118].

Six months after the trial amid further publicity, a Royal Commission was appointed on 7 March 1881. The terms of reference were to enquire into the circumstances preceding and attending the Kelly outbreak, the efficiency of the police to deal with such possible circumstances, the action of the police authorities during the period the Kelly gang were at large, the efficiency of the means employed for their capture and to report upon the present state and organisation of the police force.

The Commission held sixty-six meetings and examined sixty-two witnesses. It visited Benalla, Greta, Glenrowan, Beechworth, Se-

A petition for the reprieve of the death sentence organized by David Gaunson M.L.A.
Courtesy Public Records Office, Melbourne.

bastopol and Wangaratta, and much of the Kelly story was relived.

The eight man Board of Inquiry was headed by the Hon Francis Longmore. In the main it reported that in the north-eastern district the administration of the police had not been satisfactory with respect to numbers and distribution, and they were not satisfactorily armed or mounted. The abolition of the Glenmore Police Station and the reduction in police strength in neighbouring areas was a grave mistake. Very few of the police escaped criticism and particular attention was drawn to dissension between Captain Standish and Assistant Commissioner Nicholson, and Standish's favouritism of Hare at the expense of Nicholson. The lack of unanimity had impaired the efficiency of the Force and prevented coordinated action on important occasions. However, two members declined to support this conclusion and another protested at the denigration of Hare which drew a sharp reply from four other members of the Board.

Sadlier was criticised for errors of judgment, Detective Ward for misleading his superiors, Inspector Brook Smith and Sergeant Steele for missing opportunities of capturing the gang before Glenrowan, the hut party at Sherritt's murder for cowardice and James Wallace was recommended for dismissal from the Education Department. But Senior Constables Kelly and Johnson and Constable Bracken were praised and recommended for promotion, and Sub-Inspector O'Connor was not recommended as suitable appointment as an Inspector in the Victorian Force. Of the civilians, Curnow and Rawlings were praised.

The Commission recommended that a branch of Black Trackers be formed and that a 'thorough system of police patrol be established throughout the whole colony and more especially in the North East District' and that the force be armed with Martini Henry carbines.

In August 1881 a Board of Inquiry investigated claims by Mrs Jones for compensation for the loss of her hotel. The hotel had been erected eighteen months before and was doing a 'tidy business' with 'takings of about £7 a week'. Although Mrs Jones received compensation she was declared as an 'aider and abettor of the Kelly gang' by the Board of Inquiry, at least as far as the Glenrowan affair was concerned. Not all the Kellys trusted her. She complained that Mrs Skillion and Kate Kelly 'had a down on me because of the police coming to my house ... they used to pass my place on horseback and call me all sorts of names'[119]. Nevertheless Steve Hart's sister Julia 'in service at the bankers at Wangaratta' stayed at her place 'for holidays after the Wombat murders'[120].

The printed questions to and answers from witnesses as well as the reports of the Royal Commission are an abundant source material of 'Kellyana' and together with the Board of Inquiry into Mrs Jones' claims for compensation kept the Kelly affair in the public eye while versification and subsequently ballet choreography, film-making and rock opera carried the story into everyday language and into the mystique of folklore.

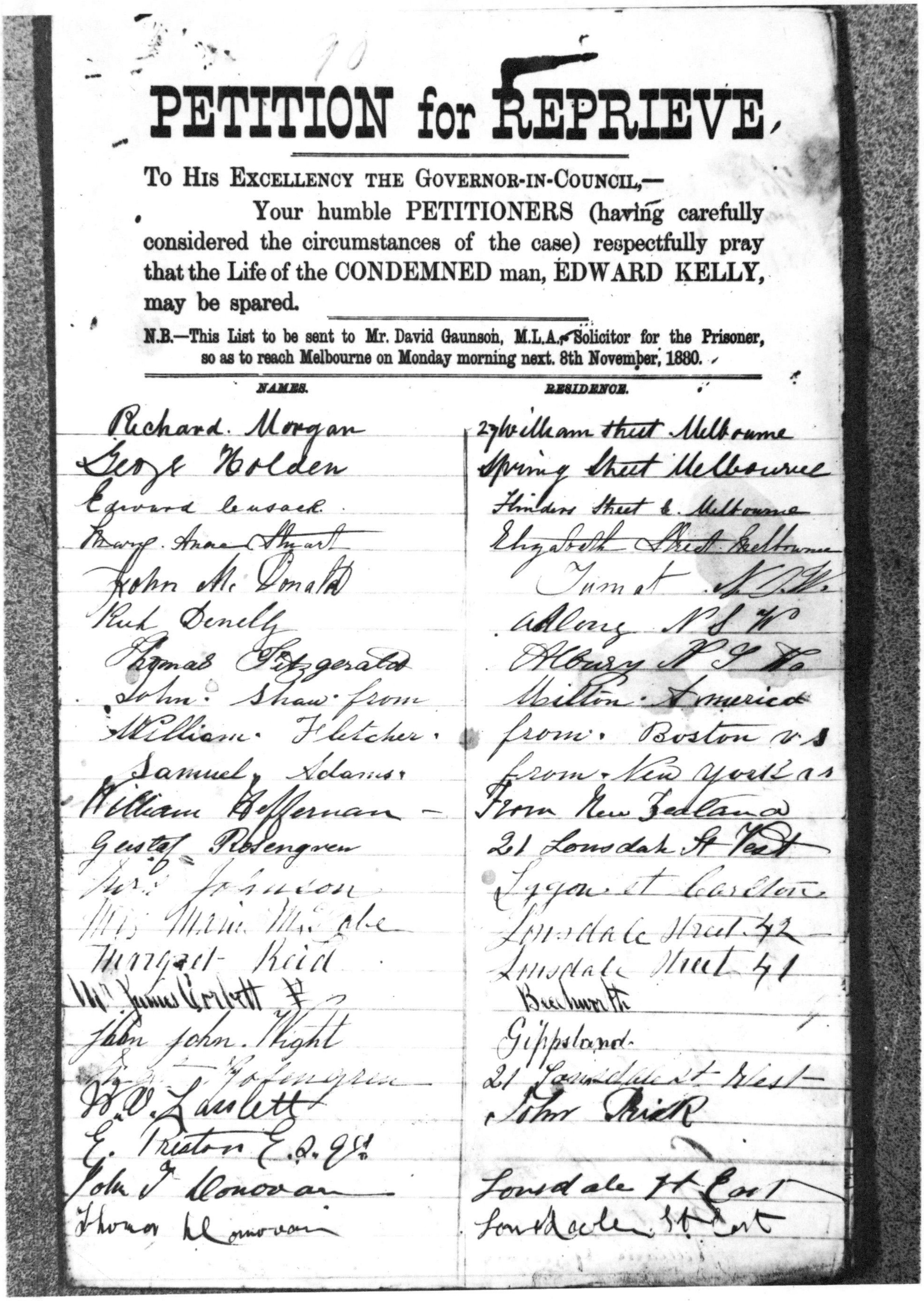
10

PETITION for REPRIEVE.

To His Excellency the Governor-in-Council,—

Your humble PETITIONERS (having carefully considered the circumstances of the case) respectfully pray that the Life of the CONDEMNED man, EDWARD KELLY, may be spared.

N.B.—This List to be sent to Mr. David Gaunson, M.L.A., Solicitor for the Prisoner, so as to reach Melbourne on Monday morning next. 8th November, 1880.

NAMES.	RESIDENCE.
Richard Morgan	27 William Street Melbourne
George Holden	Spring Street Melbourne
Edward Cusack	Flinders Street E. Melbourne
Mary Anne Stuart	Elizabeth Street Melbourne
John McDonald	Tumut N.S.W.
Rich Denelly	Albury N S W
Thomas Fitzgerald	Albury N S W
John Shaw from	Milton America
William Fletcher	from Boston U S
Samuel Adams	from New York U S
William Heffernan	From New Zealand
Gustaf Rosengren	21 Lonsdale St West
Mrs Johnson	Lygon St Carlton
Mrs Marie McCabe	Lonsdale Street 42
Margaret Reid	Lonsdale Street 41
Mr James Corbett	Beechworth
John John Wight	Gippsland
[illegible] Rosengren	21 Lonsdale St West
W. D. Laslett	John Rick
E. Preston E.Q.Q.	
John J Donovan	Lonsdale St East
Thomas Donovan	Lonsdale St East

Medical certification that Edward Kelly hanged by the neck until his body was dead.
Courtesy Public Records Office, Melbourne.

(Right) The death mask of Edward Kelly.
Courtesy Police Museum, Melbourne.

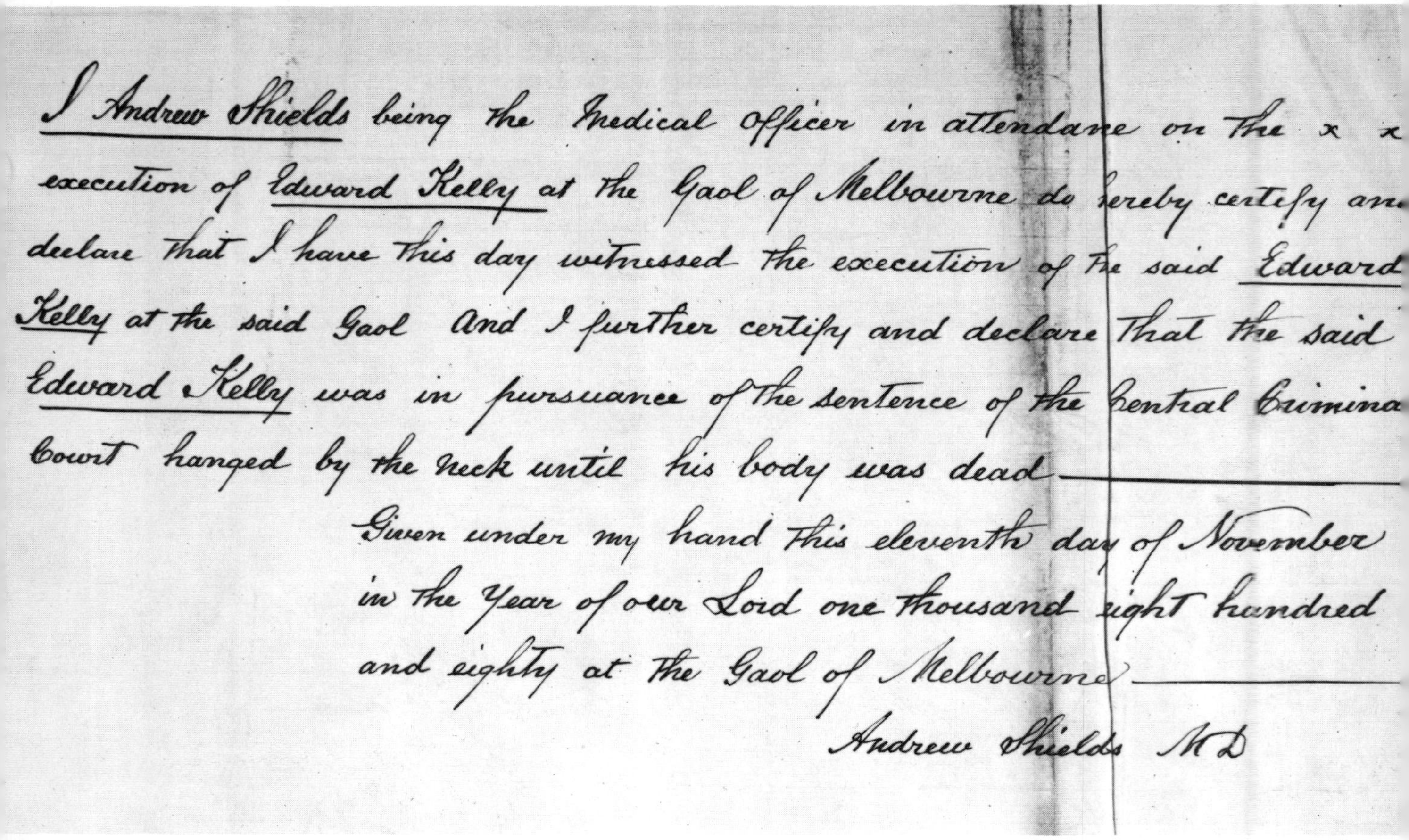

I Andrew Shields being the Medical Officer in attendance on the x x
execution of Edward Kelly at the Gaol of Melbourne do hereby certify an
declare that I have this day witnessed the execution of the said Edward
Kelly at the said Gaol And I further certify and declare that the said
Edward Kelly was in pursuance of the sentence of the Central Crimina
Court hanged by the neck until his body was dead

Given under my hand this eleventh day of November
in the Year of our Lord one thousand eight hundred
and eighty at the Gaol of Melbourne

Andrew Shields MD

Bushranging Ceases to be Popular

Interpretations of the Kelly outrages range from acts of callous banditry by murderers or crude Dick Turpins, to the view that the outbreak was symptomatic of an Irish Australian rural revolt linked with land war, depression, bad seasons and floods, the gang being 'forced' or even 'police made' outlaws, with Ned leading a personal revolt against police persecution.

This latter view sees Ned's personal revolt associated with economic and social revolution and develops to see Ned emerging as a Robin Hood who champions the underdog, distributes the proceeds of his robberies (£4,541, comprising £2,400 from Euroa and £2,141 from Jerilderie and an unknown sum from horse stealing) to poor selectors and eventually with his gang dons armour to meet thirty-four police in armed combat. His vitality as a folk hero comes from his relevance to his environment, the bush and bush workers whose influence on nationalistic feeling was quite disproportionate to their numbers.

However, in this last era of bushranging less sympathy with bushrangers was exhibited than previously and the Moonlite and Kelly gangs did not inspire the young to emulate them. In fact, bushranging ceased to be popular and came to an end.

Furthermore, apart from the heavy ninety-seven pound (forty-four kilogram) personal armour that sacrificed mobility, there appears to be no element of originality introduced by the Kelly gang; in many ways they followed the activity patterns of earlier bushrangers. It is clear that there was an unusually heavy family and clan influence on Ned and his brother Dan and a bitterness that welled from the circumstances surrounding them from which they had little chance of freeing themselves.

What is new in this last era of bushranging is the development and profound influence of the press. Earlier bushranging was a common occurrence, a small element in the colony and attracted little notice. Little had been heard of bushranging in the first era prior to the fifties, but the sensational inauguration of the second era with the plundering of Government Gold Escorts and the exploits of the vintage Gardiner and Hall gangs attracted wider notice and the press lampooned the police as scapegoats. More newspaper columns were printed about the Kelly gang than all the bushrangers of earlier eras put together.

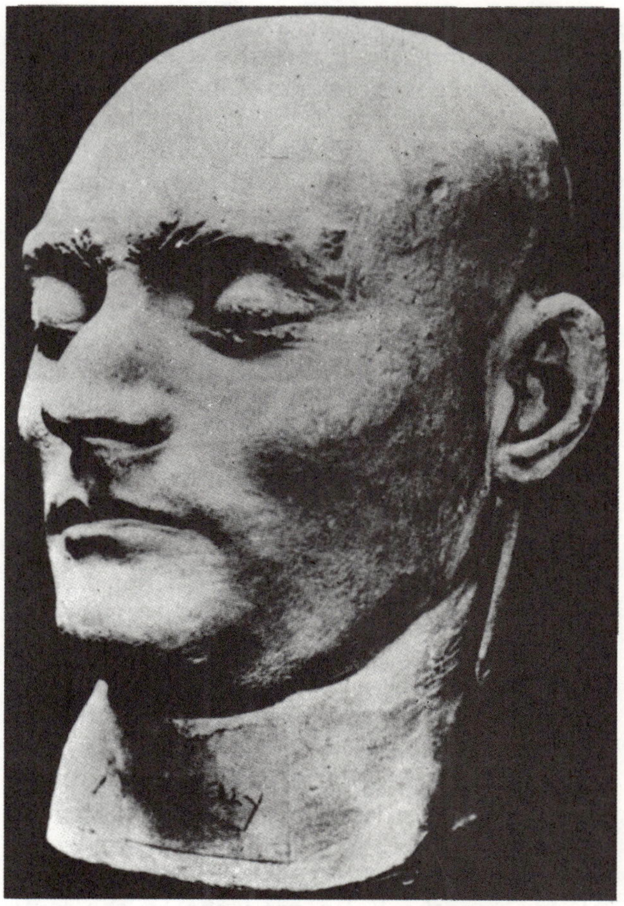

Preceded by a feud spread over eighteen years between the Quinn, Kelly, Lloyd clan and the enforcement of law in a frontier kind of

Ned Kelly, Australian legend.

situation, the Kelly gang had a short life of two years, two-and-a-half months during which their activities were responsible for the loss of nine lives, including four of their own, the tarnishing of many others at great cost to the taxpayer and providing such unprecedented press coverage that a special railway carriage was provided for journalists to be conveyed to the 'Last Stand'. Journalists were also included in the official party at the hanging of Ned.

The cold facts bereft of the media would not appear to justify a folklore figure in Ned Kelly, for as a bushman he feared that in the Queensland black trackers he had met his match and as an outlaw on the run with a warrant for murder gazetted against him he had the advantage of wide distances in which to manoeuvre and bush telegraphs both to warn him and also to lay false trails. Nevertheless tactically speaking his judgement seemed impaired when he led his gang to destruction.

In the end the electric telegraph and the railway not only closed in on him but also brought about the demise of bushranging. Police may have been mocked as traps or for being flash, insulted by Ned as a matter of course and criticised in hindsight by the Royal Commission, but like the many bushrangers before them the Kelly gang shared the same ignominious fate of those who throughout the history of bushranging inevitably failed to escape capture, imprisonment or death.

In his dictated autobiographical writings, apart from straight defence or justification of particular events of his career, in his insults to police there are outbursts which reflect attitudes about England, Ireland and America:

> the cowardly conduct of a parcel of big ugly fat-necked wombat headed big bellied magpie legged narrow hipped splay-footed sons of Irish bailiffs and English landlords which is better known as officers of Justice or Victorian Police[121]

or a further example:

> what would England do if America declared war and hoisted a green flag ... to reinstate it and rise old Erin's isle once more from the pressure and tyrannism of the English yoke ... a strapping big lump of an Irishman shepherding sheep for fifteen bob a day ... would be a king to a policeman who ... deserted the shamrock, the emblem of true wit and beauty to serve under a flag and a nation that has destroyed, massacred and murdered their forefathers[122].

An integral part of a close-knit Irish clan, Ned Kelly faced difficulties in thinking objectively but he also had a feeling for the harsh bush country of Australia and the frustration of making a living from it. But apart from those convict bolters and bushmen who like him turned to the gun and robbery, there was a vast majority of law-abiding hard-working pioneers who adapted themselves successfully to a new environment within the framework of a developing society.

In Ireland, erosion destroyed the productivity of the sloping land and siltation destroyed most of the lowland. Forced to emigrate after the potato famine of the 1840s some Irishmen tended to blame all of Ireland's trouble on oppression by the English and some of this was transplanted to Australia.

However, the deterioration of Ireland's productivity cannot wholly be blamed on England since 'Irish farmers exploited their land by farming whilst other lands enjoyed a forced rest'[123] given to 'English, French and German land by the barbaric invasions of the Middle Ages'[124]. Even heavier damage to the land occurred during the eighteenth and nineteenth centuries when 'potatoes grown for home consumption and export did what goats and deforestation did to Lebanon and what cotton did to some areas of the United States'[125].

Possibly not all Irish in Australia had successful ideas on the use of land in a pastoral economy. The Quinns, Kellys and Lloyds turned to cattle duffing and horse stealing and the Quinns' 25,000 acre (10,000 hectare) property became a transit and holding area for trafficking in stolen horses. Many Irish were inherently absorbed with the possession of land of their own, memories of English landlords in Ireland, and the bitterness from the frustration of trying to earn a living from small holdings may well have been a common bond between Ned Kelly and Irish small settlers in north-eastern Victoria.

Kelly lived in a developing society, which justified a Royal Commission on land, and when there were trends to humanitarianism, had debates on penology and a literary climate of Victorian Romanticism.

Ned had the Romantic's contempt of law and order and speaking of its representatives he declared 'I would manure the Eleven Mile with their bloated carcases' and

> by the light that shines pegged on an ant bed with their bellies opened their fat taken out rendered poured down their throat boiling hot will be cool to what pleasure I will give some of them and any person aiding or harbouring or assisting the police in any way whatever[126].

The tyrant is also present in his utterances, 'I am a widow's son, outlawed and my orders must be obeyed'[127] together with violence 'we will leave your colony, but we will not leave it till we have made the country ring with the name of Kelly and taken terrible revenge for the injustice and oppression we have been subjected to'[128].

Such words with his lament for the 'fearless, free and bold' days of Greta irrespective of the consequences, so typical of the Romantic hero and its reflection in literature and art, may explain in part why in a growing society Ned Kelly became legendary and one hundred years later is still an emotive figure.

Kelly described the police as his natural enemies but perhaps the enemy was within himself and he was unable to rise above his inherited background and the circumstances of his life. At his trial he declared 'I did not recognise myself as a great man' and in a letter a few days before his execution wrote 'I don't pretend to have lived a blameless life'.

A fortnight after Glenrowan, the *Australian Sketcher* was constrained to apologise to readers in England for the 'serious charge against the character of the colony' by the Kelly outrages and explained that the circumstances were exceptional, 'a sparse population dispersed over immense territories ... country of the most inaccessible nature ... occupants of out stations tainted with convictism who gave their sympathies to the side of the bushrangers' and referring to 'a tribe of horse thieves and cattle stealers that the four men came from' hoped that the 'Government will clear out this nest of sympathisers and abettors of crime' and prevent 'a repetition of the late proceedings which reflected so seriously on the credit of the community'[129].

Nevertheless a century later, the man and the myth are still part of legendary folklore.

References

Introduction

1 G.W. Evans, *A Geographical, Historical and Topographical Description of Van Diemen's Land* First published, London, 1882, Reprinted Heinemann Pioneer Series, 1967.
2 Bertrand Russell, *"History of Western Philosophy"* London, 1946, p. 658.
3 ibid. p. 656.
4 ibid p. 656.
5 ibid. p. 651-2.

The First Era

1 Cesar de Saussaure, *A Foreign View of England in the Reigns of George I & II (1725-1730),* quoted L. Radzinowicz, *A History of English Criminal Law,* London, 1948, vol. II, The Movement for Reform, appendices, p. 172.
2 B.L. Muralt, *Lettres sur Les Anglais et Les Francais,* quoted ibid., p. 712.
3 Delemare, *Traitė de la Police,* 2nd edn., Paris, 1722, quoted ibid. vol 3.
4 *Letters of Horace Walpole to Sir Horace Mann,* 2nd edn., London, 1833, vol. 3, p. 9.
5 Smollet, *The History of England,* London, 1848, vol. 2., pp 279-80.
6 *Memoirs of Charles Lewis, Baron de Pollnitz,* 1738, vol. 2, pp. 27-80, quoted L. Radzinowicz, ibid. vol. 1. p. 29.
7 Coke., Inst. 197, quoted L. Radzinowicz, ibid, vol. 1, footnote 2, p. 50.
8 Gilbert White, *The Natural History and Antiquities of Selborne in the County of Southhampton,* quoted ibid. vol. 2. p. 50.
9 J.B. le Blanc *Letters on the English and French Nations,* 1737, quoted ibid., vol. 2. p. 191.
10 Jonas Hanway, *The Defects of the Police: The Cause of Immorality, etc* 1775, quoted ibid. vol. 3 (London, 1956) p. 17.
11 "Report...on Education in England and Wales", 465, Parl. Papers, 1835, vol. 7, p. 836.
12 *Annual Review and History of Literature,* 1805, vol. 3. p. 225., quoted L. Radzinowicz, ibid. Vol. 3, p. 179.
13 P. Colquhoun, *Treatise on the Police of the Metropolis* pp. 348 & 625, quoted ibid., vol. 3., p. 275.
14 "Letters to Sir Horace Mann", 18 Oct., 1750 in *Letters,* ed. Mrs P. Toynbee, 1903, vol. 3, p. 21, quoted ibid., vol. 1, p. 168.
15 ibid., vol. 3, p. 5, quoted ibid., vol. 1, p. 140.
16 ibid.
17 Villette, *The Annals of Newgate,* 1776, vol. 3, p. 26, ibid., p. 191.
19 *A Journey through England and Scotland to the New Hebrides* Geike (ed.), 1907, vol. 1, p. 60, quoted ibid., vol. 1, p. 703.
20 d'Archenholz, *A Picture of England,* p. 182, quoted ibid., vol. 1, Appendices, p. 705.
21 ibid.
22 *Historical Records of New South Wales,* vol. II, p. 758. (From the *Gazetter,* 29 December, 1790.)
23 General and Garrison Orders by David Collins Esq. Lieut-Col., Royal Marines, Lieut-Governor of Port Phillip. (16 Oct., 1803-10 Feb., 1804).

24 *Bobby Knopwood and His Times* Mabel Hookey (ed.), Hobart, 1929, p. 65.
25 G.W. Evans, *A Geographical, Historical and Topographical Description of Van Diemen's Land,* 1822. Fascimile Reprint, William Heinemann, 1967, p. 15.
26 ibid., p. 137.
27 ibid., p. 101.
28 ibid., p. 141.
29 Ernest Scott, *A Short History of Australia* London, 1916, quoted p. 168.
30 A Maconochie, *Norfolk Island,* 1847, quoted C.M.H. Clark, *Select Documents in Australian History, 1788-1850,* p. 143.
31 ibid.

The Second Era

1 Garryowen, *The Chronicles of Early Melbourne, 1835-1852,* Melbourne, 1888, vol. 2, p. 787.
2 *Eureka Documents 1,* Public Record Office, Victoria, 1977, p. 4. Hotham's Despatch 112, 18 September, 1854.
3 ibid., p. 4.
4 ibid., pp. 11-15, "Deputation of Miners at Ballarat to the Government of Victoria", Government Shorthand Writer's Notes, 27 November, 1854.
5 Eureka Documents 1, ibid., p. 10.
6 "Report by Chief Commissioner of Police to the Hon. the Chief Secretary", Chief Secretary's Office File 69/U8455, Box 729, Public Record Office, Victoria.
7 ibid., 69/U2213, 6 December, 1869, Box. 729.
8 ibid., 70/W5922, 31 May, 1870, Box 729.
9 ibid., 73/W6735 & 73/D2591.

The Third Era

1 George Boxhall, *The Story of the Australian Bushrangers* 1899, Fascimile Edition, Penguin Books, 1974, p. 276.
2 "Report of Detective 1st Class No. 947 to Superintendent of Police, Beechworth (A. Winch)", 12 April 1861, Chief Secretary's Office, Police File L3700, Box 193, Public Record Office, Victoria.
3 "Report of Board Appointed to Enquire into the Circumstances Connected with the Mutilation of the Remains of the Bushranger Daniel Morgan as well as the Persons who directly or indirectly took Part Therein." Mss Chief Secretary's Office, Police File 65/M4750, 18 May 1865, Box 153, Public Record Office, Victoria.
4 ibid.
5 ibid.
6 ibid.
7 ibid.
8 Rex v. Scott, 10 June 1872, Exhibit B, Court of General Sessions, Ballarat, Law Department Files, Public Record Office, Victoria.
9 ibid.

10 Report by Detective R.S. Kennedy, 3 June 1872, also statement of evidence by J. McDonald, splitter, All Nation's Gully, Egerton, ibid.
11 Report of Detective D.S. Kennedy, re Hawthorne, ibid.
12 Rex v. Scott, ibid.
13 Mr. G. Sly, Solicitor, 112 Pitt St., Sydney to L.W. Brunn, Geelong Grammar School, 10 June 1872, ibid.
14 Superintendent E. Wardley to G. Sly, also statement Superintendent Wardley to Mr. Gurner, Crown Solicitor, 10 June 1872, ibid.
15 A.G. Scott to Rev. Thomas Scott M.A. Coromandel, Auckland, New Zealand, 2 March 1872, ibid.
16 H.W. White, *Crime and Criminals or Reminiscences of the Penal Department in Victoria,* Ballarat, 1890, p. 195.
17 Royal Commission of Enquiry into the Circumstances of the Kelly Outbreak, Second Progress Report, Parliamentary Papers, no. 22, 1881, p. 9.
18 ibid., Minutes of Evidence, Parliamentary Papers, Legislative Assembly, 24 December 1881, p. 6.
19 Edward Kelly to Marquis of Normanby, Governor of Victoria, 82/1957, Law Department Files, Public Record Office, Victoria.
20 Jerilderie Letter (MSS) copy, Law Department Files, Box 1, Public Record Office, Victoria.
21 ibid.
22 Report by Senior Constable Hall, Greta Police Station, Benalla District, 17 November 1870, Chief Secretary's Files, Public Record Office, Victoria.
23 Jerilderie Letter, ibid.
24 Edward Kelly to Donald Cameron M.P. 14 December 1878, Box 16, Chief Secretary's Files, Public Record Office, Victoria.
25 Report by Senior Constable Hall, 17 November 1870, ibid.
26 Jerilderie Letter, ibid.
27 ibid.
28 ibid.
29 ibid.
30 Reports to Sergeant Mountford, Benalla Police Station, 1866, Chief Secretary's Files, Public Record Office, Victoria.
31 Jerilderie Letter, ibid.
32 Jerilderie Letter, ibid.
33 Royal Commission, 1881, quoted *Ned Kelly Bushranger,* Brian Carroll, Lansdowne Press, 1976, p. 47.
34 Jerilderie Letter, ibid.
35 Royal Commission, ibid., Minutes of Evidence, p. 467.
36 ibid., p. 464.
37 ibid., p. 464.
38 Jerilderie Letter, ibid.
39 Constable Fitzpatrick's Deposition, 17 May, 1878, Box 1, Law Department Files, Public Record Office, Victoria.

40 ibid.
41 ibid.
42 Depositions, Beechworth Assizes, 8 October, 1878, Box 1, Law Department Files, Public Record Office, Victoria.
43 ibid.
44 Letter, Edward Kelly to Donald Cameron, ibid.
45 Assistant Commissioner of Police Nicholson to Superintendent Sadlier, 13 August 1881, File 3798, Police Files, Box 3, Public Record Office, Victoria.
46 Williamson's statement re Fitzpatrick, 12 August 1881, File 3798, ibid.
47 Letter "Bricky" Williamson, 6 August 1881, File 3798, ibid.
48 ibid.
49 ibid.
50 Edward Kelly to Marquis of Normanby, Letter, 3 November 1880, Capital Case 82/1957, Law Department Files, Public Record Office, Victoria.
51 Royal Commission, ibid., Minutes of Evidence, p. 467.
52 Petition to Chief Commissioner of Police by Citizens of Lancefield, 3 May 1880, Miscellaneous Kelly Files, Public Record Office, Victoria.
53 Jerilderie Letter, ibid.
54 Edward Kelly to Marquis of Normanby, Letter, 3 November 1880, ibid.
55 ibid., Letter, 10 November 1880.
56 ibid.
57 Letter, Edward Kelly to Donald Cameron, ibid.
58 Jerilderie Letter, ibid.
59 Constable McIntyre's Deposition, Rex v. Edward Kelly, Box 1, Law Department Files, Public Record Office, Victoria.
60 ibid.
61 ibid, also Miscellaneous Files, Box 22, Chief Secretary's Office, Public Record Office, Victoria.
62 Jerilderie Letter, ibid.
63 ibid.
64 Edward Kelly to Marquis of Normanby, Letter, 10 November 1880, ibid.
65 Constable McIntyre's Deposition, Beechworth Assizes, p. 27, Box 1, Law Department Files, Public Record Office, Victoria.
66 Jerilderie Letter, ibid.
67 Constable McIntyre's Deposition, p. 46, ibid.
68 ibid., pp 27/28.
69 Jerilderie Letter, ibid.
70 Rex v. Edward Kelly, Crown Depositions, Beecroft's evidence p. 70, Box 1, Law Department files, Public Record Office, Victoria.
71 Rex v. Edward Kelly, Capital Case 82/1957, Notes of Evidence, 80/5433, p. 64, Law Department Files, Public Record Office, Victoria.
72 ibid., p. 65.
73 Edward Kelly to Marquis of Normanby, Letter 3 November 1880, Capital Case File 82/1957, ibid.

74 ibid, Letter 10 November 1880
75 Mansfield Police Occurrence Book, October/November, 1878, Copy only, Box 4, Chief Secretary's Files, Public Record Office, Victoria.
76 Sergeant Steele to Superintendent Sadlier, Miscellaneous Files, Chief Secretary's Office, ibid.
77 Rex v. Edward Kelly, Notes of Evidence, ibid.
78 Superintendent Hare to Chief Commissioner Police, 9 July 1880, File S6875, Police Files, Box 3, Public Record Office, Victoria.
79 ibid.
80 Byrne to Sherrit, 26 June 1879, Police Files, Box 15, Public Record Office, Victoria.
81 Assistant Commissioner of Police Nicholson to Chief Commissioner Standish, 7 February 1880, A2057 Police Files Box 3, also 80/5122, 21 May 1880 ibid., see also Box 11, ibid., Public Record Office, Victoria.
82 ibid.
83 ibid.
84 Superintendent Sadlier to Chief Commissioner Standish, Y11475, Box 3, Chief Secretary's Office files, Public Record Office, Victoria.
85 Detective A. Wilson to Detective Inspector F. Secretan, Detective Office, Melbourne, 3605, Capital Case File 82/1957, Law Department Files, Public Record Office, Victoria.
86 Detective Meade to Secretan, 31 May 1880, ibid.
87 ibid.
88 Superintendent Hare to Chief Commissioner Standish on capture of Kelly Gang, 2 July 1880, File 80/S6875, Box 3, Chief Secretary's Office, Public Record Office, Victoria.
89 "Board appointed to Inquire into Claim for Compensation by Mrs. Jones for the destruction of the Glenrowan Hotel", MSS Minutes of Evidence, p. 114, Box 4, Chief Secretary's Office, Public Record Office, Victoria.
90 Jerilderie Letter, ibid.
91 Superintendent Hare to Chief Commissioner Standish, 2 July, 1880, 80/S6875, Box 3 Chief Secretary's Office, Public Record Office, Victoria.
92 Board of Inquiry into Claim for Compensation by Mrs. Jones, Minutes of Evidence, ibid., p. 36.
93 Detective Eason to Superintendent of Police, Benalla, 26 July 1880, R7629, Box 3, Chief Secretary's Office, Public Record Office, Victoria.
94 Board of Inquiry into Claim for Compensation by Mrs. Jones, Minutes of Evidence, ibid., p. 96.
95 ibid. p. 120.
96 Detective Eason to Superintendent Sadlier, 26 July 1880, R7629, Box 3, Chief Secretary's Office, Public Record Office, Victoria.
97 Board of Inquiry into Claim for Compensation by Mrs. Jones, Minutes of Evidence, ibid., p. 43.
98 ibid., pp. 44-5.
99 ibid., p. 48.

100 ibid., p. 49
101 ibid., p. 47.
102 ibid., p. 48.
103 ibid., pp. 141, 2.
104 ibid., p. 177.
105 ibid., p. 139.
106 ibid., p. 111.
107 Constable Phillip to Superintendent of Police, Benalla, "Relative to the capture of Ned Kelly the Outlaw", A6244, Box 6, Police Files, Public Record Office, Victoria.
108 ibid.
109 Superintendent Sadlier to Chief Commissioner Standish, 1 July 1880, Y6055, Box 3, Chief Secretary's Office, Public Record Office, Victoria.
110 *The Australasian Sketcher,* vol. VIII, July 1880, page 101.
111 Superintendent Sadlier to Chief Commissioner Standish, 1 July 1880, Y6055, p. 44, ibid.
112 ibid., p. 43.
113 ibid., p. 47.
114 *The Australasian Sketcher,* vol. VIII, July 1880, p. 106.
115 Memorandum Crown Solicitor 10 November 1880, Capital Case 82/1957, Law Department Files, Public Record Office, Victoria.
116 Assistant Chief Commissioner Nicholson to Chief Commissioner Standish, 30 June 1880, R26501, Box 2, Police Files, Public Record Office, Victoria.
117 Chief Commissioner of Police to Chief Secretary, 24 July 1880, G6609, Box 2, Chief Secretary's Office, Public Record Office, Melbourne.
118 Sub-Inspector O'Connor to Chief Commissioner of Police, 7 September 1880, 80/R9050, Box 2, Chief Secretary's Office, Public Record Office, Victoria.
119 Board of Inquiry into Claim for Compensation by Mrs. Jones, Minutes of Evidence, ibid., p. 38.
120 ibid., p. 32.
121 Jerilderie Letter, ibid.
122 ibid.
123 V.G. Carter and T. Dale, *Topsoil and Civilization,* University of California Press, p. 184.
124 ibid., p. 183.
125 ibid., p. 183.
126 Jerilderie Letter, ibid.
127 ibid.
128 Edward Kelly to Chief Secretary, January 1879, Miscellaneous files, Chief Secretary's Office.
129 *The Australasian Sketcher,* vol. VIII, no. 192, July 1880, page 106.

Index